Developmental Psychology

Developmental Psychology

How Nature and Nurture Interact

Keith Richardson

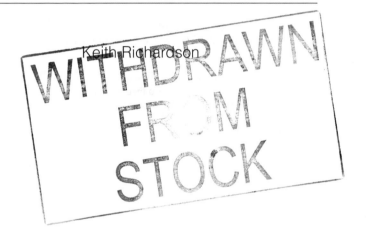

First published 2000 by
MACMILLAN PRESS LTD
Houndmills, Basingstoke, Hampshire RG21 6XS
and London
Companies and representatives
throughout the world

ISBN 0–333–74042–4 hardcover
ISBN 0–333–74043–2 paperback

A catalogue record for this book is available
from the British Library.

This book is printed on paper suitable for recycling and
made from fully managed and sustained forest sources.

10   9   8   7   6   5   4   3   2   1
09   08   07   06   05   04   03   02   01   00

Typeset by Cambrian Typesetters, Frimley, Camberley, Surrey

Printed in Hong Kong

Contents

List of Figures

Preface

Development psychology has made huge progress in recent years. The child is now recognized to be an active agent in complex interactions with a multi-layered social and physical environment: transactionalism rules. But underneath this liberal gloss a set of traditional assumptions remain. We retain the belief that causes of development are due either to the structure of genes or to the structure of environment, the ancient nature/nurture, organism/environment dichotomies. These and related assumptions have massive implications for theories of development. I will show how they are delaying and distorting theory-building in human development. They obstruct a properly ecological, systems perspective because this requires that the organism and environment form a single system, not a dichotomy. They fail to offer a means of showing how two exclusive forms of cause could manage to combine. And most of all they preclude the possibility of an interactionism in which change is produced by interactions themselves, basic to other domains of science, not by regulators in the form of genetic instructions or environmental structure. We need a view which escapes this conceptual straitjacket.

There is one. It is based upon principles which apply to all natural processes. It shows how we do not need to invoke regulators, how we can be 'ecological' about people and can admit of the enormous complexity and uncertainty in development whilst still retaining a scientific rationale. It is an ecological, dynamic systems view.

The aim of this book is to make as clear as I can the enormous difficulties the traditional assumptions lead to and to persuade you of the value of grasping a new framework. I want to change your head, to adopt a new paradigm. My version of this paradigm, like any developmental product, emerged from a complex flux of interacting causal influences.

The first influence to mention is J. J. Gibson, for his deep, radical critique of standard thinking. He made explicit the lack of necessary connection between regularity and regulators. Susan Oyama developed this notion and her influence is important. But then so are the writings of Bower, Bruner, Goodwin, Thelen, Smith, Costall, Hendriks-Jansen and many others.

I ended up with a wide-ranging but insufficiently focused draft. Brian Hopkins was kind enough to give detailed comments and suggestions about it. They helped enormously and I want to express my particular thanks to him. Alan Costall has provided encouragement and acute comment over several years and Iain Burnside many hours of mind-sharing. Frances Arnold and her colleagues at Macmillan have inducted me into the book-writing game with great skill and kindness. I thank all of these. Last but not least I acknowledge my debt to Glen McKeown, for her unfaltering and unconditional support.

Tutor's Guide

There is a Tutor's Guide with statements of the purposes and objectives of each chapter, plus suggestions as to the main points and issues that students should consider when working on the discussion points for each chapter. It is available free to adopters of the text for use in a class with more than 12 students. Please contact the publishers direct to obtain a copy or for further information.

Acknowledgements

Grateful acknowledgement is made to the following for permission to use copyright material: Holt, Rinehart & Winston for Figure 18 from R. N. Haber and M. E. Hershenson, *The Psychology of Visual Perception*, 2nd edn (1980), figure 8.24; Houghton Mifflin Company for figures 16 and 17 from J. J. Gibson, *The Senses Considered As Perceptual Systems* (1966); Masson éditeur for Figure 23 from Amiel-Tison and Grenier (eds) *Evaluation neurologique du nouveau-né et du nourrisson* (1980); MIT Press for Figures 5 and 6 from J. A. Meyer and S. Wilson (eds) *From Animals to Animats I* (1991), figures 2.2, 2.3 and 2.4; MIT Press for Figure 9 from E. Thelen and L. Smith, *A Dynamic Systems Approach to the Development of Cognition and Action* (1994), figure 1.2; MIT Press for Figure 15 from R. Port and T. van Gelder, *Mind as Motion: Explorations in the Dynamics of Cognition* (1995), figure 2.19; Oxford University Press for Figure 22 from S. Healy (ed.), *Spatial Representation in Animals* (1998), p. 27; Psychosomatic Society for Figure 24 from T. G. R. Bower, 'The Object in the World of the Infant', *Scientific American*, 225 (1998) 30–8. Offprint 539; Steve Redwood for Figure 4.

Every effort has been made to contact all the copyright-holders, but if any have been inadvertently overlooked the publishers will be pleased to make the necessary arrangements at the first opportunity

Chapter 1

Introduction: the traditional view and its alternative, a summary

Is there a problem?

Let's start simple. What controls, say, walking in humans? The standard view, which I expect you to agree with at this point, is that the explanation of both the universality of walking by humans and the variation in forms of it is relatively unproblematical. It involves two distinct forms of cause. There is an underlying propensity for humans to walk due to the operation of an in-built genetic programme applying to all members of the species, being independent of learning, not based upon specific environmental events, and not dependent upon interactions between internal and external factors. It is 'innate', part of 'nature'. There are, on the other hand, a variety of forms of walking to be observed, the variations being due to experiential factors, shoes worn, fitness, load carried, cultural norms and so on, the 'nurture' side of the coin. Thus any given instance of walking can be accounted for by a consideration of the relative contribution of the two sorts of causal factors and their interaction. The same general argument applies to every human ability. It is a model for all development. It is the dominant paradigm.

There are two critical features to the model. First, the two sorts of causes of development are mutually exclusive and exhaustive. That means change is due *either* to innate, internal, genetic, biological factors, *or* to learned, external, environmental ones and between them all possible forms of change are accounted for: they form a dichotomy, the 'nature/nurture' dichotomy. Second, in both cases the structure determining the changes is complete, fully formed, either in the blueprint in the genes which gets 'read out' in development or in the existing structure of the environment which becomes internalized through learning, like the route to work or the company policy on dogs. In both cases it is reformed in the brain, either as the expression of the internal genetic code or as internal representations, 'copies' of the external world. Change based on a preexisting form is called preformation, the second critical feature.

A trip to the moon allowed a natural experiment, a test of the model for the case of walking, but also turns out to pose a challenge to the assumptions underpinning the model in general. The prediction had to be that we expect to find 'odd' walking due to the 'odd' conditions, but it will not be possible to find that this form of locomotion is simply not adopted by a member of the human species generally wanting to get about in no great hurry. And certainly not when the only change to reasonably 'normal' conditions is a reduction in the value of one variable out of the huge number influencing the outcome. The variable in question is gravity. Reduce its value, to one-sixth of 'normal', by being on the moon, and what happens – the supposedly in-built, genetically fixed, independent-of-environment programme fails to operate. The astronauts found that jumping was a more suitable mode of locomotion, for the sort of bodies they had in the sort of conditions they encountered (McMahon, 1984, reported in Thelen and Smith, 1994). The prediction that walking would occur and why is based upon the nature/nurture dichotomy, walking in some form being genetically determined. But it didn't happen. It has been suggested that they had practice on earth before they went. They did, but that does not explain how what is supposedly genetically determined failed to occur.

If we can be wrong about something as relatively simple as walking, can we rely upon the validity of the two central assumptions of which it is supposedly just an obvious example, that the 'nature/nurture' dichotomy and causal change by preformation constitute a valid basis for psychological theorizing? If we can't we have a major problem, because every single textbook on development still refers to 'innate' causes, to 'biological' influences, to 'predispositions', and so on, and contrasts these with the alternative forms of cause, 'learning', 'cultural or social factors', etc., independent of genes and dependent upon experience, thus still assuming the validity of the nature/nurture dichotomy and the critical implicit assumption that causes in development are to be allocated to membership of one or other of these exclusive, preformed (not formed in the interaction) categories.

Interactionism without interactions

The situation is odd because it is not as if developmental psychologists claim to be preformationists, or to believe in dichotomies. Everyone, but everyone claims allegiance to an interactionist banner. We recognise the facile nature of single-cause, passive-child, unidirectional explanations. We see the limitations of focusing on end-points in development, stages, and the need to examine the processes of change themselves. We appreciate the pervasive influence of contexts. As a result, we all believe in multiple forms of influence, complex interactive effects and transactional, constructivist change. There can be no dichotomies here as causes of all sorts are presumed to interact with each other. Yet the newest textbooks do still use, without modification, precisely the same categories of thought and assumptions they purport to deride, as Oyama (1985) pointed out. We still read about genetic blueprints for development even though we know that a complex of structures and conditions and interactions are also essential for the usual developmental outcomes, not just genes. Where is the interactionism here? If I learn to recognize someone or to learn a language, their face and that language were preformed. Where is the interaction here? And as for some causes being a mixture of what is 'innate' and 'learned', we are never told even in the most general terms how molecular biological mechanisms involving genes can 'mix' with learning mechanisms. Thus it is that we have effects that are supposed to be due to interactions, but are also claimed to be due to fixed features, genes, faces, language, whatever. And thus it is that we are supposed to accept that different sorts of causes can and must interact, yet belong to categories which are exclusive from each other. This is what happens in the midst of a paradigm shift, confusion. Hence there is now an urgent need to put in place assumptions which are consistent with notions of dynamic, interactive change, not based upon a static, non-interactive, anti-contextual model which dichotomies and preformation demands. The lack is holding psychology back, as there is no focus on interactions themselves. They are the source of all development and the key to our understanding of the processes of change.

The dichotomies remain

Just to get a glimpse of the difficulty, consider this small sample of statements from prominent developmental psychologists. Karmiloff-Smith (1992) often refers to the innate capacities of the human mind (e.g. in the Open University course book (ED 209), edited by Lee and das Gupta, 1995). Now these are generally taken to be developmentally fixed and independent of the environment (Michel and Moore, 1995), not dependent upon contingent interactions, but it is clear from the book that Karmiloff-Smith knows this not to be true. I am not saying she is wrong, but that it is confusing. The same course is extremely pro-interactionist, yet tells us that 'Information-for-development is stored in the genes' (p. 167, Book 1). If it is stored in the genes it is surely preformed and not formed in interactions.

There is a variety of forms of preformationist explanations and of confusing uses of associated terms. Take 'biological'. The Open University Course on Foundations of Child Development, ED209, referred to earlier, tells us that there are 'biologically rooted individual differences' or 'genetic differences between children'. Here 'biological' and 'genetic' have the same connotation. But when we hear that 'there are biological effects on temperament that are not influenced by genetic differences, for example – effects of illness' (p. 196, Book 1), the terms refer to totally different sorts of causal factors as 'biological' is being *contrasted* with 'psychological'. But no explanation of this paradox is offered. Even avowed ecological psychologists (who should be united in their opposition to dichotomous thinking) are not immune to the use of such language: Claes Von Hofsten (1997) in Dent-Reed and Zukow-Goldring writes, 'though experience is necessary for developing actions, biology has also prepared the child for acquiring such skills' (p. 167). The use of this sort of terminology by 'interactionists' shows, I believe, the state of flux thinking is in. And you have the difficulty of being expected to accept a new gloss on psychological development whilst still being expected to work within the language of the old assumptions. So long as we continue to use the language of dichotomies we have an extra barrier to the adoption of a new paradigm.

Some have proposed alternative theoretical frameworks (Gibson, 1979; Oyama, 1985; Thelen and Smith; 1994, Reed, 1996; Butterworth and Hopkins, 1997; Dent-Reed and Zukow-Goldring 1997), all dynamic systems views, seeing change as the central feature of any theory of knowledge, stability as the emergence of products which inevitably become involved in new interactions and resultant flux; and they are all ecological in emphasizing the role of context as of critical causal significance in those processes. In direct opposition to basing analysis on mutually exclusive and exhaustive categories such as nature/nurture, organism/environment, biology/culture, mind/body, we are exhorted to recognize the systemic nature of interaction and development in which the boundaries between dichotomous categories dissolve.

Resistance to change

But be clear, these frameworks have, as yet, been accepted by only a minority. It is no surprise. When assumptions have dominated thinking so profoundly and for so long, it is no small matter to give them up. Nor should we do so without care. I do not expect you to release one way of thinking until and unless you are convinced that the alternative is better. My aim is to supply the grounds for that conviction. There are several obstacles. The use of 'mixed' assumptions, as I have suggested, is one, because it clouds all the relevant distinctions. But there are other sorts of impediments. In the first place, to question these basic assumptions about the nature of things is, by definition, improper, because assumptions are assumed. The reaction thus tends to be defensive, usually taking the form that no one holds these assumptions anymore. But if we do not, why are all the textbooks still using them? In any case, every conversation we ever have depends upon assumptions. If I discuss public transport with someone, I will assume the existence of people, of a variety of sorts of vehicles, trains that travel on railway lines, lorries on roads, and so on. Talk, even thought, is not possible without assumptions. The same applies to theories. So it is never a case of whether we make assumptions, but only of which ones we make.

Slightly more subtle is the way that words embody assumptions, often implicitly. For instance, the arguments against reducing the age for homosexual consent depend upon an assumption that it is not accorded equal rights with heterosexual sex, as otherwise all arguments would apply equally, irrespective of the sex of the partner. The fourth reason is to do with the circularity involved in paradigmatic change. One cannot grasp the new thoughts and the language suitable to their expression without releasing the old. But one cannot release the old without grasping the new. Change is hard and you will hear novel terms and encounter novel arguments in this book. Don't worry. The whole point of this book is to try to set out ideas in such a way that the new does not have to be the obscure.

In this Introduction I describe what I consider to be the main components of the traditional view, followed by the alternative, not because everything will then be clear, but so that you know the sort of ground we are going to have to cover. Expect it to be unclear at the moment, but equally, expect it to be clarified as you read the book. My aim, however, is not just clarification. I want this book to change your head. I want it to make you forsake allegiance to a tradition and choose an alternative. The alternative includes my personal attempt at a contribution to theory, but first, standard thinking in a nutshell.

The traditional view of psychological development

The model implies that the unit of analysis is the organism, that causal change is due to genetic or environmental factors or some unspecified interaction of the two, and that genetic causes are effective independently of experience (innate) while environmental factors are dependent only upon it. The complexity that we observe in behaviour is due to complex, genetic blueprints or to complex, mental representations. The regularity, the sameness observed in human behaviour across cultures or other sources of difference, is due to the mechanisms of genetic regulation, while the differences in behaviour which covary with experience are due to environmental regulation, learning, by which internal representations of external structure are built.

The main psychological components of the developing organism are perception, cognition and action, each of which must be clearly distinguished from the other. No complex behaviour is possible without a set of internal representations, the content of cognition, which is the essential link between the outside world and the inside mind. They are the map and the directions without which we could not intelligently traverse the mental topography, the key to complex action or thought. They and only they allow analysis and validation of the ambiguous and deceptive world of appearances, which is all that perception can provide, and enable the complex decisions which our bodies are then directed to make material. They consist in knowledge which is not limited to particular situations, but is abstract, general, disembedded, free from particular contexts. Contexts in which behaviours occur are thus not central to psychological functioning. This one is problematical because there is so much evidence now for the importance of context, for the view that all cognition is situated. But, as I say, we are in the midst of change.

Finally, a host of factors can influence any given developmental outcome but we can take refuge in the (assumed) knowledge that at least these factors have linear effects (more of a relevant independent variable has more of an effect), and are additive (pertinent factors accumulate in their effects). I will need to show why and how these views are implied, but more, I need to demonstrate that they are incorrect, every one of them. But that is only a start. For the aim, as I say, is to help you embrace an alternative.

The ecological, dynamic systems view

This view could hardly be more different. It is based upon the assumption that the unit of analysis is decidedly not the organism, but the single system comprised by organism/environment; that the structure and functions of the organism can be understood only in relation to its fit with the environment. Adaptive action, on this view, is action coupled to specific situations, to environmental contingencies, and that means that organisms must have up-to-date knowledge of the environment as they act and think, which itself means that cognition cannot be decoupled from perception, or from action, as if it were it would not be sensitive to change. Perception becomes critical to intelligent thinking and action.

The traditional position assumes an initial lack of coupling between organism and environment and thus requires the construction of a map or representations of the outside on the inside so that the mind is coupled to the external world. Complex action thus depends upon complex representations. The ecological position assumes that psychological systems evolved to inform action in the real, complex world (not the conditions of the laboratory) and were tested and thus selected by their results in action. This argument applies to selection over evolutionary time, and over ontogenetic time, learning. It implies that representations are not the prime consideration in considering how action can be explained. Rather than complex representations being the condition of complex action, perceptions, cognitions and actions organized together, interacting in the most effective way, are the condition of complex thought.

Development is then that progressive emergence of new relations between the two main components in the system, organism and the environment, as a result of interactions between them. It follows from this position that the components, whether these be internal to an organism, like genes, or external, like social norms, could never be accorded the status of a necessary and sufficient causal condition because it is only in the *interaction of all the factors* that behavioural outcomes emerge. But these component factors are a mixture of those that have evolved over evolutionary time, like having arms, knee joints, etc., those that have arisen more recently, like practices which have been regularly used for several generations, even those that happened but 10 seconds ago, like learning someone's name. This implies that every time an act is to be carried out it will be constrained by, informed by changes that have taken place over a continuum of time extensions, phylogenetic, ontogenetic, and many others. Thus, both sorts of factors, those from phylogeny, 'nature' and those from ontogeny, 'nurture', are necessary, but only part of the total causal flux from which every single change ever emerges.

In summary, rather than factors causing development coming from two exclusive categories, all developmental and behavioural outcomes emerge from the causal interactions of both sorts together. No developmental change or behaviour is ever preformed, not in genes, nor in the structure of environments. It always arises from interactions in the developmental system. We can account for the regularity observed in development only in terms of the regularity of interactions comprising the developmental system, and the regularity of these interactions depends only upon the regular co-occurrence of the components which interact. That means that to understand how development occurs we need to identify the components of the interactions and the outcomes.

The adoption of the tenets of dynamic systems views entails that we do not expect gradual, linear or additive characteristics of change. On the contrary, we predict that we will find that causal change is characterized by discontinuities, sudden shifts, not continuous change, by non-linear movements between steady states and large, qualitative changes with little change in input to the developmental system. Such change is non-additive and unpredictable in that pertinent variables may have no effect, or a huge effect, depending upon the stability of the system.

We can only adapt to the structure (dynamic and complex in its ways of change, but structure nevertheless) of the environment and of ourselves in relation to it. I call structure invariance, after Gibson (1979). It refers to any regularity to which it would be useful take account of, or which informs adaptive action of thought. Any aspect of the environment which is structured, and almost everything is, thereby must have some invariant properties. Does language have structure? Does a ladder have structure? Does a snail, a thunderstorm, bath time? They all do, of course. This does not mean they are completely fixed, it means they are not random, so we can utilize the pattern, the predictability, the invariance. If you feel uneasy with the word 'invariance', 'structure' will generally do the same job. I argue, crucially, that invariance is a property of the environment or the organism and is thus a component in interaction, while information is what is gained from invariances only if the organism involved has the relevant internal structures, perceptual, cognitive, to utilize the invariances.

Interactions, then, are the basis of development. But development is a long, gradual process involving multiple changes and interactions. The relative stability we observe implies a systematicity to the process, hence the developmental system: a system of interactions which are functionally related to each other, so that earlier events provide opportunities for interactions from which new events will occur, new interactions, and so on.

Now, we need to add another factor: all systems are composed of sub-systems, they are nested, so that the body, for instance, is made up of the immune system, digestive system, circulatory system, etc., each of which is itself sub-divided, and the total external environment made up of the cosmic system, within that the solar system, the earth system, and more local ecologies and effects. The sub-systems always have to function within the constraints of the general system of which they are apart. All organisms and all their adaptations are constrained by the broader system of physical laws that operate, like gravity. All the physiological sub-systems are designed within the general constraints that organisms are self-promoting, active, exchanging energy with their environment, reproducing, etc. That is, no organism is fixed in its design by those constraints (all organisms would be the same if they were), but none are designed other than within the constraints. The point is that the larger system constrains in a generic way the organization of the sub-systems, while the sub-systems have a more specific function and a more differentiated effect. Hence developmental explanation must take account of the nested hierarchical nature of the organism and its environment and the two together.

I will make the case that human development consists initially in generic systems of knowledge production, which constrain in a general way the psychological structures which exist, channelling them in certain directions and limiting the sorts of problems the infant has to deal with, and that the solution of such problems gives more differentiated knowledge. Each successive set of solutions affords new problems to be tackled with the ever more powerful and differentiated structures at its disposal. The organism becomes more differentiated, as does the effective environment and as does the coupling between organism and environment.

This will not yet be clear. If it were I would not need to write this book. But one example might help a little here. Neonates detect and preferentially attend to the regular use of exaggerated rise and fall of tone of voice (invariances in prosody) used by 'mothers', apparently everywhere, called 'motherese'. The 'motherese' is an undifferentiated, generic form of communication, and its effects are pretty undifferentiated, as they do not specify any specific facts will be learned, but the preferential attention to 'mother' does typically ensure that learning about how prosodic features relates to other aspects of mothers' behaviour, and to the infants' feelings, about how prosodic features co-vary with words, etc. does occur. Preferential attention to 'motherese' constrains learning in that attention is focused on these limited aspects of the world, not on others. The broad system, species-typical in this and many cases, produces relatively undifferentiated information, but it serves to organize what sorts of learning will occur, and this learning is more specific and differentiated. The more generic interactions afford the more specific ones. This is how knowledge develops.

Organization of the book

In order to achieve my aims I have to start at a place most of you will recognize. Then we can embark on a journey in which you are invited to view familiar sites from a different perspective

and thus to be able to look at the same world but see it differently. I want, as J. J. Gibson (1979) wrote, 'to educate your attention'. If I succeed you will have a more critical attitude to
traditional thinking about development and a better appreciation of an alternative view.

I do not see how you can come to agree with the new ideas
unless you see clearly what they are an alternative to. Hence
we need to be clear about the deepest assumptions and about
how they interrelate, depend upon and support each other,
creating a bit of a monster which resists attack, not by denying
new ideas but by swallowing them whole, hence the claim that
we are all interactionists now. If only. Thus, I begin with a brief
description of Darwinian theorizing because it reveals the
basic arguments and assumptions about the dichotomies and
preformation. Once I have outlined the basis of dichotomous
causes, I identify some of the immense difficulties that maintaining the present assumptions requires. This provides the
opportunity to follow the alternative line of enquiry, beginning
to introduce two interrelated notions that are emerging from
the initial critique: ecological thinking and dynamic systems as
the twin perspectives upon which a radical alternative can be
built. I start with dynamic systems theories, showing how they
are based upon precisely the assumptions about causality and
change that we will be finding are necessary. Such a perspective may prove to be central to developmental psychology in
the future, but first it will need to be specifically related to a
systems perspective on the origins and development of human
knowledge, or as I prefer, information. The key to this coupling
lies in the ecological psychology of J. J. Gibson, and so it to his
view that I then turn.

In my view Gibson made one significant error, in not distinguishing between 'invariance' and 'information'. It is central to
my overall thesis that this distinction is elaborated and clarified. I argue that invariance is a property of the environment
and thus a component in interaction, while information is an
outcome of developmental interactions, and I describe a variety of cases where the two are simply not found together.

Because broader systems encompass narrower ones, I then
look at broader and narrower sorts of structures, invariances,
from which information is derived. Gravity, as I mentioned, is

an invariance that has constrained human development in powerful but undifferentiated ways, while structures, invariances of lesser extension, like my mother's face, constrain them in lesser but more specific ways.

There is an end-product to the elaboration of this emerging paradigm, as I then put some of these ideas together to produce my own version of ecological systems thinking. I have not tried to be comprehensive in my empirical evidence, but illustrative, and the focus is clearly on the earliest processes of development. In Chapter 8 I look at two areas of dispute to show how this paradigm creates a position on important areas of discussion: cognitive and social development. Have fun.

Discussion points

1 How do adherents of the innate/learned dichotomy account for what is typically found in a species, and how do they account for the variation between individuals? Suggest how they might account for the flying in formation that many species of birds show.

2 Provide arguments for and against the traditional view of development.

3 In what way would the role of culture in development be seen differently by evolutionary psychologists, cultural psychologists and ecological psychologists?

4 Why is it difficult to question assumptions and how does language use affect our thinking about assumptions about development?

5 What is a paradigm? Do they matter?

Chapter 2

Darwinian dichotomies and their dissolution

Our journey starts with Darwin and his voyage on *HMS Beagle*, because the theory of evolution which emerged from it provided the grounds for a view of development as based upon two alternative forms of cause, natural selection and learning, which has underpinned theories of development ever since. As others have pointed out (e.g. Morss, 1990) the dominant paradigm is not a faithful reflection of what Darwin wrote. Nor is he the only source of influence. Dichotomies are common and they were not invented by Darwin. It could well be that this one is due in part to the writings of philosophers, such as Descartes, who believed that all organic nature was determined, but that the 'thinking I' was not, and Locke, who believed that some human characteristics like personality, were inborn, due to 'nature', but experience, 'nurture', was the only source of knowledge, or Kant, who set apart 'living things' from the laws of physics, the material world. What matters here is to show the influence on thinking that the dichotomy has exerted and continues to exert in developmental psychology. It dominates, the newest textbooks still using versions of the same dichotomous terms that Darwin's theory popularized, reinforcing the maintenance of the assumptions underpinning them. If it is wrong, as I believe, it has to be confronted and replaced. But we must start small, with a short account of the basic thinking used to justify the assumptions.

Natural selection

Darwin's original theory argued that the natural variation that occurs among members of a species meant that some had characteristics that better enabled survival in the environment they lived in and thus offered more opportunities for reproduction and thus more off-spring. This is the principle of natural selection. As off-spring inherit the characteristics of parents, the principle of heredity, the combination of natural selection and heredity ensured the optimization of characteristics that fitted the environment. Once Mendel's laws of inheritance were discovered, it was argued that it was the variation in genes that directed the variation in characteristics or traits. Thus, one mechanism for change in species starts with natural changes, usually mutations, which occur to genetic material inside the organism. Those changes which lead to traits or phenotypes which better enable survival are selected and, so long as the typical environment for the species remains relatively constant, those members with the mutation tend to survive more often, thus to reproduce (which is, by definition, normally possible for all members of the species) more often, with the result that the new genes will spread through the gene-pool of the species. As the gene spreads, so does the product, the trait. The process is 'selection' and the products 'adaptations'. At any given moment we would have a developing species-typical gene-pool, a species-typical internal environment (bodily structure and component systems) and a species-typical external environment, the ecological niche for the species. As a result of this development of a species (phylogeny), when we observe the earliest stage of development of a frog, a cuckoo, a human, we know we can predict the changes and the final form of each because of the stored genetic information specifying its general form and functions.

On this view the selected traits or capacities which aid survival can be seen as full or partial solutions to problems facing the individual and the species, like how to digest food, control temperature, detect prey or predator, identify a potential mate. These are specialized problems requiring specialist adaptations. Selection thus takes the form of increasing the efficiency of an adaptation, not in broadening its function. We would not expect the eye to become an ear as well, or the lungs to aid digestion. Thus, over evolutionary time qualitatively different sorts of discrete-function adaptations would emerge to 'solve' discrete 'problems'. As a result species develop and can even lead to differences that get emphasized and by which new species arise, but only over huge periods of time because the process is gradual, incremental, linear. The same logic of selection must apply to all adaptations, and thus include psychological ones: they will help solve specific problems concerned with survival, but in this case they will do it by the use of evolved perceptual, cognitive and motor structures which are used to guide action. Remember, all such change is based around changes in genes and results in a gene-pool which contains all the information for the adaptations to emerge in development. Where this process is responsible for developmental change it is said to be genetically determined.

Learning

Such adaptations are an efficient way of coupling action to general aspects of the environment which are typically encountered for the species. However, sometimes a much more differentiated response is required which itself requires more differentiated perceptual and cognitive knowledge, like the location of salmon today, or the state of one's brother's temper, etc. For the human species, like millions of others, there has also been an evolution of means of acquiring knowledge about specific, locally varying states and events which enables action that is coupled much more precisely to those contexts. It is called learning, traditionally taken to involve the development of internal representations of the world that are related to the specific external form or structure of environment encountered, rather than to general, species-typical features. One learns particular routes, to use particular tools, to relate to specific individuals with their idiosyncrasies, all forms of adaptation to the environment which involve more individualized coupling than merely to generic, species-typical features.

The dichotomies

The nature/nurture dichotomy

Change in the form of new knowledge can thus arise from one of two sorts of causes, genetic selection, based on internal structure, leading to relatively undifferentiated knowledge of species-typical conditions, or learning, based upon external structure, affording a more differentiated and sensitive adaptation to individual states and events. One process is adaptive in virtue of what is universal, typical for the whole species, the other is adaptive in virtue of what is particular, individual, local. The two processes are exclusive, they form a dichotomy, and exhaustive, all change is accounted for by them. This is the 'nature/nurture' dichotomy.

The organism/environment dichotomy

The reach of the dichotomy extends to the physical location of the cause of change. Changes due to 'nature' come from within the organism, changes due to 'nurture' come from outside it, but both lead to changes in the brain and thereby in behaviour. Causes thus have a single direction, from the body to the brain or from the environment to the brain and we can look inwards for one sort of cause and outwards for the other. The dichotomous nature of the relation between nature and nurture is reflected in the view that the organism be seen as independent of its environment, not part of a single system. In fact the relative independence and stability of the environment is seen as a condition of being able to adapt to it.

The ontogenetic/phylogenetic dichotomy

A related distinction is made between the changes that occur within the life-time of one member of the species, ontogeny, and the changes which have occurred to a species during its history, phylogeny. Phylogenetic change occurs through the selection of new adaptations and thus involve a changing gene-pool and a changing species. The process of ontogenetic change, on the other hand, depends on an organism with a fixed set of genes changing through experience. Thus gene change is the basic mechanism of change for phylogeny but not for ontogeny. However, many changes in ontogeny did not appear to be due to learning, like the propensities to crawl, to walk, to talk. The response of the 'dichotomizers' is predictable. Even within ontogeny there are two exclusive categories of cause, experience on the one hand, or genetic determination directing when maturational, biological change occurs.

Recapitulation, the view that the changes that have occurred over the history of the species are seen in individual development, recapitulated in ontogeny, is again not allowed to disturb the dichotomous equilibrium as, even if it occurs, which is arguable, such change is due to 'nature'. As with maturation, if learning does not seem to be involved, it had to follow that genetic programmes were.

The biological/learning or social or cultural dichotomy

The split is very commonly encountered in the form of a counterposition of biological explanations of change with change due to learning of various sorts, e.g. socialization. 'Biological' development refers to the changes in an individual due to the operation of species-typical, genetically regulated programmes that apply equally to all members, while non-universal changes are due to culture-specific influences which vary between societies, classes, etc. The distinction also serves to contrast fixed, pretty immutable influences, the biological ones, from contingent environmental influences. Hence the former are supposedly reliable and change only through adaptations, while the latter can and do change in a (contingent) moment. 'Biological', 'maturational', 'innate', are just versions of one half of the single dichotomy.

The mind/body dichotomy

The function of the 'mind', the seat of concepts, is to represent the external world inside us. It is the means by which we are connected to that world and has to develop through learning. Behaviour, on the other hand, is simple. It is either the direct result of the unfolding of genetic programmes, like being able to walk, or simply the enactment of the decisions the mind has made about what is out there and what to do about it. The body is only a vehicle for the mind. Again, the distinction is clear and dichotomous.

Other means of change

Variations on means of evolutionary change need mentioning. Baldwin (1902, 1906) established the principle of organic selection, whereby adaptive changes during individual's development which were due to their individual qualities or traits would result in their greater likelihood in surviving, thus reproducing, and thereby reproducing the characteristics of the individuals concerned until natural selection did the job in the 'normal' way. Thus, rather than selection being carried out only by 'nature', it could involve 'nurture'. Another variation comes initially from Mayr (1963), who argued that if some members were isolated and thus could not contribute reproductively to the gene-pool for the whole species, then random fluctuations in gene frequencies (called genetic drift), together with natural selection in what was presumably not an identical environment, could lead to a sub-species or new species. This view was developed by Elderedge and Gould (1972) and called 'punctuated equilibrium'.

A more radical view of evolutionary change is described by Stewart (1998) and uses the same principles underpinning much of this book. He argues that all natural systems that change over time are dynamic systems, therefore evolution is a dynamic system. Dynamic systems are based upon complex interactions leading to non-linear change in qualitative leaps, thus we should expect evolution to proceed in this non-gradualist way and the development of new species would be expected to be abrupt, not gradual. Research at the level of molecular biology has inclined towards this dynamic view, showing that genes interact with each other, suppressing or enhancing, delaying or promoting action, and that the biochemical environments of genes interact with the genes to affect their function. Richardson (1998, p. 56), quotes Rollo (1995, p. 80):

what is being uncovered . . . is not some fundamental level of invariant, ultimate control [preformation, blueprint – my addition], but complex, interactive systems with cascading levels of organization and numerous feedback systems.

Richardson himself (1998, p. 58) asserts:

We now know that the rhetoric of genetic determinism is quite wrong. Genes by themselves do not 'make' proteins, 'self-replicate', 'control', 'constrain', 'programme' or issue 'instructions' for anything; neither do they 'express' them-selves . . . Genes are best thought of as resources utilised by a dynamic system in a regulated manner. What we inherit from parents is not just a set of genes, and not a genetic programme, but a whole developmental system which utilises genes as resources.

At the level of molecular biology, then, the unqualified assumption that genes determine developmental outcomes is accepted as wrong. This broader version allows that the contexts can cause changes in the genes, that it is from *interactions* between genes and their contexts that developmental change at this level occurs. Now this could mean that a new psychology based upon the idea of development as occurring only through complex, interactive systems principles that Stewart and Richardson refer to, could and should have emerged. But if it had the textbooks I referred to would be full of dynamic systems theory, full of studies based upon ecological assumptions wherein systems are the unit of analysis, and not replete with dichotomous language. But they are not full of dynamic systems views and they do retain dichotomous language. The systems thinking that has occurred at the level of biology has not extended to the field of psychology. Nor have the views of Baldwin led to the dissolution of the dichotomies. Nor those of Gould. The simplicity of the causal dichotomy is maintained even when more complex explanations of the processes involved have emerged. The basic assumptions of the nature/nurture split remain. Questions are raised about which behaviours are due to which form of cause but that the distinction is plain wrong and unhelpful is still not on the agenda for the majority. As a result we are stuck with the problems they cause.

Whose side are you on?

One effect of accepting this dichotomous thinking is that it has polarized opinion as to the relative importance for development of these two sorts of factors. This is not implied by neo-Darwinism, but is commonplace nevertheless. Some place over-riding emphasis on the importance of the information in 'inner', genetic factors. They attempt to explain the nature of external organization, like culture, in terms of the preformed nature of the humans in it, which itself is due to the information in the genes. This view is popular at the moment, having its own name and its own professors, of evolutionary psychology. Well-known proponents argue that

> Culture is not causeless and disembodied. It is generated in rich and intricate ways by information-processing mechanisms in human minds. These mechanisms are, in turn, the elaborately sculpted product of the evolutionary process. (Barkow, Cosmides and Tooby, 1992, p. 3)

Alternatively, many have focused upon the external structure and dynamics of the environment as being the main determinant of mental organization:

> The normal adult cognitive processes ... were treated as internalised transformations of socially prevalent patterns of interpersonal interaction. (Cole, 1985, p. 148)

The dichotomy in sorts of causes, sorts of explanation, thus allows the two camps to exist, with fence-sitting not generally seen to be an option. The general confusion about alternative forms of explanation and interactionist views is indicated by the fact that both these sorts of views are enjoying a tide of support, yet interactionism cannot be about one or the other.

An interactionist alternative?

It is certainly *de rigueur* to claim allegiance to the interactionist camp and the most common – well, simplistic, to be honest – way to do this is to claim that development consists in a mixture of the two sorts of causes. Mithen (1996, p. 197), for instance, writes:

> A strict division between these – between 'nature' and 'nurture' – has long been rejected by scientists. Any behaviour must be partly influenced by the genetic make-up of the animal and partly by the environment of development. Nevertheless, the relative weighting of these varies markedly between species, and indeed between different aspects of behaviour within a single species.

This sort of view is taken to be a standard interpretation of interactionism. The reader needs to understand, and hopefully will, well before the end of this book, that this is a version of the traditional position. Why do I say this? Look at the wording. It still presumes that there are two forms of change which exist as alternative categories (the dichotomous assumption) and it still presumes that information resides in, either 'genetic make-up' or 'environment' (the preformationist assumption).

Beginning the dissolution

Preformationist forms of explanation

Environmental states exist and they contain information in that they too have structure. I may learn the route to school, but the route was already there. The same applies to dynamic structure. Early social routines, for instance, like 'round-and-round the garden' exist independently of and prior to each baby learning to play them. Genes exist and they contain information within them in virtue of their arrangement on a length of chromosome. Thus, according to the dichotomous, preformationist tradition all change in all species is the result of processes in which either internal, preformed information produces external change in phenotypes, physical states or behaviour, or external, preformed structure, information, is internalized in the form of representations. The information for change is already formed, preformed, before it affects development. It is not formed by interactions. Hence, when one asks for an explanation of how a particular behaviour or way of thinking developed, the form of the answer will be either that it was learned because the relevant external structure was there, or because the relevant genes were, the shorthand of which is to say that the behaviour or knowledge is 'innate'. Now consider this latter form.

The pernicious function of preformation

When we are told a behaviour is innate, we are supposed to accept that we have received the explanation of its origin, its cause. The trouble with this is that, as Johnston (1997, p. 88) points out:

> instincts, innate categories, predispositions, constraints, blueprints, plans, programmes, and so forth. Why do I say these are all nondevelopmental? Because they all presume what they are supposed to explain, namely, the origin of order and organization.

That is to say, each term is supposed to function as an explanation in itself, thereby obviating the need to inform us *how* anything happens. It implies we should not ask for the origin of the plan, etc. or of how it comes to have its effect. A poor explanation is one that does not offer a description of the mechanisms involved, but the poorest 'explanation' of all is the one which implies that it is improper even to ask for a developmental explanation. I suggest the use of these terms is an admission of ignorance, which is fine, but also a claim that it is not our business, or theirs. Why not? Easy, because it is the province of biologists. Such subject boundaries have no more substance that the initial dichotomies. If developmental psychology is about the means by which behaviour arises, then it has to be the job of developmental psychologists to give a developmental answer to questions about the origins of a behaviour. Whatever else preformationist thinking about human change is, it is not *developmental* psychology.

I suggest that the logical status of all preformationist explanation is exactly the same as many forms of thinking now regarded as primitive, irrational, unscientific. Consider, we (science students in an advanced industrial, capitalist culture) deride animism, wherein anything that moves must have a mind or soul, so that the cause of the sun's movement must be due to some preformed 'mover': a fiery chariot pulled by winged horses. We laugh at vitalism, the idea that every living thing must have a special substance inside it, to give it its active nature. We patronize anthropomorphism, the attribution of human-like intentions to a non-human thing to explain its behaviour. In all these cases the form of explanation is preformationist. When we observe that the sun rises, we do not posit winged horses or any preformed programme as being responsible, however regularly it occurs. Instead we recognize that relative rotation emerges from the interaction of various dynamic forces, e.g. gravity, rotational, and that a description of the component forces and their interactive effects constitutes a proper form of explanation, a dynamic systems explanation, as it happens. A properly interactionist position denies the all-powerful causal status of preformed entities of any sort, not just 'chariots pulled by winged horses', but 'genes', 'concepts', 'representations' and 'environments'. This is not to say that these are not involved in causal interactions, but it is to say that they are only component· and that it is only from interactions of components that developmental change occurs. It asserts the causal power of interaction itself as the source of development or learning. It is not possible to over-state the importance of this distinction. Much of what you will read here is intended to illuminate this properly interactive position.

'Genes' or 'environments' as separate and sufficient causes?

To say something is genetically determined means that genes are necessary and sufficient for the change, which implies, of course, that no other factors are required. Replace the word 'genetic' by 'environmental' and exactly the same argument applies to that form of cause. But do we find such cases in psychological development? Well, we do know, for instance, that genetic changes are associated with some syndromes involving learning disability: different genes, different outcomes. Conversely, we also know that prolonged disruption to or privation of human contact leads to impoverished and deviant development: different environments, different outcomes. However, even for cases like these the existence of the change does not explain the outcome. Having an extra copy of chromosome 21, the genotypic change in Down's syndrome, does not specify what any individual will or will not be able to do. There is a vast diversity of ability within and between domains of ability for people with the syndrome. Yes, it is a factor in development. But there are many others we also know to be influential like home conditions, school environment, themselves shorthand for a multitude of factors. Similarly, it is well known that the effects of separation of a child from significant caregivers are unpredictable for any given individual, that separation is but one factor among many which interact with each other and with the history of the individuals involved. Again, genetic factors can be relevant, but again, so can environmental factors. The fact is that these supposedly isolated causal agents are factors, often important ones, in development, but they are always simply part of a causal complex of interactions of factors of both 'genetic' and 'environmental' origin. In a similar vein, Hendriks-Jansen (1996, p. 226) notes that

> a genome arrived at by selective breeding in one environment may have quite different phenotypic characters in another environment, and an environmental change that has a profound influence on the developmental outcome of one genome may have no effect at all upon that of another.

Again, multiple factors are involved, and their interaction is of significance.

This interactivity, this involvement of multiple factors mean that, at the least, the traditional view has to be restated as the claim that different genes lead to different effects, except when they don't, and the same gene has the same outcome, except when it doesn't. This position might be tenable, but only if there is a clear identification of when and why the exceptions occur. What is required is a statement of the conditions under which a change to genes will be both necessary *and* sufficient for a given outcome. Without such a specification it is not possible to test the claim and if it cannot be tested it cannot be wrong and if it cannot be wrong it cannot be right. There is no such clarification from the traditional position.

Regularity does not imply a regulator

The situation has arisen because of the invalid preformationist assumption, as I will now show. Regular, predictable developmental outcomes are observed, for all species. That much is agreed. What explains such regularity, such order? There are two possibilities. We could make the preformationist assumption that the regularity must be due to preformed regulation, blueprints, in which case the logical status of this explanation is equivalent to the 'winged horse' explanation. Alternatively, we could conclude that the regularity of the developmental outcomes is contingent upon the regularity of the *co-occurrence* of all the components of interactions by which development occurs. No magical essence, or internal key is required or justified. Development proceeds when typical internal and external states and events which interact in typical ways are encountered. It is not inevitable, or predetermined or preformed. The ecological psychologist, Gibson (1979, p. 225) realized this:

> The rules that govern behaviour are not like laws enforced by an authority or decisions made by a commander; behaviour is regular without being regulated.

In one line, 'behaviour is regular without being regulated', the claim against preformationism, and the implicit claim for an alternative theoretical starting point is made. When all the relevant components are present, all the relevant interactions by which development proceeds can take place. The mistake is to assume one component can do the job on its own, without interaction and thus that it does it through preformed regulation.

Phylogenetic or ontogenetic factors as separate and sufficient causes?

This dichotomy is no more sustainable than the last. Consider this example. The general form of argument could apply to any member of any species in any situation. A falcon surveys the scene below. It has learned the most likely locations of small prey and where occasional larger prey can be found. It also has knowledge of telephone lines up the valley, and a damaged wing from hitting them last week. It is very windy, but the falcon is very hungry. These sorts of factors will inform the behaviour that results, will be necessary parts of a causal explanation of behaviour. But some more basic factors will also influence what it does and how it does it. It will use an evolved visual system that can differentiate prey far better than the human eye. It will grip with its talons, tear with its beak, rise on thermals with its wings: its courses of action will be heavily constrained by these sorts of factors. They equally inform the actions of the falcon. Any specific behaviour that occurs can emerge only from a causal flux that includes both these sorts of factors, and, for that matter, any changes that have taken less time then phylogenetic change but more time than ontogenetic change. For instance, the falcon may be part of a family group that has lived in the area for generations, and adults may have been exhibiting hunting or other behaviours based on local knowledge and thereby may have passed on that knowledge from generation to generation, by accident. It is silly to try to argue that the falcon does what it does because of one set of factors alone or another alone. Behaviour is always a function of interactions, and these always involve interactions that have been selected both over ontogenetic and over phylogenetic time, and others in between. Behaviour emerges from a combination of and interactions between all manner of factors, irrespective of whether they are the result of processes taking a million years (it has wings), two days (lack of food) or two minutes (experience with telephone lines).

Dissolving the organism/environment dichotomy

It is pretty obvious that when we focus on the environment we see that it is inhabited by organisms. If we want to study one of the organisms in the environment of an organism we have been studying, then what was part of the environment becomes the organism and, conversely, what had been the focus, another organism, now becomes part of the environment. Thus, something is always 'organism' in relation to a given context, but is itself context in relation to another organism. Now if the terms are defined in relation to each other, if they are only to be mutually understood, they are not going to be involved in causal disconnection or independence. This is just the start of the difficulties in sustaining the dichotomy.

A more compelling argument against the organism/environment or genotype/phenotype dichotomy can be built upon the work of someone celebrated for their exposition of a gene-centred view, Richard Dawkins. Traditionally, a phenotype has always been taken to refer to part of the organism side of the organism/environment couple, either a state, like a beak, or an event, like pecking. In no way could it be construed to be part of the environment, until that is, Dawkins wrote, *The Extended Phenotype* (1982). As he explained, the critical feature required for attributing the term 'phenotype' is that it is an adaptation. The lobster's shell, for instance, is an adaptation because it is a construction developed by natural selection which functions to protect the lobster, acting as a shield, a house. It happens to be a part of the body of the lobster. The caddis fly larvae, on the other hand, build their own 'house' for protection in the marine context it occupies, from small stones stuck together. As Dawkins (1982, p. 198) notes:

> The house of a caddis is strictly not part of its cellular body, but it does fit snugly round the body . . . it is easy to see the stone house as a kind of extra protective wall, in a functional sense the outer part of the vehicle.

The crucial aspect is that it is an adaptation and has come into being through the process of natural selection. Extending this thinking, if the house of a caddis is a phenotype, then so is a spider's web, the dam of the beaver family, the badger's sett, the sparrow's nest, because all are adaptive expressions of the evolved capacities of the relevant species. Dawkins calls them 'extended phenotypes'. Once he stopped concentrating on which side of a supposed organism/environment divide a phenotype is on and focused on its biological function, he could appreciate that here was another route for adaptation. The point is that selection of the extended phenotype results in better survival of the species in just as direct a way as, for instance, a beak.

The concept of the extended phenotype is particularly relevant to the human species because the human environment is dominated by its own phenotypic expressions. *But all extended phenotypes are parts of the environment, not parts of the organism.* Thus, not only can organisms be part of the environment of another organism, as argued earlier, but phenotypes can be part of the organism or the environment. His own example shows how irrelevant the organism/environment distinction is when we actually look into the processes involved. In fact it simply takes attention away from the interactions between the organism and environment, which as I will keep repeating, should be our focus. And when it is, we observe complex causal chains which flow within and between bodies such that, once again, the notion of causal *systems* inevitably comes to mind, in which components interact in a systematic manner and produce overall effects which cannot necessarily be tied to one organism in one environment, let alone one organism or one environment.

Systems and relations

Systems only work because of the functional relations between the components comprising the system. If the organism in the environment is one system, then change to one part should often involve a succession of effects and a reorganization of the system, a process called 'self-organization'. Here is an example. A rise in local temperature due to more sunshine can lead to oak trees producing leaves earlier, and caterpillars emerging earlier. The food (the oak tree leaves) have a defence mechanism against predators and produce tannin, which toughens the leaves and makes them less digestible. With warming the process is speeded up and as a result the caterpillars cannot eat enough. Fewer survive, there is less food for song birds, fewer of them survive, leaving less prey for sparrow hawks. So more sun causes fewer sparrow hawks. One changed relation amongst the many component factors can imply many changed relations and one small change in conditions and thereby interactions can lead to massive reorganization of the whole system. On the other hand, precisely because interaction is critical, we cannot know that a change in components will entail any change in outcome and indeed, sometimes no reorganization occurs at all. Now we find this ecological perspective a comprehensible and indeed the only sensible sort of model for studying flora and fauna in their habitats. Why is it suddenly irrelevant when the fauna are human, that is, when it is ecological human psychology that is proposed? There can be no justification for treating humans as not part of the ecology, yet the organism/environment dichotomy demands that we must.

In the example of deprivation of social contact and its effects, the research shows that organismic and external environmental factors interact with each other, so the outcome for any given individual is not predictable, and only tendencies for samples studied can be observed. The fact that this unpredictability is the result of the interactions of factors which are supposed to lie on different sides of a dichotomy, not the result of preformation, means that no useful purpose can be served by maintaining an artificial dichotomy.

Stable but changeable genes, stable but changeable environments

In the traditional view of evolution, incremental changes are gradually and progressively selected so that the organism comes to have characteristics which better fit an environment

which must be assumed to be stable, to have reliable characteristics. Otherwise it would be like dieting to make clothes fit
when the clothes changed size themselves. The assumption of
constancy allows the notion of adaptation to a particular niche
to appear reasonable, if static. But we all know that environments change. Just as in the case of Down's syndrome it was
convenient, in order to maintain the dichotomy, to under-
estimate the influence of environmental factors, and in 'attachment' to under-estimate individual characteristics, so it is
convenient when thinking about change in evolutionary time
to focus on changes in genes, not changes in environments.
That focus does not so much lead to certain views as simply
reflect those we already have. But given that environments,
and changes in them, are no more and no less reliably encountered than genes or internal phenotypes, what we need is a
form of description which does not try to ignore the complexity, the amount of variation and dynamism that we actually
observe.

I want to be perfectly clear. Genes are a universal (to a
species) and necessary part of internal structure, and they do
have the characteristic of remaining relatively constant, which
is just as well as there would be no species otherwise. But
equally they have the characteristic of change, which is just as
well, as it is supposed to be the starting point for any evolutionary change, remember. At the same time, niches are a
universal (for the species in question) and necessary part of
external structure and they do have the characteristic of
remaining relatively constant, which is also just as well as there
would be nothing to adapt to, according to natural selection
theory. But equally they too have the characteristic of change.
In other words the stability of both the internal and external
environment are of equal import. And the instability or change
is just as important. That is the crux of the matter. As organisms change, so does the relevance of different aspects of a
stable environment. As environments change, so the relevance
of existing characteristics of the organism changes. If both
change, the relation is even more likely to change. But in all
cases it is only the *relation* that matters. Change that and the
interactions may change. That is the key.

Genes are necessary conditions for some sorts of change,

and they play this part because they are reliably encountered elements of the internal context for all organisms (In fact it is not just genes that remain relatively constant but can change. All internal phenotypes, bones, muscles, ligaments, gall-bladders, etc. have this dual nature). Environmental states and events are necessary conditions for some sorts of change, and they play this part because they are reliably encountered elements of the external context for all organisms. But only the contingent (not necessary) co-occurrence provides the sufficient conditions. As Gottlieb puts it, 'genes do not make behaviour happen, even though behaviour won't happen without them' (1997, Preface, p. xiii). Exactly the same is true for environments. The point is to find forms of explanation which take due account of the need for all the interacting elements to co-occur and which do not take their contingent occurrence for granted.

There are simpler arguments. Genes do not become more complex so they cannot explain the increasing complexity we see in development. Further, as every single cell in an organism contains the same genes, then if the genes alone are the instructions the changes in every cell must be identical. It follows that there could not possibly be differentiation of any sort between cells. And that hardly makes for any sort of organism, let alone one capable of complex behaviour.

The generation of generic forms: not a job for genetics

You may have realized that this account does not directly challenge the role of genes as being generally crucial for explaining evolutionary change and specifically responsible for the generic developmental forms encountered in biology and psychology. Such a challenge has been spelled out by, amongst others, Brian Goodwin (1995). He describes the development of organisms in terms of morphogenesis, the development of form and structure, in ontogeny or phylogeny. He describes how, despite the great variety in plant and animal life, certain forms are incredibly robust, appearing again and again in a huge variety of species. For example, we can look at a variety of forms of the bones of the limbs of four-legged vertebrates.

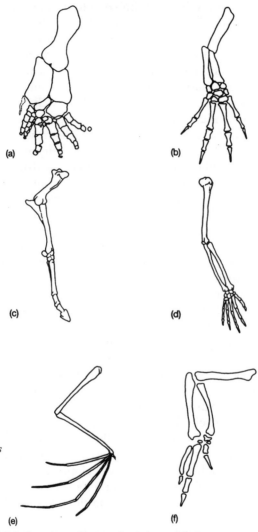

Figure 1 Variations on a theme: the tetrapod limb
a Ichthyostega
b Necturus
c Horse
d Human arm
e Bat wing
f Chicken wing

Source: Goodwin (1995), p.130.

Figure 1 shows the hind-limb of a fossil species of amphibian, (a) *Ichthyostega*, (b) a salamander, (c) the front leg of a horse, (d) a human arm, (e) the wing of a bat, and (f) of a chicken. What diversity of species and of function of limbs involved. Yet all have a basic similarity of form. As Goodwin describes, each starts at the shoulder with a single large bone, then two more major bones followed by a cluster of smaller ones and then digits (and there is a variation, as you can see, in the number of these).What can explain the major similarities? It is not as if they are used for the same purposes. One is for scratching, another for galloping, others for drinking, swimming, flying, walking, kicking. The crucial point is that according to the traditional view of natural selection we simply should not find anything remotely like this. Recall that adaptations are task-specific solutions. The differences in solutions between species, even for superficially similar problems, like how to avoid predators, will be of completely different sorts, involving such diversity of acts as attack, flying, burrowing, camouflage, etc. Even within one species problems of completely different sorts need to be solved by completely different sorts of adaptations. Thus, Darwinian theory predicts fine-tuned specialized adaptations to solve species-specific and context-specific problems. But the generic form of the tetrapod leg across species and functions is not species-specific or function-specific. It is just about the opposite of these. How is this to be explained? As Goodwin notes, the usual response is to claim that selection did operate, but on the already existent ancestral forms, which were then changed by selection to species-fitting versions of the prototype. We are bound to ask, as developmentalists, *how* things develop, what is the origin of the basic, ancestral form, why and how was *it* selected? There is no satisfactory answer to this question from the traditional position.

The fact is that it looks very much as if these legs, arms, wings, number of digits at the end of the form, are but variations on the generic form of the tetrapod limb. The same argument applies to a vast number of other generic forms and variations on them, many of which Goodwin describes. This strongly suggests that the variations can indeed be attributed to the sort of incremental change that does characterize genetic selection, but that the origin of the original generic form has to involve a different sort of selection process. As Goodwin (1995, pp. 133–4) explains:

> Darwinian biology has no principles that can explain why a structure such as the tetrapod limb arises and is so robust in its basic form. This leaves a very large hole in biology as an explanatory science ... However only in this century have the mathematical tools ... been developed ... complex, non-linear dynamic processes that give us some insight into the origins of the structural constraints that can explain the distinctive features of biological form, such as tetrapod limbs.

Further (1995, p. 154):

> The main proposal is that all the main morphological characteristics of organisms – hearts, brains, guts, limbs, eyes, leaves, flowers, roots, trunks, branches, to mention only the obvious ones, are the robust results of morphogenetic principles. There is also a lot of variation of these structures in different species, and it is in these small-scale differences that adaptation and natural selection find a role.

It seems that generic forms emerge from the interactions in dynamic systems and that such forms are then subject to genetic variation, a sort of fine-tuning to fit specific organism/niche systems. Now this is an observation, not an explanation, but given that we know a multitude of interacting factors are involved, and that basic forms are observed to arise in many different sorts of interacting systems, a name is required for this creation of order from disorder. Dynamic systems theories give us such a term, as well as a host of others and of empirical findings for a diversity of systems. It is self-organization, which emphasizes that order is not imposed from outside, is not preformed, but created by and in the dynamic interaction of the multiple and interacting components of the system. We will explore something of the properties of these systems in Chapter 4. Goodwin has started by identifying a problem for 'genetic', i.e. traditional explanations, but ended by proposing a solution along the lines we are just beginning to move towards.

Now Goodwin is writing about physical form but exactly the same argument must apply to psychological form, that is, movement and thought. He writes about the emergence of a fixed structure, a tetrapod limb, but the emergence of jumping as a preferred mode of locomotion on the moon, is just as much a (relatively) stable form. In both cases the form of thinking is identical. Just as jumping, a stable form of action, emerged, was selected, from the incredibly complex sum of interacting forces, so the tetrapod limb emerged as a stable form of organization of bones, etc. from the complexity. And that is how all developmental processes work and developmental products emerge.

We had in genetic programming a form of explanation which in some measure accounted for the differences between species. What we did not have was an explanation which accounts not only for differences between species but for what is shared between them as well. That is what Goodwin gives us. And that is an awful lot.

If you still want to believe that genes have always been the source of evolutionary change, I have one last argument. If genes are the key element by which evolution is to be explained, then what did genes evolve from? I take up this point as well in Chapter 4.

I want to move the critique on now by showing how the very notion of species and gene-pools for them are both incapable of being understood in the traditional way we have been led to believe. Rather, they both need to be seen in terms of dynamic systems, showing elements of self-organization, but not being comprehensible in terms of static, dichotomous thinking.

Species-typical?

Take the case of humans. Wherever humans first lived, it is not in doubt that for a million years or so they lived in a variety of parts of the earth, dispersed, a tiny population on a relatively huge globe. But this tiny population, whether or not they had

started together, in Africa and then migrated, or started separately in different places, had ended up in places where they
were isolated from each other. They were isolated in that they
could not reproduce with more than a tiny part of the population of the human species. Further, as their habitats varied
enormously, the environments to which they were adapting
also had different qualities. In this situation what was adaptive
would vary with the 'niche' and the spread of the genes would
be limited to puddles rather than any species-typical gene
pool. Variations in the genes of isolated sets of groups could
drift (the 'genetic drift' mentioned earlier) from the 'main'
species, especially as they were adapting, as I say, to different
conditions. Thus the accepted notion that the evolution of
species consists in the 'essential' sources of these adaptive
changes, genes, spreading through individuals till they were
species-typical, could not have occurred because the mechanism for the spread, sexual reproduction, was not available
over the whole population in question. The effect would be
that many sub-species of humans evolved, with different gene-
pools, the implication being that there is no such thing as a
human species. This is clearly nonsense and needs clarifying.

Goodwin and his observations of generic forms, self-organization across species, can help. What we commonly find in
practice, and which we will look at in Chapter 4 on the properties of dynamic systems, is the maintenance of robust,
generic forms irrespective of specific contextual variations. We
even see the same generic forms maintained across thousands
of species. That is, they continue to be the typical result of self-
organizing principles in action, even in the face of internal or
external contextual variation, as in the case of the tetrapod leg.
In short, self-organization is a source of stability in the process
of change. This means that generic forms of self-organization
account for a maintenance of the main form of a species,
despite contextual variation, like the contextual variation that
would have been characteristic of the differences in environ-
ment/organism relations between 'human' reproductive
groups. This form of explanation explains why non-reproduc-
ing groups in different environments have not become different sub-species from each other.

There are differences between humans according to their

historical niches, for instance in pigmentation, which we would expect as adaptation has to include sensitivity to local variations, but these consist only in variations to the main generic form. This form has been retained precisely because it is the outcomes of robust principles of self-organization across contexts of all sorts. As I try to argue throughout the book, our accounts have to predict both stability and instability, and to account for sameness and difference, without reference to preformationist dichotomies. This explanation does.

So, 'species-typical' is to be understood as 'that set of generic structural invariances in physiology and functional invariances in behaviour that a set of organisms which could in theory reproduce with each other robustly display despite variations in local conditions'.

I want to end this chapter by emphasizing that Goodwin's argument that the mechanism of genetic selection is nested within that of the broader mechanism of self-organization at the level of morphogenesis, is an important example of the principle I mentioned in the Introduction, that generic, high-level systems constrain – that is, organize within limits – lower-level systems. The generic form of the tetrapod limb is a basic, relatively undifferentiated form, but the variety of such limbs in different species is due to genetic selection within the generic constraints. These latter do not imply variations in the basic form of adaptations but a fine-tuning of them. Morphogenesis in general may be construed as providing a generic, relatively undifferentiated but partial solution to the problem of the selection of adaptive living form or structure, while genetic change provides an extra level of differentiation in the process in the form of incremental refinement of the generic form. The two mechanisms are thus subordinate systems which are combined in a superordinate mechanism for evolutionary change. I have already suggested and will later argue that precisely the same integration of systems of development describes many of the changes we observe in the development of psychological knowledge in humans, and indeed, in a huge variety of species: generic, self-organizing interactions produce knowledge at a relatively undifferentiated level, such knowledge enabling new interactions at successively lower levels which provide more and more differentiated and specific knowledge. Chapters 6 and 7 are devoted to an analysis of and evidence for such systems.

Discussion points

1 Explain how the various dichotomies relate to each other to form a coherent whole.

2 How do the views of a 'gene-centred' biologist, Dawkins, lead to arguments against gene-centred views?

3 How does the the evidence for generic forms across species and functions relate to 'genetic' explanations of development?

4 What are the assumptions underlying preformationist explanations, and how is the view that 'behaviour is regular without being regulated' relate to them?

5 'Information is produced in interactions.' Discuss possible traditional and ecological systems interpretations of this statement.

Chapter 3

Towards the alternative: ecological, dynamic systems

Internal and external structure: equal partners

In this chapter I use two different techniques to try and convince you of the need to change. I start by continuing my description of an alternative way of thinking but then adopt a different way of illuminating the differences in assumptions that the traditional and alternative methods are based upon, describing some case studies which I think let me really draw out differences in the two sorts of thinking involved. One involves an important attempt to dispense with the nature/nurture dichotomy, but it is particularly instructive because we can identify, even within the attempts to change, the forces of traditional thinking restraining the attempt. I hope to clarify both the old and more importantly the new ways of thinking by emphasizing the failure as well as the success of the attempt.

The other two involve contrasting computational metaphors of human thinking and change. One you will be familiar with, to the extent you may not realize it is only a metaphor: the mind as serial computer. The other is a connectionist model, a simple robot in which 'perception', 'cognition' and 'action' are closely coupled. I describe them to show how the different assumptions about dichotomies between perception, cognition and action, between complex mind and simple body, make all the difference to what 'psychology' can be demonstrated by these computers. The aims are again the same, to highlight the way in which assumptions control our thinking, and how different assumptions lead to very different outcomes.

But to prepare the way, some further analysis of ecological and traditional thinking. If the traditional position were valid, we would not find cases where a developmental outcome or behaviour was not attributable to either form of cause. But when the man walked on the moon, or rather, didn't, the assumption that walking was due to 'nature' was violated. But nor was the change in preferred means of locomotion the result of learning. Neither of the traditional explanations work. But they are supposed to form not just exclusive categories, but an exhaustive category system; no other form of explanation is possible. The traditional position cannot be correct. But there is a form of explanation which does account for the observation. We encountered it already when considering the properties of internal, organismic structure and of external, environmental structure. This section is critical.

I observed that genes and indeed many internal products are a universal and necessary part of internal structure for every species, that they display properties both of stability and of change, but that for developmental change to occur requires that exactly the same properties are displayed by the developmentally relevant external conditions with which the internal ones are in interaction. Development thus depends upon the interactions between two sorts of contexts, one internal to the skin and one external to it. At every moment it is in the interactions between and within these two contexts that change occurs and thoughts and actions are selected. Both are necessary for development but only their joint occurrence over the period of the selection of adaptations is sufficient for the change to get established. If and only if the components co-occur can the interactions reliably occur and a system of developmental products reliably emerge. The two contexts in interaction form one system, the developmental system.

In Chapter 7 I briefly consider factors involved in migration and we will see that external factors, like the movement of the stars, and the changing light/dark cycles, and internal factors, like hormonal changes and muscle development, are just a few of the many influences in the interacting complex from which the adaptive action of migration, to the right place at the right time, emerges. When humans walk and how, emerges from the complex interaction of the biodynamics of the body (which have been selected over millions of years) which enables some actions, like arm flexion and alternate leg movement, and prohibits others, like flying, from the external structures and forces, air containing oxygen, gravity, surrounding fluid (gas or liquid) which may afford swimming in but not walking on, and from the psychological structures, motives, intentions, fears, etc. which affect what we would try to do, be scared of, feel obliged in respect of, etc. Which aspects are relevant for a given situation depend upon the relation of organism, context and task at any given moment. If walking up a hill is the task, a change in terrain, mud (increased deformability of surface), altitude, attitude are a few of the many factors involved.

Thus the organization of our bodies affords (makes possible) actions of certain sorts but not of others, as a result of phylogeny, and the organization of the environment affords certain actions or uses but prohibits others. However, the form of influence of each does not act separately of the other. In fact the opposite is true. What the body can or cannot do is totally relative to the conditions, the environment encountered and what the environment affords or constrains depends upon which species or individual we are referring to. Humans can run, but when we say this we are stating a shorthand for 'run if there is a sufficiently rigid surface, oxygen is reliably encountered, etc.', conditions which can change. When attempting to describe the affordances of the external structure the same applies – they mean nothing till we specify the organism as well. The affordances and constraints of a mountain hillside in Rwanda are very different for me than for a gorilla, and even more different for a conifer, or a human infant on their own. The dynamic structure, the organization of the external environment matters, but for understanding and explaining development it is the *relation* of that dynamic structure to the internal dynamic structure that determines developmental and behavioural outcomes. And it cannot matter how long the structure took to develop (talons, brains), only what its characteristics are in relation to those of the environment. Thus the interaction of a structure that just came into being two seconds ago, like my foot on this piece of earth, with one that has been around for a hundred million years is a common event. It does not matter if one was selected in evolutionary time and one in a moment, all that matters is the relation between two interacting structures, just as in the case of the falcon I described in Chapter 2.

Further, what we can and cannot do with an environment is as much to do with psychological factors as internal or external physical ones. These affect what we perceive – what you 'see' depends upon what you need or what you know, and they hugely influence what you think, remember, understand, value, plan – thereby what you may do. Put all three sorts of factors together and we have the following scenario: a human organism which is a specific physical realization, having legs, fingers, joints of various sorts, plus a level of fitness, fatigue, etc., operating in a specific physical ecology which both enables and constrains actions of different sorts, with specific psychological resources and impediments which equally both enable and constrain what thoughts and actions can be chosen. Each of these is meaningless except in relation to the other two. Thus every act we ever carry out occurs only as the complex outcome of interactions between all these sorts of factors. And each of these has a phylogeny and an ontogeny.

In the Introduction we saw that a change in the value of one variable was indeed sufficient to dramatically alter the outcome from the whole pattern of influence: walking was replaced by jumping as the more efficient, preferred mode of locomotion for that internal/psychological/external set or system of affordances and constraints, for the total pattern of forces in interaction at that time for that individual. It was not replaced because of a bodily reason or factor, or a psychological reason or an environmental reason. Nor could it ever be. It was replaced because the overall pattern settled into a different state, self-organized differently. It becomes irrelevant to the ascription of causal power to try to place the origin of the outcome in one part of the causal flux or another. It is only from the whole pattern of forces and constraints that the most efficient pattern of action emerges. This is self-organization.

The organism/environment dichotomy makes no sense in

this world. The inner/outer dichotomy is no help. The biological/learning/social offers nothing. All any of these dichotomies does is to try to break apart what is a unity, to artificially categorize the world. It is the total pattern which matters. Change that pattern, that set of relations, and the action, the functioning of the organism is itself likely to change.

Types of interaction and the integration of nature and nurture revisited

When a young gull pecks at the spot on the beak of the parent herring gull the adult regurgitates food. It is typical for the adults to have the spot, typical for the young to see it, to need food, and to have internal brain structures which interact with the visual input from the spot to lead to pecking at it. This little dynamic, self-organizing system involves species-typical components, of which some are part of the external context and some part of the internal context, in interaction, and has evolved to generally ensure the chick gets food. It 'knows' how to do this in the sense that it does not require practice at specific beaks to learn it. But the beak that was pecked at was a unique beak, and so was the beak pecking it. And of course they were bound to be. There aren't any other sorts of beaks in the material world. These species-typical interactions are thus also necessarily acts of individuals and thereby affected by the individuals characteristics, their particular shape, size, strength, vision, but also their learning, of how to move, given the young gulls relatively weak muscles, of when, given their appetite. Similarly, the gull will be learning various things, which involves interactions between specifics in the external context leading to changes in internal contexts, brain organization. But these changes are totally constrained by what learning and what behaviour is possible for the species. There are separate sorts of interactions, ontogenetic and phylogenetic, in theory, but all necessarily involve the other sort in practice.

Remember the caddis fly that has the evolved capacity to build its own extended phenotype. The larvae typically locate, pick up and manipulate individual stones during their unique life, stones which may not have existed when the extended phenotype first evolved. But the action of the caddis must be tailored to the exact position and weight of individual stones, fitting their species-typical action exactly to the unique contexts they are encountering. The construction of this extended phenotype thus only emerges from the combination of knowledge afforded by species-typical interactions, knowledge of action in the species-typical context, and knowledge afforded by individual interactions between the individual larvae and the individual contexts they encounter, knowledge of size, location, and adaptive action in respect of the individual stones under analysis. That stones have locations and extension is species-typical, but the particular locations and size are not. Production of the adaptive phenotype is dependent upon using both sorts of knowledge together. As we will see, this ability for systems to arise in which products of interactions over phylogenetic time and those in ontogenetic time are integrated together is of great import for the evolution of developmental systems.

These are not special cases. Behavioural outcomes will always be a function of phylogenetic (contingent interactions which have been selected over evolutionary time) factors and ontogenetic factors (contingent interactions selected during an individual lifetime). It is impossible for an individual organism not to be operating within its phylogenetic context. But it is equally impossible for a species to change in any other way than through and in the individual lives in individual contexts of individual members of the species.

Selection of cognition and action ignores the origin or location of factors

Again, however long these interactions have been going on, irrespective of whether they arose over evolutionary or ontogenetic time, the outcomes depend upon the contingent presence and thereby interaction of the relevant components, like beaks and visual input and brains. For instance, cognitive impairment to the herring gull chick, a contingent state, can immediately stop the species-typical interaction of internal and external structure required for the peck to occur, however long that adaptation had taken to evolve. The loss of the (contingent) value of gravity species-typically encountered on earth immediately led to the start of a self-organization of loco-motion. In this case (and in all others) it matters not one iota that the physical structure of the human body has taken evolutionary time to develop and has done so in ways heavily constrained by the invariant force of gravity on earth, etc., while the contingent interaction of a human body trying to get around on a surface which afforded walking but with a changed force of gravity for the first time in the history of that species (apart from simulation), had only just occurred seconds before. The phylogenetic context and the immediate gravitational context interacted and produced a novel outcome for the history of the species.

What is selected in natural selection?

Darwinian explanations of adaptations did not specify the precise circumstances, the specific context in which a behavioural phenotype would be adaptive. They would identify some general connections, such as between type of beaks and types of food available. With no detail of context the explanation that a change is adaptive is bordering on the preformationist, 'If it exists, it must have been adaptive', being given as the explanation of the adaptation, with no independent evidence of adaptive value. Even a view like that of Gabora and Colgan (1991), in which it is claimed that adaptations are relatively specific solutions to specific problems, like avoiding predators or obtaining energy, is wide open to criticism because although 'avoiding predators' is an understandable logical category, it is a meaningless ecological category because it is an abstraction. It is not grounded in the material world of specific events as it specifies no particular predator in no particular contexts and therefore no real material situation in which success or otherwise could be an outcome. Ideas cannot be selected, only material states and events in particular contexts.

Consider a prey trying to escape by running down a burrow. A successful outcome depends upon it being able to perceive when the predator is nearby, where the burrow is, being able to navigate quickly and accurately towards the burrow, not to mention being small enough to fit, having means of locomotion, etc. But it also depends upon the characteristics of the prey, the fact that it cannot go down burrows, that it can perceive you and catch you, etc. Both sorts of capacities are a mixture of phylogenetic and ontogenetic considerations, as the evolved visual powers of the predator, for instance, are brought to bear, while the particular experiences of this escaper aid or inhibit survival. But even the skills, attributes, limitations of each are only part of the story because what is critical here is the relation between the powers of the prey and of the predator, for a given physical situation. Suppose our predator is a fast digger, or comes to be able to get down burrows, the whole 'game' may change. Just as the reliable co-occurrence of genes and external contexts has been identified as crucial for development, so we can now begin to see that what is selected in this scenario has to be the reliable co-occurrence of all the relations between predator and prey. Change one aspect, the rest may have to reorganize. The means of avoiding predators is thus determined by the powers or affordances the predator has, those the prey has, and these include those arising from the relations of the prey and the predator to the physical geography. The physics of the body of the prey and of the predator and the geography combine together to determine whether a given sort of behaviour will be adaptive. The unit of selection is all of these.

Look what happens if it is not, if one factor is changed. We could have an animal that was brilliant at disappearing down burrows, but not when the predator appeared, or brilliant at running when it appeared, but not down burrows, or brilliant at perceiving predator and burrow, but failing to run. None of these are of any use, none can be adaptive, and thus selected, because the only thing that can be adaptive is the *systematic combination* of the perception of the predator, the perception of location of burrow, and the act of getting down it quickly, given the predator dynamics.

A different species has different characteristics and so even if preyed on by the same bird of prey may need to make use of different affordances, e.g. camouflage, because the pattern of relations is different. If burrows disappeared it is surely clear that the whole system by which predator avoidance (and thus prey capture by the bird as well) for this species of prey and predator could completely change. It would become reorganized to 'take account' of all the sorts of factors we have been talking about. The developmental system itself evolved in the face of this dynamic complexity.

Mixed paradigms: case studies in confusion

One: orientation to faces

As I wrote above, I now adopt a different method of making the assumptions underpinning the alternative paradigms clearer, by describing case studies in which the embeddedness of traditional assumptions within a study or a metaphor can be teased out, hopefully showing more clearly how a whole way of thinking must be subject to clear critique if we are to adopt an alternative.

The first case involves the use of studies of attention to 'faces' and subsequent learning about them. This work is described in an important book by Johnson and Morton (1991) *Biology and Cognitive Development: The Case of Face Recognition*, a book that helped me a great deal. First I outline their position. They had reviewed and carried out research which showed the operation of two distinct mechanisms in chicks, one involving preferential orientation to a 'mother' chicken before there had been opportunities to learn what it looked like, and the other involving learning to recognize the individual chicken, typically the mother in the natural environment. As it is generally necessary to attend to an object to learn to recognize it, the function of the first mechanism is to enable the second, with the result that the chick learns to recognize 'mother' at the earliest opportunity. Johnson and Morton hypothesized that a similar mechanism operated in human infants with respect to orientation to the human face. They replicated the studies of Goren, Sarty and Wu (1975) and Dziurawiec and Ellis (1986), and performed their own experiments which indicated that infants as young as 42 minutes and up to four weeks of age would track a two-dimensional model of a face on a 'bat' as it appeared at the periphery of their visual field and was moved across it, more often than they would track a non-face or scrambled-face 'bat'. Figure 2 shows the stimuli used, and Figure 3 those used in a similar experiment with older infants, based on Maurer and Barrera (1981).

It was argued that there was no time for the infants to have learned about the shape of human faces (we shall question this

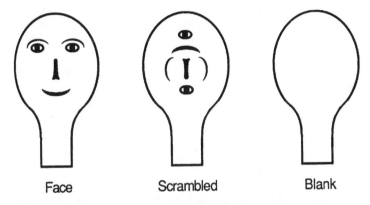

Face   Scrambled   Blank

Figure 2 The three stimuli used in the replication of Goren, Sarty and Wu (1975)
Source: Johnson and Morton (1991), p. 31.

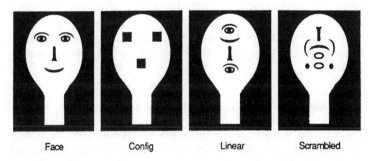

Face   Config   Linear   Scrambled

Figure 3 The four stimuli used in the attempted replication of Maurer and Barrera's study
Source: Johnson and Morton (1991), p. 34.

later), yet they turn preferentially to any human-face-like visual input. The appearance of a conspecific, a member of one's own species, is a species-typical event. Turning to the face is independent of learning (again we will question this later) and appears to be itself typical. The orientation involves species-typical input, and it is an act, an event, not in any way like a face, a state. Orientation to the conspecific allows the infant to start to learn to recognize the individual involved, the mother, and like all learning, the representation is like that which it is a representation of. Thus the first part of the mechanism appears to have several species-typical, unlearned features. Within two months evidence of a preference for mother's individual-specific face began to emerge.

Johnson and Morton used the distinction between the species-typical and individual-specific inputs to identify different levels of interaction in development without recourse to the nature/nurture dichotomy. Instead of having to use terms like 'innate', with its connotations of fixed behaviour independent of experience, they proposed that there was a system of interactions based upon species-typical external environmental input interacting with the brain, and that this constituted the developmental system. Such interactions were termed primal. A mechanism for what had been inadequately termed 'innate' had been supplied. Then other sort of interactions, learning, take over based upon taking account of individual-specific input. The two sets of interactions together thus form one mini-system of information-production. The only proviso, but a critical one, is that where the learning is itself basic and typical for the species, e.g. learning to speak, individual-specific input must count as part of the developmental system.

The retention of preformationist thinking

I want now to offer some thoughts about the ways in which their thinking appears to be constrained by the traditional assumptions, and to offer an alternative. First, the location of information. This is what Johnson and Morton (1991, p. 85) have to say about the primal mechanism. It is:

a cognitive mechanism *in the neonate's brain* [emphasis mine] with the following properties:

1 The mechanism contains structural information concerning the visual characteristics possessed by conspecifics. By 'structural' we mean that the information is concerned with relative spatial position of elements within a pattern . . . We . . . use the term Conspec for the device, since it specifies conspecifics in the context of the species-typical environment.

As the relevant biological event that occurs is the movement of the infant face to see and follow the species-typical face, and it occurs after an interaction, between the external species-typical input and some part of the (species-typical) brain, we should conclude that information arises from the interaction, and is not usefully said to be preformed in the brain, or anywhere else. Johnson and Morton are de-emphasizing the need for coupled internal and external structure to co-exist and interact for relevant outcomes to occur and emphasizing a preformation of information. They are writing as if there is a preformed internal structure against which external structure is compared (how?) till a match is made and as if one component of an interaction could produce information on its own.

Lack of appreciation of the equal status of interacting factors

Johnson and Morton refer on many occasions to the 'species-typical environment'. They always mean the external environment. But the internal species-typical environment, part of the brain in this instance, is equally important. The adaptive movement of the head is the outcome of the interaction of aspects of the external and internal species typical contexts. The focus on just one component in this interaction inhibits the appreciation that it is in and only in the interaction between organism and environment that adaptive outcomes emerge and that both sorts of components have equal status in this interaction.

The coupling of perception and action and the issue of representation

There is also an undue emphasis upon the purely perceptual aspects of the process. The description of Conspec refers only to the visual characteristics of a human face. But without the infant tracking the moving image, no adaptive change can accrue. For an adaptive outcome, movement was required and movement was duly produced. As I have tried to emphasize, a perceptual ability on its own could not be selected, as it is only action-in-context which works or doesn't. Johnson and Morton may be led to describe what goes on in terms of the neonate having a built-in knowledge of the human face because they accept the basic assumption that representations are the key to action. And they may be committed to that view because they conceive of perception and cognition and action as separate – first there is an act of perception, then the brain makes a decision about what is really out there, cognition, then it makes a decision about what to do about it, action. This is still standard thinking, consistent with a view of psychological processes as independent of each other, not coupled as an ecological view would assume. Later in this chapter I examine this encapsulated view of psychological functioning in an attempt to show why the serial computer metaphor of successive, discrete processors and processes is not useful or empirically based. In my view we cannot infer that there is a representation of a face in the brain. And we don't need to. What we can infer is that some structure, some invariances are 'picked up' by the neonate and that these are directly coupled to action in respect of that input. There is no need to speculate about the nature of inner processes, what matters is to state the relation between what is in the environment and what the infant does about it. What has been selected is the turning of head to a specific contextual item (face-like thing, no awareness implied) when that item is encountered. It is initially no different to a gull chick's peck. It becomes different, because, as we shall see later, humans can de-couple action and thought.

The failure to explore the dyad as the unit of analysis

Johnson and Morton also pay little attention to the actions of the mother in this scenario, focusing completely on a structure in the head of the neonate. But the 'preference' for the species-typical face may be just as much due to actions by the mother to manipulate the attention systems of the newborn, her positioning and actions affording highly interesting and information-rich input, as Bushnell (1998) suggests. Certainly her actions are important, though the fact that the neonates did track a two-dimensional model of a face on a 'bat' moving, hardly the ultimate in salient input, suggests that is also not the whole story. Rather, if the dyadic system is the unit of analysis, it follows that we see the actions of both parties as equally important. Remember, we cannot reasonably infer that the main causal power resides in the organism or the environment. In this case the main element of the environment is an organism, usually mother, but the logic is the same, causal outcomes only emerge from the flux of interactions involving organism and environment, and the system of dyadic interaction is the unit of selection here, not the acts of a component.

Change as continuous, not dichotomous

Johnson and Morton also appear to retain a dichotomous view of the sorts of changes that occur in the process of development: either the change is species-typical and unlearned, or it is individual-specific and learned. There is no recognition that the process may involve a gradually increasing differentiation of the environment. But consider this evidence. Walton, Bower and Bower (1992), for instance, obtained higher amplitude sucking to produce a video of mother's face at 12–36 hours, compared with a face that was not mother's, and Bushnell (1998) reports several other studies showing recognition of something that functioned to discriminate between mother and another. But these results are explained by realizing that it is probably only differences in shape of head and hair that are the basis for differentiation in the first days. At two months physiognomic differences are the basis of preference (de Schonen, Mancini and Liegeois, 1998, p. 115). That is, it is important to see development as a gradual increase in differentiation, as changes along a continuum, rather than in terms of an unlearned/learned dichotomy.

The 'generic/specific' continuum of knowledge

Johnson and Morton seem to focus on the unlearned species-typical aspect of the first primal interaction, as if its relation to 'innateness' was important. Given what I have suggested about the importance of generic constraints or effects on sub-systems, I suggest the orientation should be mainly regarded as involving relatively undifferentiated perceptual, cognitive and motor abilities which result in limiting learning, focusing in certain areas, without specifically determining exactly what is learned. The learning that does occur will involve a variety of more specific, differentiated information, for example about particular aspects of communication, about self and others in interaction, about intermodality. These are more differentiated sorts of knowledge than is involved in the generic preference for faces, but all afforded by, made possible by, the constraining effect of the narrowing of attention, the limiting of what is perceived and thus available for learning about. This is our first concrete example in human development of the principle that generic interactions produce knowledge at a relatively undifferentiated level, such knowledge enabling new interactions at lower levels which provide more differentiated and specific knowledge.

The multiple affordances of primal interactions

Johnson and Morton focus on only one function of the primal act, to aid recognition learning. But systems are messy. Attention to the face of a significant caregiver affords the best opportunities for the infant and the caregiver to gain maximal information about the state of the person they are with; it affords viewing of the movements of the face, the eyes, the mouth, movements in space and time; it does so for the caregiver as well and as this means the two can perceive their own and the others acts, it means learning about contingencies in interaction can occur, the perception of 'turn-taking', for instance, being afforded; it also affords the chance to notice contingencies between the different behaviours of the 'other', such as the changing shape of their mouth as they speak, the changing of their expression as their voice changes (in tension, in relaxation), etc. This single example of a primal interaction shows how a simple movement, orientation to a face, can afford significant and complex development opportunities. It also points to the dangers of the interaction not taking place, though it may be that there are other means of obtaining the preferential attention.

Different extensions of invariance within the same 'stimulus'

There is a developmental aspect to this research which is again not focused on by Johnson and Morton. They refer to the species-typical input of a human face, but the fact is that what is perceived itself follows a developmental pathway. Figure 4 shows roughly how the 'face', the 'effective environment for just one aspect of the world', changes with time. In addition, as I have made clear, every species-typical input is necessarily also a unique, individual-specific instance, though the perceived face varies.

Figure 4 shows how the same face might appear to a newborn compared to how it appears to someone with high visual acuity, which is the same as saying how it will normally appear to the same person later in their development. The external invariances constituting the species-typical face are less differentiated than those required for personal identification in the individual-specific interactions. At one point in development the former invariances are informative while the latter are not, but the operation of the former enables interactions by which the latter become informative. The process of development itself transforms the external environment. It becomes what it was not. Again, there are not two faces, but a continuum of them, the differentiation gradually emerging. The 'same' face is many faces.

Moreover, further thought again demonstrates the integration of what is 'species-typical' (related to nature) and what is specific (related to nurture), as follows. A species-typical face has invariances which are not specific to an individual, so what to look at can be known by the undifferentiated interaction, but where to look can be known only by a differentiated interaction, because the face is in an exact position. Part of the mechanism must thus be sensitive to this aspect of local context, position and movement, and part to the species-typical context. For successful completion of the first part of the task, the infant must not only utilize the invariances specifying that there is a

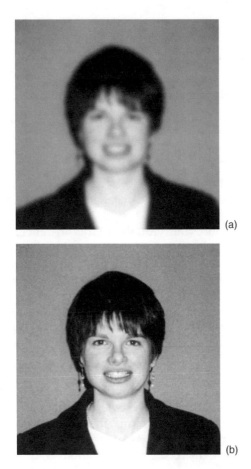

(a)

(b)

Figure 4 A face, as it migh. appear (a) to a newborn, (b) to us

species-typical human about, that is, the 'what' problem must be sorted, it must also specify where it is in order to attend to it, thus solving the 'where' problem. The 'what' is dependent upon utilization of extensions which have lasted over species-typical space and time, the 'where' by extensions of seconds and centimetres. This is another example of phylogenetic and ontogenetic factors being integrated, of 'nature' and 'nurture', interacting in systematic ways to utilize the invariances in the environment. Species-typical actions have to include this 'sensitive-to-this-moment' aspect for them to work.

Variations in faces and the interacting factors involved

I will devote some time to this topic later, but here I mention it as the differences between faces constitutes a nice example of how there is no dichotomy between faces as 'species-typical' or 'unique'. It is not only the phenomenal face that varies with development, actual faces also vary to some extent according to racial origin, an extension of invariance between species-typical and individual. But then we will think of family resemblances, another extension of invariance. But faces also vary according to age, an interesting case in that there is a species-typical aspect to the change for the species during life (the change is relatively invariant for the species), and an individual aspect. You may well now be thinking that there are gender differences as well, and then move on to conjecture how species, racial, age, gender, familial, aspects of facial invariance interact with each other and with external environmental contingencies. Thus, there are great variations between instances of what is still invariant enough for it to be recognized by all, a face, and variations in the extent to which we can extract invariances coupled to ones developmental level, not mention quality of vision, etc. This is what dynamic theories appreciate, the nature of complexity, the amazing amount of variation, of interaction and yet of stability as well. The emphasis on a simple learned/not learned dichotomy signally fails to do justice to what we actually encounter.

The effects of non-obvious early experience

Johnson and Morton seem to suggest that nothing relevant to preferences or to other primal interactions occurs before birth. This itself may be linked to the traditional idea that the neonate is incompetent and that nothing useful for cognitive development could have previously occurred. Far from it. Prenatal experience is particularly relevant in so far as it involves the first searches of task spaces, the first attempts to act in and on their world – which, of course, the developing infant does not know is going to change dramatically at about nine months. All such motor and perceptual (especially but not only auditory) experience, and thereby reorganization, learning, are precursors to and conditions of, later differentiation. Given also that we shall find strong evidence that information in one mode is informative for other modes, so that, for instance, movement of one's own face in the womb can be 'recognized' when the infant sees another face, the conclusion has to be that a great deal of relevant experience has already occurred before birth and that again the notion of a continuum of differentiation is more relevant than the dichotomy between what is learned and what is not.

Gottlieb (1997) and others have found evidence in birds which demonstrates the significance of prenatal, perceptual experience. One case involves wood ducklings. He found they failed to show a preference for their mother's call after hatching unless they had heard, whilst still in the egg, the alarm call of their siblings, and that it was a specific aspect of that call that was critical, a drop in frequency towards the end of the call, which was very similar to the adult mother's call. With mallard ducklings it was their own call they needed to hear, but in both cases he found that the function, the effect of the initial auditory experience, was to reduce the range of frequency of input to which the duckling was sensitive. Because 'mother's' call was within this range, whilst other ducks calls were not, this effectively meant that they normally heard their mothers call, but not that of other species and thus did react to mother and did not react to the calls of other species.

Sleigh, Columbus and Lickliter (1998) found that bobtail quail chicks which were exposed to species-typical, maternal auditory input (mother's call) but not simultaneously to species-typical maternal visual input (sight of mother) did not develop a preference for the sight and sound of 'mother' over the sight of a different species of quail hen emitting the bobwhite call. The experience of concurrent maternal auditory and visual input was necessary for the later preference to be shown. These cases show that 'primal' interactions may depend not only on upon relevant environmental input at the time, but on earlier, even more undifferentiated (even more primal) interactions. So even interactions which we are only just coming to accept as requiring relevant input, not being 'innate', may depend upon previous, non-obvious experience. These results are discussed in Chapter 7, but I raise them here to show that even when the earliest experiences are of a relatively undifferentiated nature, their developmental effects can be of great significance, and to indicate that we may only be beginning to see how far off the mark our notions of the causes of development have been.

Two: disembedded mind or embedded robot

The serial computer metaphor: why it is so powerful, but why it is so wrong

In this first case I want to show how the general metaphor of the human mind as akin to a serial computer served, serves still, to help maintain preformationist and dichotomous thinking, by itself being based upon the same assumptions. We begin with the uncontroversial notion of the human as a brilliant information processor, like a computer but much, much better. Humans process raw perceptual data, use a central set of representations to classify it and make decisions, and carry out the appropriate behaviour. So do serial computers. They input data into the appropriate format, find solutions through the application of the central programme, and decode the decision into the designated form of output or print-out. In addition, both the serial computer and the mature human mind operate with symbols, an abstract formal code, with the resultant power to classify and categorize in terms of criterial qualities and to operate in a 'disembedded' manner, not being tied to specific contexts or instances. Moreover, just as serial computers carry out separate, successive information-processing operations and sends the processed data, as so often indicated on a flow chart, to the next processing unit, so humans have the separate processes of perception, cognition and action by which intelligent action is achieved (Newell, Shaw and Simon, 1958; Marr, 1982; Fodor, 1983; Gardner, 1987; Johnson-Laird, 1988). For some years it was accepted by all but a tiny minority of stalwarts (e.g. Still and Costall, 1991) that this was a most useful way to conceive of the functioning of the human mind, that its structure and functioning was basically of the same general sort as a serial computer.

A key feature here is the relation of perception, cognition and action to each other. In human development the assumption is that individual acts of perception can only reveal appearances, while acts of cognition, using concepts (symbols and the like) reveal reality. Perception is thus totally separate from cognition, merely providing raw, basic data for the complex representational structures to analyze and make sense of. The ability to use concepts thus allows one to be sure that any particular instance of, for instance, a sexist act, or a hedgehog, can be correctly classified and not mistaken because a decision was based only upon its appearance which will include contextual, 'interfering' features. Input to computers similarly has no role in complex thinking, it merely gives the programme something to work with, raw data. There is an absolutely clear distinction between raw data and the programme, the software, just as there is between perception and cognition in the traditional model. Similarly, the output from a computer is disconnected from the complex analysis of data, being merely a form of presentation of results, a digital print-out, graphs, statistical tables, the written word, whatever. Computer output has to be the analogue of behaviour, so again the metaphor is taken to be apt because action and output are not where complexity lie, because that is back in the programme. The same sort of thinking extends to buildings, etc. We understand that when we are told that a certain bridge or palace was built by a famous individual, we know that what we are intended to understand is that the complicated, intelligent work, the design, was done by this person, and the names of those who did build it is irrelevant. The output is connected to the processing in one direction only, it is directed by it but has no direct effect on it. The 'hub', all the complexity, is based in the central programme. Both perception and action, input and output, have the same epistemological status and function in the production of knowledge – very low.

But humans and indeed many species show amazing skill in adapting sensitively to variation in the physical or mental terrain, subtle abilities to cope with unexpected environmental contingencies throughout their lives. Indeed, intelligent action is precisely that which does show the ability to sensitively adjust to new situations and which is not stereotyped and rigid in its form. This sensitivity to context, this coupling of organism and environment in action, is emphasized in the ecological view. Each organism must be able to perceive the salient features of its environment, must know what context it is operating in in order to act according to particular conditions. And as situations change, the ability to notice this and react to it must be part of the design. Now how can this be ensured? The simple and compelling answer is that there must be a strong and permanent coupling maintained between its action systems, its perceptual systems and its cognitive systems. Only in this way can the organism maintain sensitivity to change and do something about it. When this is the way functioning is organized we are seeing a system in action, the organism-in-environment system. It is systems which need to be understood and the individual organism is part of an ecosystem. This much is accepted, part of espoused theory and yet we retain a metaphor for thinking based upon the exact opposite.

The conclusion has to be that the concept of ecology simply has no relevance to this information processor. It is the only intelligent thing that ever existed that did not have to display a sensitive relation to its ecology and in which the cleverness was nothing to do with its actual effect on the material environment, but only on what was inside. It is a powerful but lonely organism. It is a mind conceived as superior to its environment, imposing order on it and orders about it through its physical outputs.

I suggest the metaphor was and is widely accepted because it reinforces the underlying assumption that the character of the internal, preformed, complex mental processes is basically unrelated to the particular contexts from which they derive, namely, material action in the material world. The computer software is the mind, the hardware is the body. In the mature mind, what the body does does not affect the complexity of the mind. In the complex programme the output does not affect the programme. The software makes sense of raw data. Cognition makes sense of perceptual data. The mind imposes meaning on an otherwise meaningless world. It is boss. The body merely carries out what it is ordered to do. In short, the metaphor reinforces the 'mind/body' dichotomy. It does the same for 'nature/nurture'. 'Nature' corresponds to the simple, bodily hardware functions, 'nurture' to the complex mental ones, distinct from the hardware. Hence we find that the supposedly archaic notion of preformation never left the serial computer – the programme is the homunculus, the 'mind' of the computer, rendering bodily action (print-out) and perception (raw material data) redundant in the production of knowledge.

None of this implies that the design of computers has to be totally different to people. I am now going to describe a computer in which perception, cognition and action are closely coupled. It is one without a complex central programme. In fact its starting points are positively feeble. In so far as it has a programme at all, it simply links its sensing (perception) to its outputs (action) and records what it does. It is a parallel processor, not a serial processor, based upon a connectionist mode of thinking. And yet its performance turns out to be pretty impressive, absolutely impossible according to the traditional view. It proves that complexity can emerge without complex built-in representations, that preformation is not necessary, that mind and body, nature and nurture, can be united.

Case study of complexity from simplicity, without the use of concepts

This case is about a robot designed by Mataric (Mataric and Brooks, 1990; Mataric, 1990, 1992), itself based on Brooks' initial work at the MIT Artificial Intelligence Lab between 1986 and 1992 (e.g. Brooks, 1986, 1991) and described by Hendriks-Jansen (1996) and Clark (1997b). Like many 'organisms', it can detect surfaces, compass direction and has a memory. The robot is fitted with 12 sonar detectors, one covering each 30 degrees of the surrounding space, detecting surfaces and their approximate distance. It will avoid walls it is approaching by the two 'ahead' sensors prescribing 'back off' when activated (a bit like a 'reflex'). It will turn appropriately at a corner by an arrangement that dictates that it turns 30 degrees away from the nearer wall, and will keep doing so until it is not nearer (which is when it has turned 90 degrees). Similarly, detectors on each side measure the distance of the surface away, and the rule effectively makes it turn away from the nearest wall if less than a specified distance away. In this way it can traverse a corridor or an irregular 'tunnel'. If the corridor is straight the changes in direction will normally be alternate, as it 'corrects' going nearer the left side and then corrects again as it nears the other side. If in an irregular corridor the record of its turns will itself be irregular. As a result of these basic sensors and rules for how to react, the robot can manoeuvre itself in the environment. Because the power source and the functioning of the sensors vary slightly, the specific route it takes each time is never identical to another, but it does follow the same general path.

In addition to this system of 'reflex-like' rules and acts, the robot records its own movement, and the sensor readings. But the combination of recording its own movement, plus this simple 'sense data', which corresponds to surfaces and their distance away, means that a record of routes taken exists, and of landmarks, and of where the landmarks are in relation to its route.

Another level displays this data in the form of a map, showing the various positions of the robot when it carried out its manoeuvres, i.e. when it reached landmarks, and the position of objects as inferred by sensor readings. It is effectively a map of action over time with landmarks picked out. The movement and the inferred objects are shown in Figure 5.

Note, these are not programmes or plans, but only records, little more complicated than say, a pen-recorder for climate data. Further, this cartographic whiz kid always records and thus checks every landmark on every journey. Hence, as the robot travels around, every time it reaches a landmark the current record either reinforces previous ones or constitutes the start of another one. The result is the robot whose only rules for action are reflexes and only extra help is the ability to sense and record what it has done when, ends up with a map of the landmarks which is continually updated.

Not only this, the robot can move to a desired location using

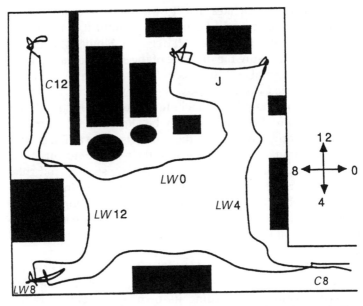

Figure 5 A robot's reflexive navigation behaviour in a cluttered office environment. Labels include landmark type and compass bearing (*LW*8 = left wall heading south; *C*0 = corridor heading north; *J* = long irregular boundary).
Source: Clark (1997), p. 48; based on Mataric (1992).

its record. The way this occurs is as follows. First, follow the route of the robot (Figure 6a). It goes from *C*8 to *LW*8 to *LW*12 to *C*12 to *LW*0 to *J* to *LW*4 and thus to starting point *C*8. There is also a direct connection between *LW*0 and *LW*12, as shown in Figure 6b. The map is electrical and current position is specified by an active node, electrical activity at a point. When a route to a destination is required the destination node is activated and the home node spreads activation through the connections to the destination node. So, from say, *LW*0 to *LW*12 there are three possible routes, via *C*12, via, *J*, *LW*4, etc., or straight to *LW*12. The shortest path defines the best route.

A map is an internal representation. Yet our robot was not even given an internal representation of a wall, let alone corridors, corners and the like. It has no purposes, no goals, no

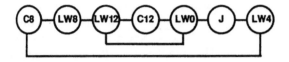

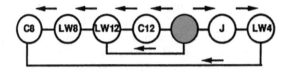

Figure 6 A map constructed by a robot in the environment shown in Figure 5

a Topological links between landmarks indicate physical spatial adjacency.
b The map actively carried out path finding. Shaded node is goal node. Arrows indicate spreading of activation from goal.

Source: Clark (1997), p. 48; based on Mataric (1992).

programmes. It ends up with something very like representations, but this one was built totally from simple action in context. The complexity only emerged *from* that action in those places and was in no way responsible *for* the apparently intelligent action and mapping. This robot has a space–time record of its perceptions (of own movement and surfaces) and this is sufficient to navigate efficiently. It has no master plan, in fact no plan at all, and no symbolic representations. It works from the bottom-up, from personal experience, dealing with local issues, not from the top-down, obeying the orders of some central authority divorced from local conditions. There is no need for a map separate from the action of the robot, one that the 'mind' looks at. The map controls action because it specifies directly action-in-context.

It is important to realise that different sensors, or slightly different rules for what to do when they are activated, or a different environment, would *all* have led to different actions by the robot. For instance, a more sensitive set of sensors would 'notice' smaller irregularities in a corridor, so the map of action or objects/surfaces would be a different one. It would not be a right or wrong one as any map is always determined by the relation of the sensors (perceptual ability) to the state of the environment. The 'map' is the *effective* environment, the environment for that 'organism', with its motor, perceptual and cognitive resources. Give the robot (or organism) slightly different sensors or rules, and the map, the world for the robot, will be a different one. Hence the action and the map must be seen to be properties of the robot and the properties of the environment *in relation to* each other. The explanation of the behaviour and the map that emerges involves statements about these *relations*, not about some internal controllers preformed goals and plans. The behaviour emerges from the interaction of the internal (the sensor functions and the 'reflexes') and external contexts, and so does the map, the nearest equivalent to a representation, exactly what I have been saying about how behaviour emerges for any organism, including humans. The robot develops complexity from coupled action, perception and cognition. And so do we.

Mataric's robot is a real practical example of the lack of need to assume built-in complexity or the existence of internal mental entities with powers that are distanced from real action in the real world. The traditional view, in which perception and action are not coupled, absolutely requires that Mataric's robot 'must' have had representations of left corners, right corners, long corridor, short corridor, windy path, etc., because the only way to explain it avoiding them or following them is to assume that it compares input with its pictures of the world, finds the appropriate representation of, for instance, a left corner, and thereby sends out a message 'this is a left corner, so you should produce the turn right programme at this point'. Sounds sensible, but it didn't happen.

Connectionism

I add here a note about connectionist modelling, because I think it is hard to grasp. It is based upon totally different assumptions to that of serial processing in that the computer is not given a predetermined (preformed) programme. Instead, it is limited to a few basic rules which can be varied by the experimenter to see what difference different starting points make to the emergence of the state of the model. The model consists of electrical systems with nodes, points at which inputs arrive and outputs leave. There are various sorts of nodes in a model. When exposed to input, activity results and currents flow in various directions, through various nodes. It is then repeatedly exposed to patterns of input, and variations to the 'rules' like which nodes connect to which others or with what likelihood, are made to maximize the similarity of the computer output with the input to it. What is amazing is that complex programmes emerge, exactly as if the programme had been given complex representations to start with. In addition, the development of the programme often 'mimics' the abrupt developmental transitions observed in humans. The only way this can happen is if there was complexity in the structure of the environment in the first place, because apart from some not complex rules, that is the only source of information the model has. All the complex structures, like grammatical rules, which have been found to emerge in connectionist models can be accounted for only by acknowledging that these external structures (what we shall later call 'higher-order invariances') can be picked up by models which are sensitive to input. It is like the robot. Its ability to get about and have a map and select routes were based upon its ability to detect input, from its sensors and its own movement. That is all that is required. You will find that this ability to detect external structure, to 'pick up' invariance, is exactly what the foremost ecological psychologist, J. J. Gibson, wrote that people could do. Thus, ecological and systems thinking is not anti-computational, but it is anti-compartmental, anti-dichotomies.

Enough of the case studies. In Chapter 4 we become acquainted with the key features of one of the two existing areas of theorizing and empirical research which should illuminate the ecological, systems thinking about development, dynamic systems views.

Discussion points

1 Present arguments to show the need for a dynamic, organism/environment view of development.

2 Why does the writer emphasise 'the interactive complex', rather than environments and organisms? What sorts of factor are included in 'the interactive complex' from which behavioural or developmental outcomes emerge?

3 Give examples of the selection of action which shows how it is coupled to both external and internal structure.

4 Name a strength of Johnson and Morton's (1991) ideas, and common themes in the criticisms of it.

5 Compare the utility of the computational metaphors for serial and parallel processors.

6 Consider the organization of a termite colony. Can you see parallels with the robot's functioning?

Chapter 4

Dynamic systems theories

The critique of Darwinian theory and more broadly of dichotomous and preformationist thinking about development has already led towards a dynamic developmental systems view, in which a complex of interacting factors make up the causal flux. Hopefully, my arguments already make you feel unsure about the traditional view, but the case would be strengthened if the alternative were more articulate. Dynamic systems theories provide us with with some of the means to be more explicit. In this chapter I will outline its key features, based on the work of Swenson and Turvey (1991); van der Maas and Molenaar (1992); Lockman and Thelen (1993); Thelen and Smith (1994); Goldfield, (1995); Connolly and Forssberg (1997); Dent-Reed and Zukow-Goldring (1997); van der Maas and Hopkins (1998); and Wimmers *et al.* (1998).

Main properties of dynamic systems

Dynamic systems views are a completely different sort of theoretical animal than traditional perspectives. The most unusual aspect is the generality of their application. We have come to accept that change such as involved in 'evolution' and 'development' involves genes, and certainly living things, and thus to assume that change in the inanimate world cannot be explained using the same principles. Dynamic systems theorists argue that their theories apply to everything that exists. Consider this argument. As I implied earlier, genes cannot be the source of all evolutionary change as they evolved from something that wasn't genes, but was physical matter. That is, during the process of evolution living things came into being from non-living things. So we know that in order to explain evolution we need a theory in which the principles apply both to the inanimate and animate worlds as they have to include the explanation of the evolution of one from the other. Dynamic theorists do not assume a dichotomy between the principles explaining change for the two sorts of matter, animate and inanimate. On the contrary, their position is that as the principles apply to the interactions of matter, they must apply to both. Of course this does not mean that as humans are intentional organizers and planners of their actions, then so are tornados, for instance. Precisely because humans (and other animals) are designed to be self-promoting, to continue to exist, they have evolved ways of incorporating information about the environments they encounter, unlike the tornado. But it does mean that dynamic systems should be found equally in the functioning of the heart, the atmosphere, snowflakes and psychology. And they are. Look first at Figure 7.

It shows the now famous pattern that emerges from a mixture of organic and inorganic chemicals studied by Beloussev and Zhabotinsky in the 1950s and 1960s, and now named the BZ reaction, in which, to simplify, bromous acid is produced. It looks like this because a cycle of interaction keeps repeating itself. Now look at Figure 8. Very similar, yes. Involves the same chemical interaction? No, it is not a chemical reaction at all, but shows the changes that occur

Figure 7 Spiral patterns in the BZ reaction
Source: Stewart (1998), p. 37.

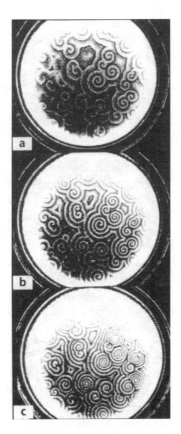

Figure 8 Aggregation patterns in the slime mould
Source: Stewart (1998), p. 91.

when individual amoebas, which themselves developed
form germinated spores, start to move and join together as
they do as part of the developmental cycle of the slime
mould, *Dicyostelium discoideum*. Similar patterns are found
elsewhere in nature. They look the same because the dynamics of their production is the same. Goodwin (1995, p. 49)
explains:

These examples show that what counts in the production of
spatial patterns is not the nature of the molecules and other

components involved, such as cells, but the way these interact with one another in time (their kinetics) and space (their
relational order): how the state of one region depends upon
the state of neighbouring regions). These two properties
together define . . . the behaviour of a dynamic system.

Dynamic models are thus especially useful because the
properties of dynamic processes are independent of the
mechanics of the process, an oscillation is an oscillation
whether it is a spring, a pendulum or a joint in motion. Thus
the descriptions it offers can apply to all sorts of behaviour of
all sorts of systems, like the development of bromous acid, an
amoeba, a snowflake, a thunderstorm, walking or facility with
calculus.

In addition, organismic development is an open system: it
exchanges energy and matter with its environment. This
property is crucial for two reasons. First, if the organism were
a closed system the second law of thermodynamics would
hold, and the energy in the system, the organism, would
dissipate, so there would be no differentiated structure, just
as ice, a result of the 'development', the self-organization of
water between 0 and –4 degrees, is the same all over.
Organisms can confound this principle only by reorganizing
internally to become more effectively coupled to the environment, more differentiated. And this is the second property.
This process of internal reorganization is the means whereby
the organism becomes more differentiated, as it develops
structures which couple it adaptively to the ecology. Indeed,
that is what development is. This coupling, like evolving a
skeleton to cope with gravity, or means of navigation based
upon complex invariances in the movement of stars, or the
sun, or learning a language, both constrains the ways in
which interactions between the organism and environment
can take place and afford others (I can walk but cannot fly, for
instance, I can speak English as a first language, but not
Japanese).

Thirdly, because dynamic models focus on change over
time they are better equipped for the analysis of process, of
how change occurs, a matter we will look into in more detail
in a separate section (p. 77 below). So as all dynamic systems

have these characteristic properties, we can apply what has already been found about the properties of such systems to the study of human development. We can thereby move away from the sterile focus on stages, to transitions, the dynamics of change.

Another obvious feature of these views lies in the unit of analysis used. It is assumed that the behaviour and function of any object, organism or phenomenon can be understood only in relation to the system of which it is a part. Systems have multiple components, so it is never assumed that any single preformed cause will determine outcomes. Rather, outcomes depend upon the particular pattern of interactions between the components, the factors. This is exactly the position we have reached both from the arguments adduced in Chapter 2 and the above point regarding the evolution of life itself; that there can be no dichotomy between organism and environment, the unit of analysis must be the system. Further, it implies that the functional relations between sub-systems is close, so that for the case of psychological development this means there must be both a close coupling between the perceptual, action and cognitive sub-systems of the organism and between these sub-systems and the characteristics of the environment and relations between them, just as we have been arguing.

A different view of causality

Because these theories start from different premises their assumptions about change will be different. The tradition in psychology is to look for linear relations, where the greater the amount of a relevant variable, the greater the effect. The reason for this tradition is the lack of belief in interaction as a force for change: it is assumed that causal impetus is limited to a preformed entity. But the nature of the relationship between sub-systems in a biological system is non-linear and the same applies to all dynamic systems: one cannot predict how the whole system will behave just by knowing the values of the inputs to it. A change in one aspect of one internal sub-system, e.g. in physiology, could make some difference, or none at all. The same is true for a change in an external environmental variable. It is often the case that a small change in conditions can lead to a massive reorganization of the behaviour of the system, non-linear and unpredictable change. The reason that this is the case is that it is internal reorganization that determines change, and changes in input are just one factor that can affect that. This process is called a phase-shift. And what follows from this interactivity and non-linearity is that the nature of the changes which do occur depend upon the interactions that occur, not being fixed by any particular value of any one variable, as in the traditional independent variable. The analysis of such forms of change requires a different mathematics than we are used to, it requires non-linear techniques. There are a variety of these, beyond the scope of this book, and the scope of my knowledge, but as an example, catastrophe theory provides the mathematics to describe the different forms of abrupt change observed in systems, and chaos theory describes changes which are not at all random, being describable exactly by differential equations, but which can look random as small changes to conditions often 'precipitate' a variety of new and different behaviours.

What is involved here is a different idea of causality. On the traditional model a significant difference in behaviour would be taken to imply a significant difference in the value or type of independent variables, because change is presumed to be linear – rate of change of behaviour is proportional to rate of change of independent variable. Without that assumption we are not forced to assume that conditions have changed significantly if behaviour has, nor that conditions have not changed if behaviour has not. There is a relation between the various causal factors and behavioural outcomes, but because it is from complex interactions between the components that change arises, where a small change can lead to a complex reorganization of the system, the relation is not linear.

This means that the whole approach to science is different. The traditional method of experimentation which assumes the linear relation between changes in independent and dependent variable, underpins the controlled experiment, where all variables are fixed except the independent one. One of the reasons for this methodology would have been the lack of a mathematical means of dealing with the behaviour of multiple complex interactions in systems. But in addition, people, especially the scientists themselves, came to consider the method to be the right and only proper way to do science. Such a procedure needs to be recognized as based upon a set of assumptions. It assumes linearity, a very similar assumption to the gradualism assumed in evolution, as it always expects that there cannot be catastrophic jumps in outcomes, that there can be no build up of dynamic energy which must be released, that various small internal changes will not eventually be followed by major reorganization. It assumes that there is not a complex of factors which has its own unique composition so that the result of the interaction of all the component factors can always surprise us. The more we actually observe what happens in development the more we see that such assumptions are simply not justified.

Rather, the behaviour of organisms and inanimate processes is characterized by two, opposite sorts of situation. We observe flux, sudden change, but we also observe periods of stability, called attractor states. The persistence is named the stability of the system and the adjustment to changing internal and external conditions its adaptability. We hear of and are not surprised by dramatic and apparently chaotic fluctuations in many aspects of life, whether it be the populations of particular species, changes in the weather, changes in our mind, for that matter. There is messiness, yet there is order. These same characteristics become ever more evident in studies of the development of organisms, including humans. Dynamic systems theories are the only theories that assume this combination of order and apparent (but not real) disorder and predict it. When there is order it looks as if the components of the system co-operated to produce it, or that the system selected it, was attracted to it. The set of factors comes to appear to act as one. Moreover, this pattern will persist even though the inputs to the system vary. The process by which it arrives is called 'self-organization'. However, just as typically, it is found that points are reached where variation to the input leads to fluctuations. These are points at which the dynamic equilibrium is disturbed, a variety of sorts of transitory behaviours, sorts of warnings of massive change, occur, and soon a new stability does indeed arise from another self-organization.

Focusing on human development

Self-organization

Because there is no external programme or fixed, internal regulator, any increasing complexity and differentiation results from spontaneous, internal rearrangement, known as self-organization. It is the process by which internal relations realign themselves in an attempt to optimize the relations between the organism and the environment. It is, as I now argue, the alternative to preformation.

We observe order as well as disorder in development. We thus have to account for it. The relative stability and simplicity of many developmental outcomes has lent weight to the interpretation that it is the effect of a relatively stable and simple cause, a preformed programme. As we have already seen, no such conclusion is justified. The common interactionist explanation is that genetic and environmental factors combine in some way. But why should combination lead to order? If there is no need for self-organization in dynamic systems, and as I say, most do not yet subscribe to the view that there is, then the interactions they refer to should lead to behaviours which are a mixture of (organized) genetically controlled behaviour and (organized) experience controlled behaviour. But why should the mixture resulting from the interaction be organized? What organizes it? Preformationism cannot do the job, as it is not about interaction. Ordinary 'interactionism' cannot, because it is not dynamic, non-linear systems theory. Only dynamic systems theory explicitly places the organization of the system itself, from within, as a major and ubiquitous feature of all developmental change.

The self-organization can involve reorganization of internal, biomechanical structures, itself a complex of sub-sub systems, as when a new form of locomotion emerges. It can involve a reorganization of the internal psychological structures, as when knowledge of aspects of language emerge. It can involve a reorganization of the relations between the external and internal factors, as when a child 'takes over' more of the task demands after scaffolding has helped their development on a given task. It can involve a reorganization of the timing of a behaviour contingent on an external factor, amount of clothing worn, as in the case when Bensen (1993), reported in Ulrich (1997), showed that babies born in the winter and spring in an area where seasonal variations were large, crawled three weeks earlier than those born in the summer and autumn. The early crawlers had had more experience of crawling because they were in less restrictive clothing, because the weather had warmed up at a time when experience would make a difference.

Despite the huge complexity of interacting factors, we do find that generic forms of behaviour do emerge, are selected by the process of self-organization. Infants do tend to crawl before they walk. They do tend to produce certain sounds before others. They do get from lying to sitting by pushing their trunk upward, leaning slightly to one side and bringing legs forward, by flexing their knee and hip joints. And despite the tendency for generic self-organization we will come across cases where a small change in conditions can change the way this occurs. Infants with Down's syndrome, who have a greater range of hip motion, just one tiny part of the internal, bodily sub-system, get to the sitting position a different way, as they can bring each leg forward on either side of the body. All these are instances of self-organization.

Collective variables (order parameters)

The characteristic behaviours of the self-organized system are said to be due to what is called the collective variable or order parameter, that regularity, often describable by a single mathematical equation, which shows the collective properties of the system under different conditions. The linear equivalent would be the dependent variable, but the difference here is that it describes the reasonably simple outcome, the 'collective dynamics' of numerous complex interactions. The order parameter is seen as typically ensuring that the sub-systems involved maintain their states so that the interactive flux remains the same, the condition for the regularity being maintained. That is to say, it looks as if it keeps them in order, ensuring that the various sub-systems do not 'upset' the overall order. This is not the same as saying that the collective variable causes the behaviour, because that variable is effective only when a given pattern of factors constitutes the causal flux.

Control parameters

Even though a vast number of factors have been involved in the interactions from which the collective order emerged (the collective variable, order parameter again), it is often the case that a small number (sometimes one) of variables or relations are particularly relevant in affecting the collective variable. These are called control parameters. It is these which are of most significance in holding the system in stability, constraining the effects of any other variation on the system. But they are also of equal significance in that when they reach a critical value or boundary condition they trigger reorganization and a phase-shift occurs. Control parameters are thus important both in maintaining stability and in evoking change.

No assumption of continued influence can be made for such variables. For instance, at birth infants produce stepping patterns if held in upright posture. These are lost when the infant is about two months old. It was thought that this was due to 'maturation'. What control parameter is responsible for this change? Thelen and Fisher (1982) found that the rapid weight gain of human infants in the first two or three months was mainly due to fat deposition, and the loss of the stepping ability in an upright posture was probably due to a drop in the power to weight ratio. That is, this was the control parameter, that variable in which variation at critical levels is associated with a phase-shift, a sudden transition in the order parameter. Recent experiments which included observing the retention of 'stepping' whilst legs are submerged (rendering the legs more buoyant and easier to lift), has confirmed the finding, as shown in Figure 9.

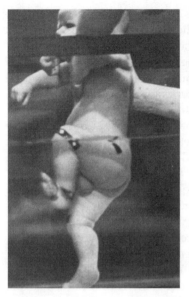 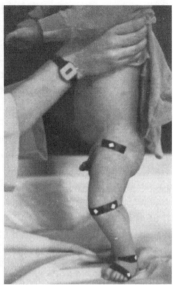

Figure 9 Upright stepping, restored when leg mass is reduced by submersion. This three-month-old infant was tested with feet on the table and submerged in warm water, as described in Thelen and Smith (1994).

Source: Thelen and Smith (1994), p. 12.

When older this will not normally be a control parameter. Similar parameters may control the transition from crawling to walking (Clark and Philips, 1993). Ronnqvist and Hopkins (1998) found that newborns may, contrary to general belief, be able to attain and maintain a midline head position, but do not normally do so because their neck muscles are not strong enough to overcome the powerful effects of gravity on the head. In this case the control parameter may be neck muscle power. Clearly, it only has this function early in development.

Here are some more examples of different control parameters. The energy applied by a horse in motion is a control parameter. As the energy increases it moves through successive boundary conditions which correspond to the abrupt transitions from trot to canter to gallop (each of which is defined by dynamic, mathematical equations relating to the phase relationships between limb movements, as is the case for all movements of all organisms with legs). When a rider 'drives' the horse on, they become the control parameter. The ratio of size and shape of fingers to size of object to be grasped has been shown to be another control parameter in motor development, affecting the order parameter, the grip pattern observed. An example from cognitive development comes from van der Maas and Hopkins (1998), who observed that short-term memory and 'field dependency' are two control parameters affecting performance on a conservation task. In the field of social psychology Dunbar (1993) found that as group size increased there was a change in the manner in which social cohesion developed. Thus group size was the control parameter. Since 1960 it has been known that infants would use the invariances which specify a 'cliff edge' (i.e. specify a sudden increase in depth of surface supporting self), to know what was there and to respond adaptively by avoiding it (Gibson and Walk, 1960). It has also been regularly found that there are large individual differences between infants in their tendency to avoid the edge. It appears likely that differences in prefrontal lobe development, which controls inhibition of motor activity, underlies the difference (Rader, 1997) and are therefore acting as one of the control parameters. It is as well to remember that in all these examples there is no fixed plan, no preformation. The controls work in some situations and become irrelevant in others.

There are three sorts of constraints, as Newell (1986) pointed out, which can act as control parameters, organismic, environmental or task-specific. For instance, the strength of muscles, an organismic factor, sets limits on what actions can be performed, as does the oxygen level in the blood; the carrying out of a task in water, an environmental constraint, will alter performance, as could being able to use a tool; learning to communicate depends upon task-specific contingent responses from another, while sorting a pack of cards, by suit, would involve and require different abilities, like dexterity, again task-specific.

A control parameter has very different properties from an independent variable and without the benefit of its appropriation from dynamic systems views, I rather doubt if its significance in development would be appreciated. We would not be looking for variables which have this amazing mix of qualities, being dependent upon the rest of the interactive flux in so far as they operate only for given patterns of that flux; constraining change up to a boundary condition; effecting change when they reach that point, and furthermore, ceasing to be relevant at a later point in the emerging developmental system, when the interactive flux has changed again. It is part of the dialectical character of systems change and once we appreciate this we can accept the fluidity, the dynamism involved in interactive effects. With the benefit of knowledge of its role from other systems it has been possible to see something of its potential role in human development. And it is very early days yet. To make real progress using dynamic systems theory it will be necessary to identify different control parameters for different conditions, and to identify those conditions, rather than simply to argue that a complex of interacting factors is jointly responsible. But you must understand that without such a recognition of the relevance of dynamic systems views to human development, we would not even be able to identify the relevant questions. Such views are important for this reason alone.

Control parameters and the production of levels of knowledge

I want to link this discussion of control parameters to the notion of greater extensions of invariance constraining lesser ones. Because some of these parameters have been invariant over the life of the species, while some only arise during ontogeny, they play a different role in development. Those that are species-specific control parameters, like the extent to which a human arm muscle can flex and extend, or the range of movement of a joint, or maximum and minimum levels of oxygen in the blood compatible with life, constrain development in generic ways (I will never be able to flex my knee by more than 180 degrees, for instance, or lift a bus with my finger), but do not specify exactly what actions or thoughts will be selected. They have generic effects in that they set boundary conditions. Individual or task-specific control parameters, like aerobic efficiency, will have more specific effects, but still, of course, within the species-specific boundary conditions. So what, you may ask. The matter becomes significant when this argument is applied to the development of knowledge. The questions become: what are the generic, species-specific constraints on information extraction? How do these relate to specific learning, or selection by experience? In dynamic systems terms, what are the control parameters for knowledge production, both species-specific and individual, and how do these systematically relate to each other? We return to this issue in Chapter 5.

Types of attractors

An attractor is a stable state, like walking, or reaching and grasping accurately. It represents a solution to a problem of how to achieve something. There are four sorts of attractors. The first is called a fixed-point attractor, and refers to the existence of a single, stable equilibrium point, like the end-point of a reach or a grasp, where action consists in a trajectory (the reach) terminating at a point (location of object) and an accurate form is roughly the same for everyone, there not being alternative stable forms. At first there would be errors in reaching too far, and not far enough, and both of these would reduce over time till the error was minimal. Look at Figure 10. Amplitude refers to amplitude of error, which gradually reduces, for both positive (overreach) and negative (under reach) instances over time, till the attraction of the fixed point prevails. Figure 11 shows the same information in a different way. The meeting of the axes corresponds to zero error in any direction, so the circular trajectory, gradually homing in on zero, corresponds to the decreasing error in reaches, over time, anywhere about the point to be reached. Figure 11 also exactly describes the motion of a real pendulum swinging past the vertical, but gradually reducing in amplitude, because the dynamics are identical. Similarly, the dynamics of the control of the various muscles and joints is exactly the same for an arm as for a spring, involving flexion of the various muscles at various times, in relation to each other, and variation in the angles between limbs at joints. In both, account has to be taken of inertia, a property of all dynamic systems, and the laws of force, mass and acceleration have to be obeyed, because the

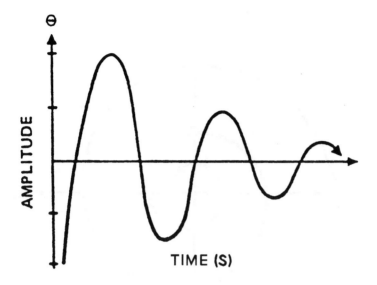

Figure 10 Amplitude
Source: Thelen and Smith (1994), p. 57.

arm is matter as well, and thus subject to its laws (Zernicke and Schneider, 1993, in Goldfield, 1995, pp. 98–9).

The second sort of attractor is a limit cycle or periodic attractor, where a continuous oscillation with a fixed amplitude and frequency occurs. Walking, in which various oscillations of parts of the body occur, which are repeated with each stride, is one case. Two examples are shown in Figures 12 and 13. Amplitude (from top of peak to bottom of trough) is length of stride and time for a stride is the time, on the horizontal axis, between peaks. Hence you will be able to work out that the person in Figure 13 has a stride which is exactly half as long as the other, but that they stride twice as often (so, as it happens, a graph of velocity alone would be identical). Third we have quasiperiodic or taurus attractors. These arise when two attractors are both having an influence, but neither is dominant. They interact to produce a novel pattern, such as in Figure 14. The pattern of activity in non-nutritive sucking in the neonate is described by such an attractor, based upon the interaction of sucking and swallowing factors. Finally we have

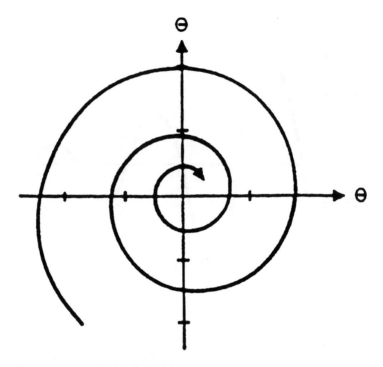

Figure 11 Amplitude of pendulum
Source: Thelen and Smith (1994), p. 57.

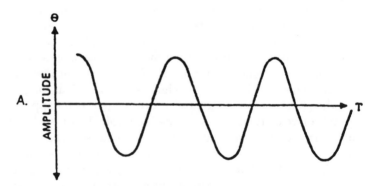

Figure 12 Amplitude of stride: 1
Source: Thelen and Smith (1994), p. 57.

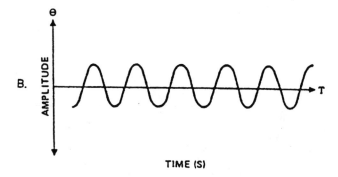

Figure 13 Amplitude of stride: 2
Source: Thelen and Smith (1994), p. 57.

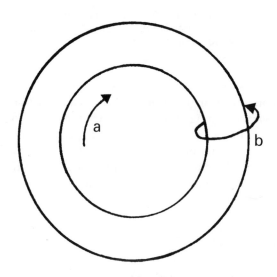

a attractor one
b attractor two

Figure 14 A torus attractor
Source: Goldfield (1995), p. 25, based on Newell, Kugler, van Emmerik and McDonald (1989).

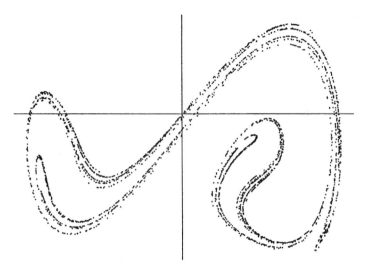

Figure 15 This chaotic attractor shows how points will converge to this complex shape under iteration, yet within this general pattern nearby points diverge from one another
Source: Port and Gelder (1995), p. 67.

the chaotic or strange attractor. These show patterns which tend towards certain regions more than others, but do not cross the same point twice, and most of all, depend for their 'shape' on the exact nature of the starting conditions. A small difference can lead the outcome, defined by the shape of the curves, to be very different from earlier behaviour. An example is shown in Figure 15.

Changes at transitions

Wimmers *et al.* (1998) describe how catastrophe theory can help in understanding the development of action and Hartelman, van der Maas and Molenaar (1998) discuss the criteria for transitions. When change is imminent, dynamic systems show the signs. Catastrophe theory specifies the various conditions which can be met when a phase-shift is going to occur. If human development is describable by this particular dynamic systems theory, we should be able to observe the same sorts of conditions occurring in human behaviour. Gilmore (1981) identified eight criteria, or flags, as evidence for the existence of transitions. All of them must involve a sudden change in behaviour, taking the form of a jump of some sort, like divergence, when two similar trends diverge widely, or an increase in variability of a behaviour, a greater sensitivity to perturbation near a transition, or a slowing down of the system in returning to its stable state after perturbation, regressions, etc.

A wonderful example of transition and speed of change at a phase-shift is seen in certain weather conditions we have all observed. Differences in air density lead to hailstones being formed, with the smaller, lighter hailstones moving to the top of the growing cloud, forming 'the anvil' shape and the bigger, heavier ones not being able to rise so much and being held in the main body of the cloud. As the stones pass each other the lighter become negatively charged and the heavier positively charged. Over time the forces of repulsion grow bigger and bigger. Then, with no change in rate of action, the system collapses, huge amounts of electrical and sound energy are released, until the system reorganizes into a new stability. The phase-shift, the self-organization, is called a thunderstorm, and the energy release is thunder and lightening. Ulrich (1997) provides another example, less familiar in Britain. When there is a sufficient temperature difference between the earth and the atmosphere, and the pressure and humidity are within certain limits, 'the collective interplay of multiple factors results in the emergence of a distinctly recognisable pattern, a funnel cloud' [part of a tornado or water spout – my addition] (Ulrich, 1997, p. 324). As Ulrich points out, no one feels the need to posit any preformed instructions, any 'plans of action', to account for these events. We accept both that novel outcomes emerge, novel in the sense that the cloud did not exist a few minutes before, and that this is the sort of thing that happens in weather systems, that 'recognizable', stable forms emerge, like funnel clouds, that huge changes do occur, and that these are marked by predictable 'flags'.

Some of this, certainly the terminology, may sound disconnected with your ordinary experience. Yet I believe we all already understand at a common sense level how pervasive dynamic non-linear transitions are. In normal conversation it is quite in order to refer to changes of heart, to violent changes of mood, to sudden rows, to inexplicable and uncontrollable changes in our mental states or physical states. We do not have difficulty with the notion of 'the last straw', just a simple example of non-linear change as it is the tiniest change – the last straw – which leads to the large change. We all know and accept that as water goes through temperature changes it changes qualitatively in form, from water to ice, and can just as easily vaporize at a given point. We know, using another example from Thelen and Smith (1994), that we take utterly for granted the abrupt locomotory phase-shifts that characterize the changes between different gaits of a horse as it walks (one attractor state), then shifts abruptly (a phase-shift) to a trot, a qualitatively different mode of locomotion, then a canter, then a gallop. The gait is the collective variable, the phenomenon which shows the collective properties of the system, under different conditions. Energy applied is the control parameter. It looks as if locomotion is under very simple control, because the attractor states observed are simple. This is a mirage, due to the self-organizing properties of this particular dynamic system in action. By the way, here is an experiment for the future. Take one horse. Place on moon. Observe how self-organizational processes affected its emergent modes of locomotion in the same reduced gravity that radically altered human locomotion.

We accept dynamic systems change in our non-academic lives even if we do not u'e the associated language. We know that when two friends ta.k to each other before they talk to you it can make a difference, but we do not normally call it the complex interaction of external factors. We know that anxiety at a nervous eye-twitch (the anxiety being both a cause and an effect of the anxiety) can make your neck ache, but do not normally call it the interaction of internal factors. We know that you can end up behaving very nervously and your friend reacts to this, but do not normally call this the interaction of external with internal factors. And we know that a stable state may arise from this mix, or a huge change may take place. However, another dichotomy we have been brought up with, theoretical/practical, induces those of us not concerned with theory to regard our knowledge as inferior, so our common sense knowledge of dynamic interactions is not accorded the validity it should be, not even by ourselves.

How is skilled action possible?

One of the important advances in dynamic systems came from the work of Bernstein (1967), who was the first to point out that all behaviour appears to involve setting the values of so many variables that it looks, on the face of it, as if even simple action is impossible. As Hopkins and Butterworth (1997) describe, the human body has nearly 800 muscles, 200 bones and more than 100 joints. Every one of these is always in a given position in relation to all the others, and has a certain velocity. This musculoskeletal system can only operate because of the links to the nervous system, which involves 10^{14} neurons and 10^3 varieties of nerve cell. Walking directly involves 3 joints and over 50 muscles in each leg, but also involves setting and varying the action of various other muscles and joints which are less directly involved but still need organizing if we are not to fall over. All this assumes no variation in external context, an ideal which is not encountered. It seems absolutely impossible that the execution of action could be organized by the brain separately controlling every single one of these components, including the effects of their interactions. Nor could a preformed, central, executive plan take account of all this vast complexity, interaction and accommodation to varying conditions. There has to be a way of simplifying the problem.

Bernstein argued that the only way it could be achieved was by constraining the action of a whole group of muscles at once so that they were set at certain amounts of tension, not allowed to vary, and thus could be 'forgotten' about. We can in fact see this happening in the development of, for instance, leg movements. Thelen (1985) described how the leg joints are kept fixed in the initial kicking that babies exhibit in the first week of life, an obvious form of constraint for one of the many movement sub-systems. Later, between one and five months they relax the fix and kicking is practised while the joints allow the attached feet, lower legs and upper legs to vary with respect to each other (under the evolved constraints of the human body). At about six months, the more controlled organization of these joints is reassembled, this time with the capacity to use the limbs for crawling. Bernstein argued that at first the 'freezing' of the relations between some groups of muscles or joints takes place which simplifies the complex problem of motor control by not having to take account of some possible variations. The infant explores this constrained system, seeing what can be done within it, realizing its opportunities for action, its affordances. It finds out what actions and effects it can have. The constraints lead to affordances. Once there has been sufficient experience with this arrangement, the restriction is released and the movement sub-system can be reorganized. Exploration of this arrangement then begins, and so on. Of course this applies to many coordinative structures, as these sub-systems are called. As a result, 'impossibly' complex acts are possible, based upon the initial restriction of possible variations through organized constraint at a sub-system level.

Dynamic systems and development

We can describe the process of the development of leg movements in terms of my central hypothesis. As the infant of less than one month explores a particular configuration of restraints to reveal what it can do, it is effectively exploring a task-space. Initially the 'space' is highly constrained in the sense that the task is simple, as not much can be varied. But so is the behaviour, as skill is limited. The task and the exploration and the information produced are thus all relatively undifferentiated. Then that particular set of constraints can be relaxed and exploration about how to control parts of the body in a new, looser and thus slightly more complex and differentiated arrangement can begin, but only because of the information gained in the previous phase. The infant only learns to crawl because it learned to kick, etc. This information then gets used to aid the next form of constraints, of self-organization, and so on.

A surface behavioural pattern exists, which appears as stability, transitions and phase-shifts, but underlying each period of 'stability' is dynamic exploration of a given arrangement. The exploration of the initial, constrained task-space produces undifferentiated information, which is then used to inform self-organization into a more complex set of constraints which affords more complex exploration and produces more differentiated information. This is exactly the same as we have already suggested as our main principle for the production of knowledge, and it is completely different to saying that the system is preformed, because each stability enables new, different interactions and it is only from these that new developmental products emerge. The developmental system can thus be construed as the process of successive constraint and release of system variables so that the affordances of each system can be explored. Though it is not emphasized in the theory, change which has this character, where reaching a stable state is also to reach a set of conditions from which change will inevitably emerge in both components and their products because of their mutual interactivity, is the core of dialectical theory. Development is just that complex of interaction over time, between the organism and environment by which these processes and products emerge and dissolve.

So what does 'biological' mean?

There may be some confusion over the fact that I have suggested that dynamic systems cover both biological and non-biological processes. That does not mean there are not special sorts of questions that biologists ask. To make clear that I am not distancing myself from a biological perspective I will set out now how I perceive the relation between what is biological and what is the subject of a dynamic systems perspective. In the first place, biological explanations of behaviour, because they are explanations, must specify the necessary and sufficient factors involved for the behaviour to occur. In systems terms the relevant factors and the role of control parameters in the development of attractors and phase-shifts in behaviour need to be identified and the manner of their interaction revealed. In the second place, because the specifically biological assumption is made that organisms behave in the way they do because it has a function for them in the contexts they typically inhabit, it becomes necessary to locate the functions of behaviour within their phylogenetic and ontogenetic contexts, that is, systems. This is a long-standing emphasis in ethology, but should become a new and crucial one in psychology, as some have argued already (e.g. Locke, 1996; Rovee-Collier, 1996).

I think a clarification of what the typical contexts for humans are and have been will clarify what 'biological' means. First, it is impossible to ignore the evolutionary context, so questions of evolutionary fitness are relevant. Bodies and behaviours represent the history of a species. Humans really do have arms, birds do have beaks, etc. and this has a significant effect upon what they can now do. This applies both to explanations of the immediate value of an act, such as the clearing of an area around the nest that results from picking up the shell pieces and depositing them elsewhere (Michel and Moore, 1995), and the long-term fitness of this tidying-up process in aiding survival chances of offspring. It is equally impossible to ignore the ontogenetic context, as behaviour must be sensitive, as we have seen, to idiosyncratic contingencies.

The immediate function and the evolutionary value of behaviour are both about coupling. Both sorts of coupling fit action to its context, so coupling through learning or coupling by evolution are equally biological. History is represented, whether the history is five minutes or 5 million years old. It also obviously follows that what is learned cannot determine whether it is to be counted as biological or not, only its function can. Thus, caretaking, bus catching and reading are all just as much parts of our biological environment as food and drink. In all cases coupling involves the selection of changes which provide a better fit between the physical and psychological form and functions of the organism and those of the environment. All such changes and all such processes are biological. But the forms of change, and the relations between organismic change and the contextual conditions, both follow laws which describe a wide variety of natural systems. Development is thus the change in dynamic, biological systems by which a co-ordination of the organism and environment occurs. Biological accounts must include all sorts of adaptation to all sorts of structure, invariance, whether these be of food distribution, prey habits, fashion fads, social norms or language rules, whatever. The model is thus explicitly ecological in character and is generic in applying to all ancestral and present forms of invariant, environmental structure and levels of them, between the humans and those environments and within the humans.

But I am not being clear about what it is that travels in these dynamic systems. What is used? What is transformed? To move towards an answer I now have to introduce you more thoroughly to the ecological psychology of J. J. Gibson.

Discussion points

1 What are the main properties of dynamic systems? Give examples of such systems.

2 Use dynamic systems terminology to describe the changes that occur in the development of a butterfly. In what sense could the process be said to be dialectical?

3 What was the problem Bernstein addressed? Evaluate his 'solution'.

4 How might dynamic systems thinking and concepts help direct research in developmental psychology?

Chapter 5
The ecological perspective: Gibson's legacy

Gibson's critique of traditional thinking

I need to make the tradition of ecological psychology clearer because it is central to my claims that the work of J. J. Gibson (1950, 1966, 1979) is understood. This is the case both because he was right about important matters and because he was wrong about one. Gibson's conception of psychology was radical in that it proposed a completely different view of how humans come to know about their environment, a different view of the relation between the structure of the environment and the structure of evolved perceptual/cognitive adaptations to it, and a different view of the relation of the psychological systems of perception, cognition and action to each other. Gibson opposed any thinking which was not premised on the assumption that to understand the nature of the organism one had to understand it through its relation with its ecology. This put him at odds with existing theorists:

> The ecological approach is a new approach to the whole field of psychology, for it involves rejecting the stimulus–response formula. This notion . . . helped to get rid of the soul in psychology, but it never really worked. Neither mentalism on the one hand nor conditioned-reflex behaviourism on the other is good enough. What psychology needs is the kind of thinking that is beginning to be attempted in what is loosely called systems theory. (Gibson, 1979, p. 2)

In taking this contextualist position, Gibson was bound to be critical of any methodology which intentionally avoided natural complexity. He observed that the dominant method used to study human psychology, controlled experimentation, meant that normal behaviour in normal environments was never observed, let alone explained. There is a place for such work, but what it cannot do is to locate the function of the behaviour of organisms within ecological systems. One example: studying the grip of infant monkeys in isolated experimental, controlled conditions may reveal much of the physiology and mechanics of grip, but nothing of its function or origins. Observe the animal in the wild clinging to its mother as the nomadic band move through the undergrowth and all is immediately made clear: hang on for dear life.

Dynamic invariance

Gibson appreciated the power of ecological thinking and was thus able to ask the right questions. To understand the human perceptual system, for instance, he considered what problems it would have to cope with 'in the wild', to be useful, and what 'information' might be available. We know that light from the sun, from electrical sources, etc., is scattered from all surfaces, including clouds, as well as birds, trees, walls, people, etc. At any given point there will thus be light approaching an observer from all angles, called ambient light. Thus, in Figure 16, we see light projected from a radiant source being scattered in all directions. An observer at X in Figure 17 would be receiving ambient (surrounding) light, light reflected from the various surfaces. Here we are shown just the light from the boundaries of objects. But there will be large differences in the light from, say, A than from B, owing to the amount of light hitting the different surfaces, the colour and texture of the surfaces, etc. This means the observer, having a visual system, may pick up these differences, having a differentiated view of the surroundings, the various surfaces in the visual field. It is also easy to see that contrasts between the light arriving correspond to edges, and variations in texture will correspond to distance away. It

Figure 16 Scatter reflection of light from surfaces. Light projected from a radiant source stimulates the emission of photons from illuminated surfaces. These photons scatter in all directions from each point of each surface. A dense space-filling network of reverberating rays results from the scattering shown.
Source: Reed (1988), p. 225, based on Gibson (1966).

is beginning to look possible that the structure of the patterns of ambient light might be extremely informative for an organism that had the relevant capabilities to utilize the structure.

Now imagine the observer to move, as in the movement from P_1 to P_5 in Figure 18. Obviously the pattern of light reaching the (moving) observer varies as they move, as shown in the pictures at the bottom of the figure. Now we can see that the act of movement itself creates the conditions to gain even more information, because there is a fixed relationship between the movement and the change in ambient light. Of course, observers do not generally move, stop and perceive, move, stop and perceive, etc. On the contrary, movement is normal, we are hardly ever completely stationary whilst awake, and as

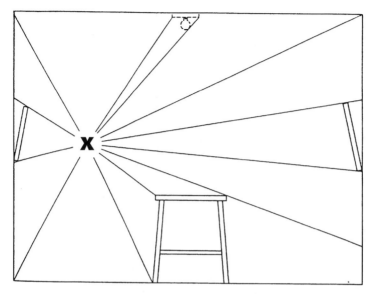

Figure 17 Ambient light and the main boundaries of the stationary optic array. The lines in this diagram represent borders of visual solid angles, not rays of light.
Source: Reed (1988), p. 51, based on Gibson (1966).

we move we see the flow of a changing pattern. The crux of the matter is that the change in flow is mathematically related to the surfaces out there. The physics of light defines the psychology of vision, to the extent that the observer has the relevant apparatus operating at the relevant level.

The mouse in Figure 19 is approaching its mousehole. As it does so the apparent size of the mousehole increases. The nearer it is the faster it increases. At A the angle the size of the hole subtends on the retina is <JAK, about 7 degrees. Halfway to the hole, after travelling 3 units, AB, BC, CD, the angle JDK is 14 degrees. However, in travelling just I1/2 units more, the angle is doubled again, and that angle is doubled in just 3/4 of a unit between F and H. The relation between the distance from the hole and the size of angle of hole is not linear, but it is invariant, so it is possible that the mouse could use the changes in size of hole to 'know' how long it will take to reach the hole. It will need to, because the cat picks up invariances which give

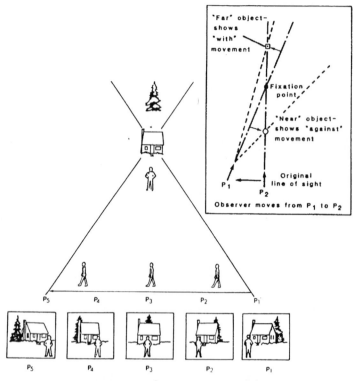

Figure 18 Changes of the relative position of objects in a moving visual field. As one moves from P_1 to P_2 the visual field changes accordingly because of the gradient of motion parallax (assuming a constant fixation point).

Source: Reed (1988), p. 170, based on Haber and Hershenson (1980).

it the same information. As the mouse passes from A to B to C to D, moving at a constant speed, the amount of head turn the cat needs to keep the mouse in focus must increase in speed as the mouse comes nearer to the perpendicular to the cat, at D, and decrease again after that. But the relation between mouse speed and cat head-turn speed is invariant. In these and in most cases, the motion of the organism is part of the covariation. Such covariations exist everywhere and they are a necessary condition of knowing what is going on. The behaviour of thousands of species attests to the fact that these dynamic

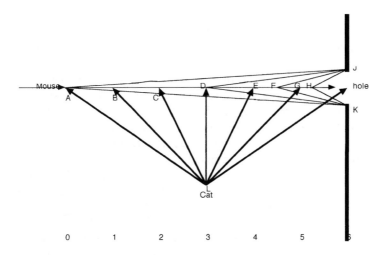

Figure 19 How mice and cats use physics

invariances in the changing structure of the ambient light (or other form of energy), corresponding exactly to the relative distance, movement, texture, etc. of the external world, are indeed picked up. The physics of energy becomes the psychology of information 'pick-up'. It shows, as Gibson put it, the specificity between action and information.

Now because movement is accompanied by dynamic invariant changes, we can move in order to produce them, that is, as a means of obtaining information. In fact it is a main basis for exploration. We approach things, walk round them, maybe pick them up, move our head from side to side, bring objects close to our eyes or nose or tongue, feel their texture. Exploration, Gibson observed, which is of course action, is fundamental to perception and much of it consists in the use of movement to create dynamic invariances which specify the structure of the ecology.

But it is not just organisms that move. Parts of the environment do, including other organisms. On a traditional view such motion should have constituted noise, interference for the perceptual system trying to detect stability, invariance. But dynamic invariances are revealed *only* when motion is occurring. These are the higher-order invariances (by which I mean that they are not described by a point on a graph, but can be described by a mathematical (non-linear) equation) which are the basis of perception. As action has to be coupled to the conditions encountered, the detection of such invariances is also the key to intelligent action. This is the stuff of real-life perception, rather than idealized notions of it, based upon motionless humans in sterile laboratories. All exploratory action involves movement, and it takes time. Given such a reality, a perceptual system needs be able to deal with continuous flows of information and take account of relative motion whilst so doing. This makes theoretical sense but Gibson showed it actually happened for a whole variety of experiments detailed in his books and articles.

Here is one example of dynamic invariance. It is a fact of physics that the size of an image on the retina is proportional to its distance away and also, that the rate of change of size is proportional to the rate of change of distance away. But rate of change of distance is speed. Thus a dynamic invariance specifies relative speed of observer and object. In Figure 20 looming, or zooming in, is the phenomenal appreciation of the proportional changes in size of image over time. Obviously the opposite phenomenon, zooming out, results from the opposite mathematical invariances as the object speeds away. If an object has a texture, the same finding applies to the rate of expansion of the discernible parts, so the dots on an approaching object would become further and further apart, as would the dots on a surface surrounding an aperture one was approaching, while dots on a distant object seen through the aperture would only be expanding more slowly, as they are much further away. Humans, indeed many species, accurately estimate distance away and time to contact with structures in the environment by effectively utilizing the laws, the dynamic, physical invariants. They can do this only because they are capable of detecting the invariant dynamic relations between the changing input over time – it gives them information. This process involves having developed brain structures which enable them to 'pick-up' the changes in external (dynamic) structure, invariance. Such change is a condition of any perception. This can happen over

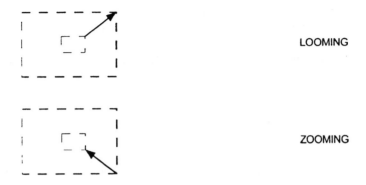

Figure 20 Events and their corresponding invariants
Source: Goldfield (1995), p. 61.

evolutionary time, in which case the result of the adaptation is that undifferentiated species-typical invariance is 'picked-up' by all the members of a given species, or it can be learned. Exactly the same mathematical relations hold for change in acoustic qualities, or pressure changes, so, for instance, bats can use sonar information instead of vision to estimate time to contact. The invariances are thus not tied to a perceptual mode. Exactly as in dynamic systems, the properties of dynamic processes are independent of the mechanics of the process. This intermodality of invariances, and thus of information when interactions are involved, will be seen to be important later in the chapter.

Why invariance is critical

The concept of invariance must be clear. Gibson focused on the light rays reflected from objects, and how these changed in an invariant way, and on changes due to occlusion, interposition, etc., but invariance is obviously not confined to the properties of light rays. It applies to all forms of energy, but even more, it must be appreciated that however dynamic invariances are, there can be no adaptation to randomness. Development is about change to increase coupling to dynamic structure. No structure means no development, no adaptation, no learning, no sense, nonsense. The mistake of traditionalists was to emphasize a static view of invariance, but dynamic invariance and thereby predictability and regularity there must be, and that is what coupling must be to. Gibson's term 'invariance' covers all such regularity.

The effective environment

But despite invariances being invariant, the world for a developing infant of all species is ever-changing. The 'effective', the phenomenal environment, is different for different species (I do not perceive the same world as a dog or a bat), different for the same species at different points in its phylogeny (the earliest human ancestors could not perceive the structure of spoken or written language) and different for each member of one species during its individual development (babies can perceive all 'human' speech sounds, when older they cannot). The environment is thus not one 'thing', does not exist independently of the organism, but exists only in relation to the perceptual, cognitive and motor capacities of the organisms involved. It is completely defined by the relation of the invariant properties of the environment to the invariant properties of the organism – how it moves, explores, detects, etc., but as the organism changes so do the relations and so does the effective environment. The organism/environment thus has, once again, to be understood only as a single system because each part of it exists as real only in relation to the qualities of the other.

Concepts are criteria: an infinite regress

Further, as the point of perception is to inform action, and all intelligent action is based upon adaptive utilization of the environment, perception must be deeply utilitarian – detection must be for use. Thus perception must be 'rich' in the sense of giving information about what can be done, not what 'is'. This is in total contradiction with the traditional notion that perceptual input was about mere appearances, not informative, while only concepts (the work of cognition) were about reality, and valid knowledge was gained only from the latter, not the former.

Gibson asked simply: what criteria were used to build the concepts which are used to judge the perceptual data? The answer cannot be perceptual as these are, according to the traditional view, unreliable, but they also cannot be conceptual because if they were, we are bound to ask by which process they gained their powerful status. The argument is circular. In the end some criteria cannot be conceptual and so the sufficient evidence for some knowledge of the world must be perceptual. As Gibson (1979, p. 253) put it:

> The fallacy is to assume that because inputs convey no knowledge they can somehow be made to yield knowledge by 'processing' them. Knowledge of the world cannot be explained by supposing that knowledge of the world already exists [in the form of representations, concepts – my addition]. All forms of cognitive processing imply cognition so as to account for cognition.

Gibson is referring to a logical fallacy here. The key element of the theory is thus that some perception involves the direct picking-up of dynamic external invariance which acts as specifications of states or events, e.g. presence of prey, food, etc.

Empirical evidence against the 'cognitive' position

There is also strong empirical evidence, some of it described in Chapter 6, but here is a foretaste. Butterworth (1993), in Smith and Thelen, considered the logic of the traditional position, as exemplified by Piaget's view that all knowledge has to be constructed and nothing can be directly perceived. If this is the case then learning will occur through developing associations between what is known, for instance, what can actually be touched and felt in the act of reaching, with what is not initially known, like how images on the retina from distal objects relate to the distance away of objects. In this way the retinal information gets calibrated via the knowledge gained directly by touch. This implies that infants will be better at learning to reach if they can see the object and their own hands than if they cannot. If, on the other hand, they pick-up the invariances which specify position and distance (and they should be able to do this through a variety of modes, remember) by purely perceptual means, they will learn just as quickly whether they can 'calibrate' touch and vision or not. Clifton *et al.* (1993) tested the Gibsonian hypothesis that the infants would learn to reach just as quickly when they could not see their own hands as they reached, that is, when they could not calibrate vision with touch. The object they were supposed to try and reach was either glowing, or emitting a sound. All infants were exposed repeatedly to both conditions, giving opportunities to compare progress in learning to reach in the two conditions. Success and improvement were just as good when the target was not visible. Equal performance in the latter condition strongly suggests that calibration across modalities, the crux of the standard learning explanation, is not required. Rather, information was available through sound and this equally informed reaching.

Other sources of input which traditionalists like Piaget would claim could be used to develop sensorimotor schemes would include kinesthetic feedback from active movement, convergence of eyes, and tactile experience. In interaction these sources of data would be co-ordinated with others and as a result knowledge could gradually develop, including inter-modal knowledge. Now if the argument is correct then neonates would not be able to show awareness of the distal properties of visual environments; there would be no reason for them to show a preference for complex, dynamic arrays and they would not be able to use intermodal knowledge without previously constructing it. Butterworth (1993, p. 79) reviewed pertinent evidence and concluded that 'neonatal perception ... almost certainly depends upon information carried in dynamic transitions in stimulation (potentially describable in dynamic systems terms)' and that 'All this evidence suggests that spatiotemporal information common to the various sensory systems is extracted by the very young infant to yield information attesting to the same external reality' (p. 180).

The evidence has kept accumulating for a view of psychological development as being far more in line with Gibson's ecological assumptions than one based upon dichotomies (e.g. Bremner, Slater and Butterworth, 1997; Goswami, 1998; Simion and Butterworth, 1998). When Gibson told us (1979, p. 246) that 'information is available to a perceptual system, and . . . the qualities of the world in relation to the needs of the observer are perceived directly' and 'the affordances of things for an observer are specified in stimulus information. They seem to be perceived directly because they are perceived directly' (p. 140), his views were dismissed by most. It is not now possible to disregard his appreciation of our embedment in ecology.

The concept of affordance

Invariances are crucial, but they are nothing in development until and unless they are utilized, that is, coupled to the behaviour of the organism, so that the properties of the organism and the properties of the environment 'fit' together. For monkeys, trees afford climbing. They do not for halibut. Rain forests afford good living conditions for bananas, but not for gannets. A 'strict' routine may afford for a youth who has encountered no limitations on his or her behaviour some structure which aids development. The same regime for someone requiring trust may not afford beneficial outcomes. The concept of affordance picks out the crucial fact that states and events in the environment cannot be accorded any absolute properties or qualities when we are considering the psychology and behaviour of organisms, including people. Neither can an abstract description of the psychology and behaviour of them alone specify how they can live, what they can do, because it all depends upon the environment they are in. Only the relation of the form of the two to each other matters. Those relations specify what is 'do-able', what is afforded. This relational theory demanded a new way of thinking, a new vocabulary. We got it, with Gibson's (1979) notion of affordances:

> The notion of invariants that are related at one extreme to the motives and needs of an observer and at the other

extreme to the substances and surfaces of a world provides a new approach to psychology [p. 143]. The affordances of the environment are what it offers the animal, what it provides or furnishes, either for good or ill. The verb to afford is found in the dictionary, but the noun affordance is not. I have made it up. (p. 127)

In 'making it up' Gibson broke with the notion that the organism can be studied in isolation, or that the environment can, because his central theoretical term only has any meaning as describing the functional *relationship* which an aspect of the environment has for an organism. I think that bit of 'making up' is an act of genius. It is the key term which makes a dichotomous view impossible. Dichotomies cannot tolerate relations. That is what matters about 'affordance', its relational nature, its mutuality. The 'organism-in-environment' is the only unit of analysis when affordances are the language of psychology and the search for affordance relations must be central because these specify what activities are and are not possible. The relation of information and affordances to invariances is a matter I return to in a later section.

The continuity between perception, cognition and action

Gibson recognized that his ecological systems thinking implied that the organism was a system composed of subsystems and that these must be integrated in their functioning, just as the organism must be so related to its environment. There is no place here for a complex mind divorced from a simple body or from simple perception. It is organisms which survive or do not, not genes, or perceptual systems, or brains. Thus there is no point in attempting to conceive of the functioning of the components separately, as it is the relations of the functioning of all aspects of psychological functioning to each other, as finally expressed in behaviour in relation to the environment, that is adaptive, aids the survival of the organism, or not. Thus there can be no dichotomy between thinking and perception. It is hard to know what language to use to describe this situation. Bremner (1997), a prominent developmental psychologist, writing about affordances, tells us (p. 62) that

> The notion involved in this concept is that in addition to perceiving the world objectively, individuals directly perceive the connections between features of the world and their own actions. In other words, with no need for mediating cognitive structures, they perceive the implications of environmental features of particular actions.

This view suggests that cognitive structures mediate but perceptual ones do not, that cognition and perception are still, as in the traditional view, to be regarded as separate. I doubt that such language helps. To say we learn to perceive some things is to say that new, higher-order invariances are extracted which is to say that 'mediating cognitive structures' have been used. It is two ways of saying the same thing, not one way of saying two things.

None of this means that learning is not involved in perception. Just as exploration of the motor system leads to improved performance after self-organization, so too with perception. We do learn and we do so because exploration leads to new internal structures developing which enable the perception of external structure which was previously not accessible, either by the reassembly of perceptual structures affording the detection of more complex dynamic invariances, or the reassembly of motor co-ordinative structures which afford better exploratory ability, or both. Thus, each bit of learning affords the next – there is a development of affordances because new systems for information production through integrated perception, cognition and action systems have developed.

Interactions between systems of different extensions of invariance

Humans can utilize all sorts of invariances. When the infant recognizes mother their brain has become coupled to the invariant features which discriminate mother from others. When they learn to walk their action is informed by the invariant resistance of floors, the invariant force of gravity, the dynamic invariance specifying their muscle flexions, joint positions and movement, balance, etc. When they participate in 'peek-a-boo' they are fitting their actions to the invariant order and content of the play routine. Invariance, structure, predictability, is everywhere and it is the condition of all adaptation, whether over phylogenetic or ontogenetic time. In fact when faced with the alternative people tend to get completely disoriented. It is called sensory deprivation, a lack of differentiation, a lack of structure in perceptual input.

It is a start to identify invariance in general as that which systematic adaptation takes place to, but because systems are nested, i.e. are comprised by sub-systems within larger ones, we need to identify the main levels of systems which have influence and how they relate to one another. You will see that the model I describe now bears a close resemblance to transactional, hierarchical models, like that of Hinde *et al.* (1985), Bronfenbrenner (1989) and Sameroff (1991). It is not the same though. The strength of transactional models is in demanding that we take account of the variety of contexts influencing development at a given moment, and on the interaction of these with each other as well as with the individual. But these models stop halfway as they have no clear historical component. There is a whole extra dimension to the factors influencing development, the historical dimension. It is this which I incorporate within the nest of factors influencing individual development. I focus on invariances because it is just that regularity which it implies that makes it the raw material, the components, which when mixed in a reaction, will produce knowledge. This focus also ensures that those constraints which most generally affect development, physical laws, are not omitted, and that we can more clearly see that there is a continuum of extensions of invariance.

One commonly used level of generality we talk about in development is that of species-typicality. A species-typical interaction must involve species-typical components. Systems of such interactions depend upon the existence of invariances which have been regularly encountered over evolutionary time. This level is seen as central, perhaps because it relates easily to the 'nature' side of the traditional dichotomy. But it is just one extension. We can identify a continuum of extensions of structures, in time and in space, invariances, of which 'species-typical' is but one, and can see how they all 'inform' development, affect what we can do and how. For all cases we will also see that my central principle operates that the greater the extension of invariance involved in interactions, the broader but less differentiated the effect on systems of lesser extension.

Some states of affairs and events have remained invariant over periods of time far longer than most species has existed, for instance, gravity, oxygen, water, sun, its heat, its light and its predictable movement. The laws of physics have operated and still operate on every inanimate and animate thing, on every crevasse and plain, fern and flower, mouse and minnow. Gravity itself is a self-organized product of the reactivity of matter with other matter. It has an extension in time and space far greater than 'species-typical for humans'. It is an illuminating case of an invariance of huge extension in time and space because it is easy to see how generally it constrains the development of, change to, all matter, animate and inanimate, setting powerful parameters on what sorts of ways every physical form and thus all organisms, could be designed. It is a classic example of a generic factor, as described in Chapter 1, 'informing' the development of innumerable species, and providing part of the context in which the whole of more differentiated change, including genetic tuning, has taken place. Without rigidity in organic form every organism would be effectively a puddle, pulled to the earth by the force of gravity. All the mechanisms providing such rigidity were selected in the context of gravity informing what would be adaptive. All mechanisms affording locomotion require the exertion of force against matter which already has structure (like the ground, or water) to act against. Gravity, like oxygen, water, etc. does not constrain evolved design in a very specific, differentiated way, but does so in powerful generic, undifferentiated ways. That there is a huge variety of species attests to the fact the the effects of gravity are undifferentiated, but that all species have form to 'cope' with gravitational forces shows its ubiquitous influence.

Now the way that the development of each species has been

informed depends upon the already evolved characteristics of the species, as well as all the other factors pertinent to their survival. That is, the same generic, external invariance in interaction with different external or internal invariances produces different developmental outcomes. For instance, the evolution of organisms living in water and those living on land were both informed by gravity, but the manner of the outcome, the 'information', depended upon interactions between the broadest invariances, like gravity, with narrower ones, like 'living in water'.

On a smaller scale compared with those invariances are those we may term 'species-typical' for humans. 'Humans' have always lived in groups, so all the regularities of social organization and communication are examples of evolutionary invariants, as are, for example, task-related invariances concerned with means of finding and identifying food, sharing it, means of navigation, prey capture, predator defence, child rearing, etc. These species-typical invariances provide still generic contexts within which selection of the human developmental system has taken place, but even these are constrained by the most generic of all, the laws of physics.

Within the human form, there have been three main types of organism/environment coupling over the course of human history so far, the hunter/gatherer, farming and industrial modes. Each of these may be regarded as a form of culture which has its own constraints and its own affordances, less generic then those invariants which apply to all human 'cultures'. 'Culture', here, is to be regarded as that set of relatively invariant forms of economic and social organization, communication, and associated knowledge, attitudes and values which underpin the 'way of life'. It implies a 'collectivisation of efforts' (Reed, 1996), whereby the individuals appropriate the resources (and constraints) of the culture and by which the interactions of the individuals recreate the culture. However, it is clear that the generic constraints and affordances would have been expressed in different ways according to the differences in conditions encountered. What you hunt, how you hunt, what is plucked, what is dug up, etc. all depend upon such variations.

Another 'way of life', industrial society based upon capital, with, as I say, its own constraints and its own affordances, is now a generic socioeconomic form significantly affecting the lives even of those who do not personally live by that mode. It comprises invariances with a breadth of extension, structural features, from which no country is immune. It now affects the development of individuals in more specific, differentiated ways than our history as a species of being hunter/gatherers does, but the history of that 'culture' will not be irrelevant. But within this present form of socioeconomic organization, it is just as clear that there are differences at the level of continent, and nation, etc. The American Dream is in some way different from the European 'model', or that of the Indian sub-continent and differences within these are also clear, like differences between the member states of the European Union. Nested within these we then have more regional, within-country differences, then neighbourhood and finally family systems and systems of individual relationships, with parents, peers and the like.

Now, each of these levels interacts with each other. The most generic system of invariances constrains in the most general ways the development of individuals. But they do so only through the interaction of more local invariances with those generic forms. The more local the level of invariance we are focusing on, the more we see its effects on development as an expression of the interaction of a more generic structure, the effects of the levels above, with local invariances. Most important, the higher parts of a hierarchical system constrain the lower ones more than the converse. The relationship is unequal. The experience of one individual cannot directly influence the socioeconomic factors or laws of physics affecting the individuals' development in the way that the generic, overarching factors inevitably will influence the form of the individuals' development. The argument applies to all 'cultures'. What we call cultural knowledge is an amalgam of frames of meaning for individuals and groups that has emerged from immersion in all these various levels of organization. Culture sets up the categories like gender, age, class, race, status, income, etc., as significant and sets up value systems about them. These inform development in important ways, more differentiated than the most generic levels, less differentiated than the changes due to one's regional, local or familial idiosyncrasies, but crucial in forming a framework of thought. This nest of systems of influence, of the various contexts 'informing' development is illustrated in Figure 21. In all cases, the interaction of levels of invariance leads to more specific outcomes, it amounts to a sort of 'fine-tuning' of adaptation to conditions.

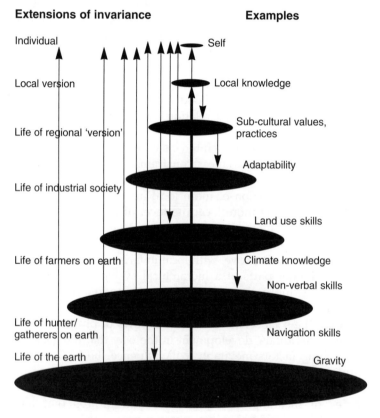

Figure 21 Influences on development

Notes: 1 The most generic invariances influence all matter (and thus all life).
   2 Less generic invariances still influence more generic ones.
   3 All levels influence individual development.

How more generic systems interact with less

I can illustrate this process with three examples. For hunter/gatherers, group living and (some) food shortage are ecological invariants. These two factors in conjunction create an invariant problem, that of how to organize the sharing of food. But though the problem is invariant for all those living as hunter/gatherers, the forms of its solution should be constrained by local conditions, lower-level invariances. Thus, where conditions, contexts, are different, the solutions should be different, but where they are the same, so should the solution form be.

The Gana San of the northeastern Kalahari were found to be less equitable in their sharing than the !Kung San. It turned out that the Gana San 'are able to buffer themselves from variability in the food and water supply in ways that other San cannot, through a small amount of food cultivation . . . and some goat husbandry' (from Barkow, Cosmides and Tooby, 1992, pp. 214–15). Living conditions were different, so the particular rules for food sharing were different.

The availability of meat cannot be relied upon (it has a high variance) for the Ache, hunter/gatherers living in eastern Paraguay, but the variance for collected plant foods is low, they are reliably found. The rule was that band-wide sharing of meat occurs, but not band-wide sharing of plants. Cashdan (1980) found that the same variation in availability of different food stuffs was typically encountered by the Kalahari San, living in a different continent, as for the Ache and that just the same rules for food sharing had developed as well. Thus we see that the generic form of the solution, having rules for food sharing, is of course still linked to the invariances of great extension, group living and food shortage, but there is plasticity in the particular expression of sharing according to the distribution of invariances in the local ecology, invariances of lesser extension. Specific cultural invariances are interacting with generic (due to farming as a culture) invariances. Here is a first example of what I mean by a continuum and a first example of how different extensions are related together.

Another area concerns parental care and nurturance mechanisms, studied by Isbell and McKee, and reported in Sants (1980). There are species-typical needs for security and attachment processes between the infant and the caregiver (referred to as mother from now on) so that infants receive the care and attention they need, but the specific mechanisms of their expression should vary with aspects of the cultural ecology. Isbell *et al.* were interested in how the physical relations between mother and child would affect what sort of communication systems developed. And let us not forget, these physical relations are themselves the emergent outcomes of the socioeconomic mode involved together with more local constraints. The outcome for many cultures is that it is typical for infants to be carried on the back or side as the mother moves around, thus receiving information about the presence of mother by her movements. The infants will also, unintentionally at first, be communicating to her something of their 'state' by movement. Here the infant knows mother is around because they feel, smell and hear her. Mother knows something of how the infant feels simply through the actions of the infant, so the infant will learn to communicate by movement, and to receive attention in the form of a movement acknowledgement. When infants are carried on the back, mothers do not generally vocalize to them, perhaps because visual contact is a control parameter for the production of vocal interaction. Infants carried on mothers' laps or side-sling receive more vocalizations (Lewis and Freedle, 1977), so learn to vocalize back.

Where there is usually a distance between infant and mother as in the USA (Ainsworth, 1977), the message will be mainly auditory (though the visual channel could be involved) and the child learns to cry out to gain attention while the adult will often need to use sound to indicate they are nearby. In addition, variations in the extent of face-to-face play, the extent of response to distress calls, the form of response, and any number of other patterns of interaction which vary between cultures will all lead to co-variations in what the infant is 'attuned' to attend to, learn about, respond to. The general conclusion is that the generic caretaker/infant system creates certain constraints and affordances, but that again variations in local systems comprising extensions of lesser invariance lead these systems to have local outcomes owing to varying local conditions.

At a slightly less generic level, Fogel (1997) has demonstrated how individual differences in the dynamic structure of mother's behaviour lead to differential forms of attention, exploration and action by their infants. Here the generic forms of interaction studied are early mother/infant social interaction, with or without interaction with an object as well. The more specific forms are the individual differences in the behaviour of the infants, consequent upon the differences in the behaviours of the mothers (which may be viewed as themselves the outcome of the generic interactional demands with their own propensities). Specifically, he found that the ways in which the mother initially behaved with an object as they introduced it into what had previously been a purely social two-person interaction with no object, made a big difference to subsequent actions by the infant towards the object in the social situation. Some mothers concentrated on making the properties of the object affordable to the infant by acting on it (e.g. shaking) or affording exploration by the infant (by bringing it near to the infant for touch, grasp). Other mothers made more short-lived attempts to bring the objects to the fore and more quickly reverted to face-to-face contact, focusing on the social nature of the event. When this latter group of infants did later reach for objects they put them straight in their mouths and continued the face-to face interaction, that is, choosing to further explore the social event, not the object. Infants in the other group explored the affordances of the objects, shaking, squeezing, and generally creating cross-modal information. The differences between the groups were maintained over time which indicates that the early mother-induced experience did continue to have the same significant effect on the children, being an attractor state.

As well as being another example of how local contexts (individual differences in mothers here) interact with more generic ones, it also appears that the outcome of the interaction of mother's 'preferred' pattern of interaction with the infant's preferred pattern (at that point in development), can lead to a system which becomes amplified and stabilized, so, for instance, the mother may use more visual demonstrations with infants who do more looking, or infants may explore by mouth more, thus gaining information about taste not otherwise available. Thus, early interactions can 'frame' later ones, providing a basic pattern which becomes further differentiated and elaborated. It is important to see that this 'frame' is the outcome of the interaction of two levels of extension, with an unpredictable developmental outcome. At whatever level we look, more local contextual structure affects development in specific ways while invariances of greater extension do so in more generic ways.

Uniqueness in the face of invariance

All humans are thus subject to the influence of a variety of levels of influence. The 'lowest' level is the individual, each of us having a unique body and unique mind. Development thus needs to be seen as a very individual enterprise because though we are all human, all in cultures, all in 'similar' contexts to some degree, every single developmental 'problem' we encounter is a function of every context that informs development, and as that includes our own personal context, all developmental outcomes are mediated via our personal characteristics. The 'problems' we face are shared, the means of their solution individual.

Different levels of complexity in invariances

Invariances also vary in their complexity and I want to indicate the different levels of complexity encountered. Gottlieb (1997) suggests that the following levels of bidirectional causal change are involved: genetic, neural, behavioural and finally environmental, itself involving three levels, physical, social and cultural. For each of these, interactions occur within that level, so gene/gene interactions and gene/biochemical environment interactions will take place at the 'bottom' level while at the behavioural level the various sub-systems comprising the body are interacting with each other, and so on. Ken

Richardson (1998) suggests a similar hierarchy, with the human developmental system comprising nested systems of development at the following different levels of complexity of regulation: genomic, epigenetic, cognitive and social. A short description of these will relate them to invariances. Genomic regulation depends primarily on the invariant presence of patterns of genes with predictable properties and a (mostly) internal environment with regular (invariant) characteristics. However, this system allows little adaptability to changing external environments. The epigenetic level of regulation gives more flexibility as it takes account of different external conditions, as in the case of a species of barnacle which develops a resistant (to predation) 'bent' form of shell only if a certain predatory snail is detected in the environs, so the relation between predator presence and resistant shell form is invariant. However, as the relevant, invariant, external conditions are usually more fluid, dynamic and complex, so adaptation to them must involve a system of responsiveness which itself has dynamic properties. Here is an example, using what Richardson calls co-variation and Gottlieb calls coaction. The sight of vultures preparing to descend on prey co-varies with the existence of prey below. Other vultures follow the first ones because their acts co-vary with food presence. They are using the co-variance of one event with another, where the co-variation is relatively invariant, to act adaptively. In other words, the sight of the other vultures flying is informative. A more complex example is of the use of the sun to navigate. The sun rises each day, moves through 180 degrees, with its rate of change across the compass greatest when the sun is high, because at other times it is moving at an acute angle to the observer (away from) in the morning and (towards) in the afternoon. Thus it could be used as a compass, but only if the organism in question 'knew' the time. But the daily pattern is not invariant, as the pattern of movement changes with season and with latitude. However, despite the number of such variations, each is rule-bound, so an organism could have changed so that its action was coupled to those invariances which were invariant over evolutionary time, (that the sun rises, sets, moves, etc.) by evolutionary selection and was coupled to local changes (due to season and latitude) by learning them, another from of selection. Dynamic equations could describe all these changes. That is what higher-order invariance is. It is predictable, but in a complex, dynamic way. That is why the sextant was invented, to utilize some of those invariances. Even insects, like bees and wasps and ants detect and use many of these complex invariances. When all such forms of variation are seen as part of one system we have 'nested co-variation hierarchies' (Richardson, 1998) and development is the utilization of the invariances underlying these. The psychology of social relations and communication involves the most complex invariances of all, including those involving social interaction, language, etc.

Given that the detection of more complex invariances will, in general, increase as development proceeds, we will examine later some of the ways in which the detection of relatively simple invariances is actually used to make possible the learning about and detection of more complex ones. That is, we examine the developmental aspect to increasing complexity in invariance extraction. The case of language will be seen to be a great example. All such work owes a great debt to Gibson.

Nevertheless, his genius does not mean he did not make important mistakes. For Gibson, invariance and information are always taken to refer to the same thing. In the next section I will demonstrate that this is a serious error, but one which, when remedied, strengthens the ecological position. A clarification of the distinction will allow us to see how the effective environment is transformed in development, just as much as the organism, precisely what we expect if they are but parts of one system. Once the developmental distinction between invariance and information is clear and the resultant thinking taken on board, I will set out the theoretical principles of my 'version' of how knowledge develops.

Information is not invariance

Recall that on the traditional position the 'solution' to the problem of intelligent adaptation to the external world lies in the gradual construction of an internal representational system of the objective, external reality. The difficulty with this account is that it signally fails to address the issue I raised earlier, of how the 'effective' environment varies with development, where, for instance, humans come to perceive what they earlier cannot (the style of a writer) and to not perceive what they earlier could (all sounds that humans make, Jusczyk, 1997).

To clarify this matter we start from the undeniable fact that the environment has an infinity of attributes. It has them in two senses. First, there are so many 'things' out there that are structured in some way that one could never even count them all. But I also mean that each of these things can be utilized in different ways, depending upon one's inclinations, skills and knowledge. Any given state, object, person, event, thus consti- tutes a number of affordances. For one person an object may be a golf club, for another a deadly weapon, for another a means of reaching something. The invariances in the structure of the object do not have to vary for the use to which it is put to vary. A board on a train platform may afford timetable posting to a human, or perching to a pigeon. Again it is the relation of organism and context which defines the ways in which action or thought are afforded. The structure of action of the pigeon and the person are informed by the affordances available to it: a given set of external invariances interacts with different internal invariances to produce different affordances and actions.

And this psychologically defined world never stops chang- ing because development never ends. Thus, as I say, even within species there is a huge difference between which invari- ances can be utilized at different points in development. Adult humans recognize individual people, places and objects mainly on the basis of invariances in their looks and sounds while neonates cannot use visual invariances to recognize indi- vidual people or any invariances to identify places or objects. Adults routinely recognize and thereby participate in complex culturally appropriate routine activities of a huge number and type, while though infants show great facility with some simple culturally defined routines like 'peek-a-boo', the invari- ances specifying complex routines are opaque to them, not meaningful or informative. The comprehension and use of language is a classical example of learned access to invariances in semantic, syntactical and pragmatic invariances which, over the course of development, become informative to the developing infant. What is invariant and meaningless stays invariant but becomes meaningful. The invariance stays the same. The relation between the invariance and the organism changes. The changed relation affords information.

The developmental question becomes that of how it is that some of the external structure comes to be 'usable' at a given point in the development of a given species or individual and some is not. How does the process of development render that which was unlearnable, unperceivable, uninformative to that which is learnable, perceivable, informative? In fact it is amazing how much 'psychology' goes on without asking these questions. But preformationism allows us not to, precisely because it is totally non-developmental in its very nature – nothing actually ever getting transformed, only getting read out from the internal blueprint or 'internalized' from the external.

The way to clarify the matter, I believe, is to make the distinction between 'invariance' and 'information' clear. 'Information' refers to any factor which informs, has some effect on, development or learning, while 'invariance' refers to any (usually dynamic) organization of the context, external or internal. All species respond to and utilize this property of pattern, predictability in the ecology, to maintain life, to solve adaptive problems. It occurs through the development of structure in the organism, in their physical form, but also in their psychological form, expressed in their behaviour. Because some problems are common there will be cases where different species will utilize the same invariances (usually the most general ones I mentioned, like oxygen, gravity, rigidity of surfaces). In the main, though, the differences between species will mean that the problems they encounter require specialist responses in the sort of things they can perceive and act in relation to: they detect and utilize different patterns. These may be the actions of members of one's own species, like dances of bees, submission gestures of wolves, etc., the actions of members of other species, usually prey or predator, or the existence of physical objects, trees, caves, flowers. It would be grossly maladaptive for a species not to have the capability of detecting those sorts of patterns which were pertinent to its survival, but to have the capability to detect patterns which would be of value only if they were a different species. The song of a chaffinch does not provide information for a wren, or the colour of a fish's flank for an octopus, however invariant those properties of the environment are. Some sharks utilize the functionally invariant structure of electrical signals from potential prey (Kalmeijn, 1974). They cannot gain information from the patterns which comprise the name of a sunken ship on its hull. Red kites in Wales can identify some patterns of movement as small mammals, but the sound of gear changes is notably uninformative. Insectivorous bats gain information about what is edible and what is not by differentiating between the sonar patterns from insects they can and cannot eat (Ostwald, Schnitzler and Schuller, 1988). They do not gain information from speech patterns. Structure will be informative only if it is relevant to actions of the organism which aid survival. Invariances thus comprise an infinite set but informative invariances are distributed according to adaptive need. The distinction is critical, but confusion is common. Cutting (1991, p. 26) tells us that

> Information is in the world; it is the measurable basis of perception . . . To qualify as information, however, it must be demonstrably used by the perceiver. Mere demonstration of the existence of an invariant, for example, does not necessarily make it information.

The last two sentences are correct. The first describes invariance, not information. It is not true and not useful. The distinction must be clear. Hence we see that invariance is a necessary condition of information, but is by no means sufficient, and that it is usually the process of development itself which transforms an invariance into something informative as the internal structure becomes coupled to external structure.

To appreciate the systemic, relational nature of this 'information' we need to remember that if any organism does not have the requisite internal structure, then any given external invariance will be non-existent or meaningless. It will not be able to perceive it, utilize it, appropriate it. Conversely, for an organism that has the pertinent evolved internal structures, but is not in the presence of the relevant external invariance, the interaction producing the information cannot take place. Thus Oyama (1985) was necessarily correct when she told us that information does not preexist interactions. The reason is simple enough: *information is a property of the system*, meaning that it is produced by system interactions, *while invariance is a property of a component of the system*, meaning that it is simply one of the interactants.

There is a debate within ecological psychology on this matter. Reed (1996), for instance, argues that affordances, which are information, exist independently of the organism. In what I think is a trivial sense this is true, chairs do exist whether I see or use them or not. But to understand chairs requires an understanding of the biodynamics of the human body and the needs deriving from fatigue. Just because this particular affordance is transparent does not mean we have a clue about most affordances involved in the process of human development. We do not. Focusing on the mutuality forces us to examine relations between the organism and the environment, and these are the key to understanding, not any 'objective' properties.

Defining information

So what, precisely, is information? Any definition of information has to include the standard notion that it is what can be gained from attention to (a form of interaction) external perceptual structure. We may gain it directly, for instance by observing the approach of a train, or indirectly, by reading the train timetable. Either way my thoughts and action are informed. The information does not cause any given action, but informs it, is part of the causal flux affecting my behaviour. In addition, we are bound also to include information from internal cognitive structures, memory, knowing where the timetable is displayed, or the route home from the station. These two senses of information both fit the following definition:

Information is any structure that informs action or thought.

But this inclusive definition also implies that many other factors must be regarded as being informative in the sense that they affect, constrain or afford, inform that is, action or thought. The systematic structure of an organism's body affects the structure of its action. This structure constitutes part of the internal context for any organism, limiting what is possible, but ensuring that many things are. So just as external structure, like the approaching train or the timetable, can inform action, so too can internal structure, as first became apparent in Chapter 2. If my use of 'information' is to cover all the sorts of influence on action and thought that the outline of dynamic systems suggest, then it must include all the influences making up the interactive complex from which self-organization emerges. It must refer to the bodily and the external and the psychological influences, and most of all it must refer to the outcome of the interaction of all of these. Certainly the phylogenetic system exerts powerful constraints on what a body can physically or psychologically do, but even within ontogeny our history cannot be ignored, it forming just as indissoluble a part of what we are, what we can do at any given moment, as the history of our species. If someone cuts my ears off I will not be able to hear, however long the phylogeny of ear development lasted.

History is represented in our bodies in both these ways, our personal history and our species history. In so far as we are products of our environments, and we are both products of it and producers of it, then the history of families, of cultures, of socioeconomic forms are all represented in our history. All these individually and collectively are our history and inform what we do. They are all information. They are all part of the unified causal system of interacting factors from which outcomes emerge. This is a materialist definition in the sense that action is the key, not idealism. It does not follow that we cannot think ahead, plan, but all such planning is based upon and in terms of knowledge initially gained in interaction. No preformation is required.

Discussion points

1 What is dynamic invariance? Give examples of some simple and complex invariances.

2 What do the terms 'effective environment' and 'developmentally relevant' mean to you? Give examples to clarify your view.

3 What is it about 'affordances' that makes them important for a non-dichotomous view of development?

4 Clearly distinguish between invariance and information. Give examples of how something can change from being informative to being only invariant.

5 Identify some of the affordances of air.

6 How might the skills required by hunter/gatherers 2 million years ago still inform human activity?

7 What is the advantage of using a 'broad' definition of 'information'?

Chapter 6

The creation of knowledge

Introduction

I have tried to make clear that the environment to which organisms are coupled is structured in a huge variety of ways; that invariances exist in a continuum of extensions, and that the broadest extensions of invariance, once involved in interactions, have a generic but less differentiated effect on development than the invariances of narrower extension. In this chapter I propose that the generic interactions have several crucial properties I have not yet identified, all related to the manner in which they aid the creation of knowledge as they form part of a developmental system which releases just the right amounts of information to the exploring child that they can cope with.

I start with the work I described and indeed criticized earlier, by Johnson and Morton (1991). Remember they proposed that species-typical mechanisms could direct attention to developmentally relevant features of the environment, like species-typical faces, and that this then offered opportunities for significant learning about individual faces. Hence the first interaction created the opportunities for the second. I suggest that what Johnson and Morton identify is but a special case of the more general claim that greater extensions of invariance in interactions constrain in more generic but less differentiated ways, and that what has been selected are systems of information production which consist in the initial production of undifferentiated information (e.g. focus of attention is informed, but what exactly will then be learned is not) which affords more differentiated information to develop (the recognition of an individual face, information about communication, etc.). The term they use for the first, generic interaction is 'primal', which I will use as a shorthand for 'species-typical interactions between invariances of great extension which have been selected over evolutionary time'. I retain the use of the term on occasion, not because of any basic, primordial connection, but because, as you will see, they have a priming function, controlling the sort and complexity of data that becomes available for learning about as a result of their action. I retain the use of the term 'species-typical' to mean 'will emerge in members of a species so long as the regularly encountered components, which in interaction comprise the developmental system, co-occur'.

A good deal of early learning includes species-typical elements, for instance much of what occurs before birth, which thus becomes relevant to this study. All such experience and its generic effects on future development would thus be part of the primal system. The generic turning to the undifferentiated 'face' is a clear case in point. The resultant attention makes data become available about 'mother's face', interaction patterns, intermodality, etc. Where any interactions produce information which coincidentally aid the production of further interactions which are adaptive, both the interactions, in tandem, are likely to be selected. By implication, where a succession of such interactions combine together in an adaptive way the system will be selected. The system is called development. In some cases the advantage is obvious, like the face orientation. In other cases the affordances may be less direct. Recall that Thelen (1985) observed how the infant explores a task space with its leg joints 'fixed', in the first month of life. These constraints limited what exploration was possible, but a variety of acts were afforded. In ecological terms, generic information about this affordance/ constraint system (the 'legs kept roughly in this position' arrangement) is being produced as the task space is being explored. All these early movements, in the foetus, are unlearned, by definition, but as soon as behaviour occurs, feedback is gained, proprioceptive, kinesthetic, etc. However limited the information arising from this early exploration, it is playing its part in enabling a reorganization to take place, at about one month, when the parameters are set differently (the leg joints are relaxed) and the exploration of this new system can begin, producing more differentiated information about body control. Each time self-organization takes place, it is both the result of the exploration of one task space, and the creation of the opportunity to explore another, more differentiated one and thereby produce more differentiated perceptual, cognitive and motor systems, that is, more knowledge. If the argument is valid, we should be able to find other evidence of such undifferentiated action, perception and cognition, action systems in the foetus, which may also be seen as initial explorations of an undifferentiated (for the foetus) environment or task space, but which are nevertheless a crucial part of the developmental system.

Prenatal experience

Recent research has not only shown that neonates are more competent than was hitherto believed, but that the developing foetus is active and responsive, raising the possibility that prenatal experience is much more relevant to development than was believed. First I summarize some of the evidence for this competence. Then I integrate it into the mechanisms for information production I am postulating. I use the accounts of Bremner (1997) and Goswami (1998) here.

Response to stimulation

Bremner reports that Hooker (1952) observed responses seven weeks after conception, as the foetus' turned their heads away from the site of stimulation when brushed around the nose and lips. Other regions produce a response only three weeks later. The response increases in complexity with time and includes pelvic rotation and arm extension. Stimulation of the palm of the hand produced the beginnings of a grasp reflex at 10 weeks which developed by 18 weeks. It is thus obvious that the external environment for the foetus, the uterus of its mother, affords a fair degree of movement, even in the early stages. This environment also affords acoustic information to travel, whether produced from internal sounds or maternal speech (Goldfield, 1995). Incredibly, DeCasper and Spence (1986) and Hepper

(1991) found that prenatal auditory exposure to a story was associated with post-natal preference for the story, even if read by an unfamiliar adult. Recognition of and preference for mother's voice was found by DeCasper and Fifer (1980) and by Hepper, Scott and Shahidullah (1993), who also found that they preferred their mother's voice to 'motherese'. Querlau *et al.* (1984) observed the same preference, having ensured no other post-natal auditory experience has been available. Bushnell (1998) reports that other studies also indicate early and comparable olfactory capability. Such studies show cognitive, perceptual and motor differentiation far more advanced than previously accepted.

Spontaneous activity

By 17 weeks mothers notice the vigorous movements of their babies. Rhythmic movements of the chest and abdomen 'simulate' later breathing and the experience helps develop the relevant muscles and co-ordination of various sub-systems involved. Head and trunk movements appear before 10 weeks and startles at 8 weeks. Most of all, studies reveal the co-ordination of movement, turning over, for instance, not being a simple activity. Moreover, the variation in activity levels corresponds to the post-natal states of sleep, quiet and active wakefulness (Nijhuis, Martin and Prechtl, 1984). It seems likely that all such experience contributes to the development of co-ordination within and between skeletomuscular and indeed neural systems as the foetus acts and thereby learns within the constraints of its external and internal environment. Remember that such adaptation involves the infant's perception of its own movements – they are a source of perceptual input, the source most often left unrecognized. The foetus is thus a perceiving, acting, and experiencing organism which is producing information about 'itself-in-environment'.

Newborn 'reflexes'?

Bremner follows Prechtl (1984) in the explanation of the origins, development and function of various, naturally found spontaneous behaviours and of newborn 'reflex' responses artificially elicited by experimental stimulation, such as the knee jerk, startle (which provokes arm flexion), the Moro reflex (a reaction to letting the head drop which consists in arm extension with the hands closed followed by flexion with the hands clenched), and lastly, the sequential 'stepping' observed when the infant is supported in upright posture with the foot on the ground. The behaviours or responses are lost or modified soon after birth. We are bound to ask the developmental questions, why they exist and why they change or disappear. As we know, the traditional form of 'explanation' is bound to invoke genetic programmes, innate causes and it is also based upon fixed reactions to fixed stimuli. But this is not consistent with the evidence for action in the womb, which appears to have rather more of a variable, almost exploratory or purposive character (the exploration of one's own bodily movements in relation to the prevailing environment). The suggestion is that alternate 'stepping' may enable turning in the womb, which may itself stop adhesion to the uterine wall, and that it could also aid engagement of the head in the cervix. The behaviours we call the Moro reflex may in fact be the results of practice at breathing before birth, interacting with the new oxygen-filled environment at birth. That is, supposedly 'reflex' activity observed is actually action dependent upon prior experience with similar environmental conditions leading to similar responses. As De Vries, Visser and Prechtl (1984) argue, the foetus may also be learning about stepping, reaching (even if only the thumb to the mouth), thumb-sucking, yawning, finger movements, turning, leg and arm extensions and flexions, etc., before birth. The prior action may be undifferentiated and species-typical, but important for the behaviours observed after birth. Certainly we need an explanation not based upon 'innateness' as that is not an explanation of anything.

I described earlier how infants who have stopped stepping would start again if their legs were immersed in water, increasing the effective power/weight ratio. An important possibility arises from this consideration. If infants are in a medium, the uterine environment, which supports them better than air, then they may be more capable of activities which depend upon muscle power and organization, like stepping, than we would expect. And the more general argument must be that a number of motor actions which are not normally observed in neonates or, if they are, are regarded as genetically determined, may actually be the result of learning in the uterus, learning as experience-based self-organization, resulting from exploration specific to the uterine environment. Further, the fact they disappear would be explained by lack of continued relevance, as the requisite environmental context in which they developed was not now being encountered – no womb, no womb-specific exploration. Whatever else is found, it is surely the case that all this activity is both a result of brain activity and a cause of changes to the brain. It follows that it has to be seen as an integral part of the developmental process.

Summary of relevance of prenatal experience

All this suggests that a good deal of species-typical movement and experience which results in developmental change has taken place by the time the neonate emerges into its new environment. The beginnings of exploration of the intrinsic dynamics the foetus shares with other foetal humans (e.g. having legs, retarded rate of development of visual system compared with auditory system, restrictions on joint movements, etc., all invariances of great extension) and of its unique qualities, what it does not share with others, will both produce information, albeit very undifferentiated, and they both inform individual action in being part of the total causal flux. The information gained during this 'generic' phase can then be used to inform the organization of further, more differentiated exploration, as the perceptual, motor and cognitive systems themselves become more differentiated. The fact that this is in a different environment only serves to make us realize that every behaviour of the neonate we observe may be, for them, an old act in a new environment. It also reminds us that exploration is of one's own body in particular contexts: never a case of being in context or not, only of which context.

The general argument is thus that these earliest forms of

exploration involve large extensions of invariance because the uterine environment is more typical and less differentiated than the external environment, that they also involve relatively undifferentiated perceptual and motor systems, and thus the exploration, itself undifferentiated, produces relatively undifferentiated knowledge. However, such knowledge then informs later exploration and thus more differentiated information develops. It is this combination of basic abilities resulting from prenatal self-organization that I will now demonstrate plays a central role in early development.

The powerful properties of 'primal' interactions

To enable the process of differentiation to start, illustrated by the case of 'kicking', is important enough; there is no development without it. To direct attention to aspects of the environment about which knowledge is particularly relevant is an additional important feature. But these generic interactions do far more than this. I shall now put forward the argument which demonstrates their crucial role.

The neonate is obviously able to 'pick out' the generic, undifferentiated features that specify a human face, others that specify 'object rushing at you', etc. This is one sort of relevant input. But infants are also shown to be able to pick out undifferentiated invariances like the variety of sounds that the human vocal system can make (they hear them all) and a variety of different variations in frequency and rhythm over time, called prosodic invariances, which are the basis of infant-directed speech and which correlate with word use. The world is being 'cut up' into units by these generic, undifferentiated 'primal' interactions. We do not yet know in detail about this world, but it may well include items like 'edges', movements, frequency changes, rough shapes, light/dark contrasts, expanding flow fields, etc. If the world were not available in this form, it really would be the 'blooming, buzzing confusion' that James thought it must be, because it would be completely undifferentiated. And that would mean there was nothing to learn about. This must be clear.

Providing the conditions for learning

Consider these examples of the conditions required for some pretty normal sorts of learning. If a sequence of conditions, *A*, *B* and *C* occur, I may be able to learn the order, but not unless I can differentiate between *A*, *B* and *C* (and have a memory, etc.). If I am to learn to associate a face with a voice I must be able to (a) differentiate between faces and (b) differentiate between voices. If human infants were incapable of distinguishing prosodic features of speech from sounds without prosodic features, how could they prefer them? If babies could not differentiate between an act of their own and an act of another, how could they learn to turn-take? And if one cannot perceive an episode as such, one cannot detect that one is in the 'same ' one at a later time. All these examples demonstrate one simple fact: we can learn about the rules governing the relations of 'bits', phenomenal segments of the world, to each other only if there *are* 'bits', that is, if psychological acts have created them. The phenomenal world defines totally what it is possible to perceive, by definition, and thereby what it is possible to learn about. Without differentiation the auditory world would either be silent, or be white noise. But so would the visual world and every other. To the extent that some things, qualities, items can be differentiated, there is the possibility of learning about them, about how they co-vary with other 'bits', what regularities exist. Only those 'bits' that are perceived are available to work with. The existence of these is a necessary condition of any learning.

The argument must apply to all forms of learning, the extraction of all forms of invariances, to all sorts of segments. Conditioning assumes stimuli and operants which can be differentiated. Piaget's co-ordinations assume certain variables and their variation are discernible in order that the co-ordinations between them can form schemas. Cultural norms and regularities implies perceivable structure in interactions and institutions. Learning a language implies the extraction of the invariances in linguistic, semantic, pragmatic and syntactical structure. This does not mean static states, in fact it is likely to involve, as I keep saying, dynamic structure.

The basic parsing varies according to species, as we would expect, but it has to occur for any species to be able to learn anything. It produces, through the interaction of species-typical external and internal input, a pretty undifferentiated 'parsing' of the world. It is direct perception. The earliest, generic interactions provide the raw data for learning to be possible because they do the initial parsing.

Reducing the problem by reducing the solution space

Equally important, when such interactions direct our attention towards something, they are partially answering a rather large question the undeveloped infant (of all species) faces, namely, of finding the most efficient exploratory strategies to gain the information required for survival. Should the neonate spend hours each day listening to car engines, preferring these to the sounds made by humans? Should they stare at stars in case they contain the secrets to adaptation? Or perhaps spend weeks looking for co-variances between nose size and loudness of speech, telephone colour and carpet texture, or taste of breakfast and noise of cars outside, etc? As Jusczyk (1997) tells us, infants can perceive the difference between male and female voices, but they do not appear to try to make meaningful distinctions between words on that basis. Nor do they use loudness differences as a basis for meaning differences. Instead, they use phonetic distinctions. Being able to pick these out helps, but not being able to pick out minute changes in nostril dilation, not for language development, anyway. Without there being preferences and without these being for states and events of developmental significance, the infant could literally spend years trying out attending to various invariances or co-variances in order to glean information about whether this was a useful thing to be looking at, listening to, whatever. There must be mechanisms by which attention is directed preferentially. The argument applies to all species. We will see later how some birds do stare at stars and as a result gain information needed for navigation. They did not stare at twigs in the nest, or at a sibling's feet, or any of a million other structures which exist, *are invariant*, but *would not be informative*. We are back to this crucial distinction. There have to be means by which attention is directed to that tiny sub-set of invariances which have the capacity to be informative for that species, have the potential to help solve their main survival-related problems. Preferential attention 'picks out' from the infinite population of invariances precisely that portion that can give the answers. Primal, undifferentiated interactions reduce the problem space to manageable proportions. Attention needs educating, but this is particularly true at the beginning of life. Search takes time and time is a crucial developmental resource.

To use an optical metaphor, in order to visually study a small animal that lived on plains, one could try and find it by training an extremely powerful telescope on a succession of tiny parts of the visual field, in the possibly forlorn hope that the animal was in the precise area pointed at, at the moment one trained the telescope on that area. One might never find the animal, as it would only be found if there was a coincidence of where the animal was and where the telescope happened to be trained. The search space is too large. What would be vastly more efficient would be to use much lower power binoculars to scan the whole field till a poorly differentiated image of the animal was found. Then the telescope could be pointed immediately in the right direction and a more differentiated image explored. Primal interactions get one looking in the right direction, or more generally, noticing the most developmentally relevant aspects of the environment, using pretty undifferentiated information. In the reduced search space exploration can then occur efficiently and far more differentiated information gained.

This issue has been the subject of discussion for several writers, for instance, Newport (1988, 1990) and Elman (1993). More recently, Clark and Thornton (1997) have addressed the issue from an Artificial Intelligence, connectionist perspective. Their views and mine converge here and an examination of them will reveal the last important function of primal interactions. They tell us that when computers are given problems without some 'framing' of the sort of solution required, the task is usually not solved. 'Uninformed learning', as it is called, is very difficult for them, so, to avoid this, programmes are designed to be able to detect, 'pick out', those sorts of inputs which are pertinent to the solution of particular problems. This design feature corresponds exactly, I would argue, to the function of the primal interactions. Just as generic, species-typical interactions 'pick out' and thereby afford learning about a restricted range of items, so efficient programming systems ensure that the problem space is reduced by ensuring that data relevant to the solution of particular problems is gained.

Coupling task demands to abilities: keeping problems simple

It is not just that problem areas are huge, but that solution mechanisms are not. The developing infant could find itself overpowered with masses of input which it was just not capable of dealing with early in development. What it needs is something that restricts the complexity of the data, the invariances that are available for analysis so the problem they have is solvable by the undifferentiated system components, perceptual, cognitive and motoric, currently at their disposal. Thus we should find that infants are actually incapable of picking up certain data, and this has to be seen to be just as important as being able to pick certain sorts out. This is precisely what we do find: the 'bits' picked out by the generic interactions have just this property, they are simple, not involving higher-order complex invariances. In this way the load upon the cognitive and perceptual systems of the infant is not too much. In fact what occurs, as we will see, is that the analysis of these relatively simple invariances leads to reorganization which provides the capability to then deal with more complex invariances.

Elman (1993) built artificial neural network models of sentence processing. He found that the networks were successful only when they began with a small memory which effectively constrained the range of data the model could operate with (only stretches of four words could be looked at for regularities), so complex connections between distant parts of a sentence could not be present to complicate matters. In discussing this work Clark and Thornton note that Elman's model was effectively able to notice what was a noun, a verb, a pronoun, and singular and plural (because these rules are generally detectable within four-word phrases) but not able to notice more complex grammatical relations (because these often involve invariances involving regularities between distant (more than four apart) words). As a result the network could 'concentrate' on learning about the rules of use of nouns, verbs, etc. without simultaneously and disastrously having to learn about complex variations in grammar use. Keeping the initial categories simple, constraining the data possible, allowed simple invariances to become clear and avoided the infant being flooded with so much data that no invariances at all could be picked out.

The initial learning avoided a great deal of the complexity, the fine detail. It was, for language learning, relatively undifferentiated, but with the simple rules that were learned the model was then able to deal with more complex input. The self-organization that was the result of the early learning constituted a new internal context, affording interactions with external invariances that were not previously possible. The initial constraints on complexity limited the task-space so the undifferentiated model could effectively search the highly constrained task-space. As a result information about that space became available. Then the model was capable of learning more complex rules – of successfully exploring a less constrained task-space (learning the rules of grammar). This is again exactly the same as in Bernstein's and my earlier examples. The system is initially highly constrained, the infant explores the simplified structures, invariances, of the system, and can thereby come to reassemble and to begin a new search in the newly arranged/constrained task space.

In similar vein, Newport (1988) suggests that the 'less is more' mode of learning will be useful where it is important to detect the relations between only certain aspects of a linguistic unit (a sign, in her work), so that the incapable infant may detect the crucial bits because they are incapable of detecting the whole complex comprising a sign. Her theoretical hypothesis predicted the differences actually found in sign language learning errors between those with limited processing capacity as they were learning, infants, and those without, adult learners of sign language.

The constraints on memory functioned as an affordance in the case of the learning of simple linguistic rules, because the complexity of the perceivable dynamic invariances was limited. Language learning is a task in which information is presented and produced sequentially. It is thus an inherent part of the task that memory is available. In fact the extent of memory acts as a control parameter for the extraction of the invariances specifying grammatical relations. We can extrapolate from this case. If we can identify tasks which have different requirements, we should expect that there are different limitations on the processing abilities involved so that the same function, of reducing the complexity of invariances, is afforded. Tasks using the visual mode are inherently different in that we can look again, or see many things simultaneously, not possible in language unless life is lived with a recorder. What the infant thus needs early on for 'visual' tasks is a limit on its ability to detect differentiated visual invariances. What do we know? Neonates are indeed quite limited in their scanning abilities, acuity, contrast sensitivity and colour discrimination (Slater and Johnson, 1998, p. 128). Simion and Butterworth (1998, Preface, p. xiv) offer a similar view as to the relative immaturity of the visual system compared with auditory functioning. Here visual immaturity would appear to be the control parameter.

This argument has an omission. Perception is based on exploration and exploration on action. Another way in which the quantity and complexity of data to be analyzed would be reduced would be through motor limitations which are involved in perceptual exploration. Once again, we find that limitations on head and eye movement, vergence (turning the eyes in or out), pursuit, saccades (sudden change in fixation) and tracking responses of infants suggest that these signals (about head and eye position), provide only simple, undifferentiated information (Gilmore and Johnson, 1998), just what is needed at that point.

Providing sensitivity to context

There is one more property this part of the developmental system must show, a sensitivity to contextual factors, so that variance in action is coupled to variance in environmental conditions. It must utilize stability but remain sensitive to change. For instance, changes in temperature or the light/dark cycle signalling changes in seasons and thereby migration start for many species, are detected. Generic mechanisms also need to ensure that such environmental contingencies are detected.

The general conclusion must be that an important function of early developmental processes is to control, effectively reduce 'effective' environmental input. We saw that the prehatching experience of ducklings had just such an effect. Here it is at least as important and as we shall shortly see, is observable in many more cases than I have already intimated. Generic interactions cannot produce an individual face, but can a generic form. We will find that they cannot produce (notice) a syntactical category, but they can produce a prosodic one. As a result the infant is not overloaded. Primal interactions thus function both to reduce the problem space in constraining what is attended to, and in making available only limited amounts and types of information to have to deal with at any given developmental point.

All this is implied by a systems approach because as I have argued, systems afford and constrain. By constraining the task demands on a developmental dimension, the child is eventually capable of gaining knowledge of highly complex invariances. No species is capable of adapting in one moment to the complexity. That is why the developmental system itself evolved. It organizes the number and quality of problems which exist for the developing infant with their corresponding solution forms into chunks. As a consequence, development can be seen in terms of the successive solution of ever more complex problems, but starting small is essential. Rather than 'nature' and 'nurture' (corresponding roughly to 'primal' or 'less differentiated' and 'more differentiated') being alternative forms of cause, they are quintessentially locked together to form one developmental system. I can now summarize these ideas about the function of generic interactions.

Summary of hypotheses

1 Where an area of learning is significant for normal development, it will be enabled by generic interactions which serve one or several of the following functions:

- to direct attention to that which needs learning about
- to reduce the enormous problem space that would otherwise be entailed in finding where to focus
- to reduce the complexity of the invariances detected so the infant is capable of extracting the regularities in the data.

2 Where variations in contextual (external or internal environmental) contingencies could make a significant difference to the outcome of an adaptive function, plasticity should be built into the emergent system such that the timing of outcomes fits the affordances of the organism to utilize them. This applies irrespective of how differentiated or undifferentiated the interactions involved are.

A note on direct perception

Perception is still widely believed to be mediated, not direct. But the crucial properties of the undifferentiated 'primal' interactions that I have just been describing hardly deserve the term 'mediated perception'. Rather, I propose that this level of extremely undifferentiated perception be regarded as a modern construal of direct perception. It means direct perception has the critical developmental functions I have identified. Time for more empirical evidence now, first animals, then people.

Discussion points

1 In what ways might experience in the womb inform development?

2 What are the conditions for early learning which make the process of development feasible?

3 'Just as Bernstein showed that the central control of motor activity was impossible, psychologists are now showing that without means of reducing the difficulty of the tasks facing the infant, development is impossible.' Discuss.

4 How does the 'less is more' principle appear to help language development?

Chapter 7

A sample of the evidence: wise owls, accurate ants

A glance at the animal world

If the coupling of interactions of greater and lesser differentiation is a powerful device for the decomposition of complex problems into simple ones, it should be found, in some form, in a variety of species and problems. It is, and here I offer a glimpse of this world, a sample of the systems which combine the utilization of a variety of invariances in problem-solving.

Barn owl prey location

Barn owls must find prey. Being nocturnal in the main, they require adaptations which make prey location by auditory means a priority. One way of achieving this might be for the owl to have evolved species-typical structures which connected auditory input with precise action to the input – simply hearing the prey would be sufficient to exactly specify its position. This would involve the detection of tiny differences in frequency, magnitude of sound and difference in arrival times to each ear for each direction. Something like this structure is found (Knudsen, 1983).

However, there are individual differences between owls' heads, which a species-typical mechanism cannot, by definition, take account of. There need to be interactions by which a more differentiated knowledge is built. On the other hand, if the undifferentiated mechanism was not 'under construction', so learning quickly led to accurate performance, the owl might die of starvation before it had learned to locate prey accurately. Thus, what is required early in hunting development is a generic interaction based upon species-typical differentiation which gets the owl to roughly the right position of the prey, and more differentiated interactions to gradually 'take over' and somehow lead to 'fine-tuning' of means of location. This is just what occurs. Each time it nears the prey visual input takes over and a new specification of prey location recorded, which is used to recalibrate the auditory mechanism that took the owl to the first 'estimated' position. Eventually sound alone specifies position to a high degree of accuracy and vision is less necessary. This second process is totally dependent on the first as one cannot recalibrate anything that is not already roughly calibrated. For the 'rough guide', the undifferentiated system, the relevant invariances have existed over evolutionary time, e.g. speed of light, speed of sound through air, characteristic features of prey and the characteristic shape of barn owls' heads (together, as ever, with the 'informing' flux of factors that barn owls can fly, see in the dark to some degree, hear, digest rodents, etc., etc.). The presence of simultaneous auditory and visual inputs is itself species-typical and is the condition for the recalibration which couples action to prey position for the individual bird to occur. Also of note is the fact that the end-result, a complex and accurate internal device for localization, was not the condition of accurate, 'intelligent' action, but the result of real action tested in real contexts, literally, in the field. As with Mataric's robot, action which is tested in context is the condition of more intelligent action emerging.

Navigation by dead reckoning and learning

Navigation is a major task for most species. I consider here just two of the numerous sorts of generic and specific interactions involved in finding out in what direction and how far to go. As navigation involves movement, which is obviously species-typical, one possible generic means of knowing where one is in relation to a base, like home, would be for the organism to record its own movement to give knowledge of distance and direction from that 'base'. Many species do appear to maintain such a record and thus know how to return to a given starting point, like their nest. This is known as dead reckoning or path integration. It involves monitoring the direction they have travelled and, separately, the distance for each direction, so that a cumulative record is developed. It does not appear to improve with practice, seeming to be the result of interactions selected over evolutionary time. The need to return to the nest is an evolutionary invariant, whilst self-movement is species-typical and feedback from it could thus act as the pertinent input for these generic interactions. However, as with the owl, the method is not finely differentiated, being based only upon species-typical invariances, so there is still a need for a second, more sensitive method of getting to the exact location. This is done by stopping when the rough destination is reached, and then conducting a visual search.

For instance, ants in search of food take a meandering, almost chaotic path. Having found it they need to return to the nest. Like bees, they take up the correct, to within a degree or two, orientation towards the nest. They note the position of the sun once they have oriented themselves and they keep the sun at this same orientation (an extra help in navigation here) to maintain this course for roughly the right distance. They do not require prior knowledge of the local terrain or nest to do this. Then they stop and begin a direct search for the nest itself. This involves using knowledge of the characteristics of the home base, the invariances which specify it, differentiated, individual-specific information. Clearly the first, undifferentiated mechanism has to operate successfully to get the ant near enough to home base that the second, local search is successful. Many species use this method (Collett and Zeil, 1998).

In Figure 22 we see in diagram A an outward and return journey, and the very obvious knowledge informing the return route. In the inset, diagram B, we observe the effect of a displacement, marked with the dashed line, the exact maintenance of the direction for approximately the right distance, and the subsequent local search around the area of the nest.

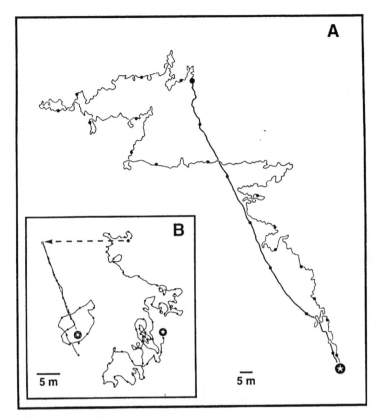

Figure 22 Path integration in desert ants

A The twisty foraging path (thin line) and straight return path (thick line) of a desert and *Cataglyphis fortis*.

B Ant is displaced after its foraging trip and walks as though it had not been moved towards a virtual nest situated 21m SSE of the release site, which is the usual distance and direction of the nest from the feeding site.

Source: Healy (1998), p. 27: A based on Wehner and Wehner (1990), B on Wehner (1982).

Invariances involved in migration

Many species of birds migrate. If there were any invariances which had remained constant over evolutionary time which specified direction, adaptations could have been selected which simply made us of them and solved the problem 'in one', at least roughly. There is evidence that at least 15 species of birds can make use of magnetic field lines which allow differentiation between 'poleward' and 'equatorward' direction but the differentiation is clearly very gross (reported in Berthold, 1998). The use of the sun to orient is plausible, and there is evidence for it in about 10 bird species but this does require an accurate clock as the sun's course changes during the year. A third possibility which does not require an accurate clock is to learn the position of stars whilst young and use these as referents. Five species have been shown to use this method (reported in Berthold, 1998). This is the logic, the constraints and affordances, of the system.

The position of the stars relative to each other has not remained constant over evolutionary time, but such change is slow, and can be ignored over ontogenetic time. In addition, though stars 'move' in that the rotation of the earth involves the 'sky' rotating each night, the whole field of stars moves as a unit. That is, the relative position of stars remains invariant as they rotate around the stationary celestial pole, over the lifetime of the individual members. That stars exist is an invariant over evolutionary time. That young birds can hold their heads up and see stars are species-typical invariants. The invariances in star movements are perceivable for a good proportion of the time. That the birds have the capacity to learn is invariant. What is required is an unlearned, undifferentiated tendency to orient to stars whilst in the nest so their relative positions could be learned about. Such a tendency is demonstrated for these species.

The first and, I suggest, impossibly large problem for these species to solve without 'help', is to find out what states or events it must attend to to gain information pertinent to successful migration. The chances of staring at stars being one of the keys to survival seems, on the face of it, no more likely than the contemplation of one's belly button. But unless this happens the crucial information for migration for these species will not be gained. What the generic interaction does is compress the problem space to a workable size.

To emphasize further the systemic nature of the process, consider some of the other invariants which must be part of the interactive complex from which this information-producing system emerged. The learning is not possible after fledging, the end, therefore, of the sensitive period. Thus, the invariances specifying readiness (when) to fly are integrated with those specifying where to fly. If the light–dark cycle is manipulated a bird will fly in what would have been the right direction if the invariant information embodied in the light–dark cycle had not been misinforming, but is not because it has been manipulated (Emlen, 1969). Other factors are internal, such as hormonal conditions, which partially specify motivational state. Martin and Meier (1973) altered the hormonal state of caged sparrows, resulting in them heading in completely the wrong direction, for the actual time of year (when their hormonal state is generally very different). Of course, in normal conditions the invariant relation between the light–dark cycle and the direction of migration has itself an invariant relation to the affordances of the destination, in terms of food available at that point in the invariant cycle of seasonal change. This invariance is itself systematically linked to many others, exactly what we predict from the dynamic systems perspective.

Berthold (1998) describes how circannual (endogenous annual) rhythms in relation to migration do not depend upon external input, as lack of seasonal cues in experimental conditions did not interfere with the timing of migratory activities in the first year. However, the fact that desynchronization was observed in later years showed that the rhythms did have to be recalibrated to 'real' seasons. As with the barn owl, the recalibration of roughly differentiated information is necessary for accurate responsiveness. This also an interesting example of how adaptation to variations in contextual (external or internal environmental) contingencies can utilize two sources of information, the species-typical endogenous circannual rhythms, or more direct, exogenous measures to 'put the clock right'.

Responses to looming

When an object is approaching on an imminent collision course we react automatically. The phenomenon we experience is called 'looming'. The changes in the size of image as it looms are defined by a dynamic invariance which potentially allows animals to know how long before collision occurs, on the basis of the distance between them and the relative speed, a function called tau (τ). Many species appear to perceive this information directly, in the sense of not having to specifically learn it, though previous experience involving the integration of perceptual/cognitive/motor processes will have been necessary to create the conditions for such knowledge to be displayed. It is part of the skilled adaptation to a variety of related tasks, like how to land (pigeons, bats, etc.), fly through narrow apertures (bats), retract wings as they plunge into the sea (gannets), avoid collisions (turtles, chicks, crabs and humans) and 'stop' at the flower for feeding (humming birds). It is thus a robust and generic form of adaptation which has evolved to deal with a general form of problem by using higher-order invariance as information.

Eleanor Gibson (1991) describes research by Schiff (1965) on the reactions to imminent collision specified by expansion of the image of the object, by infant monkeys, fiddler crabs, frogs, chicks, kittens and humans. The crabs ran backwards, flinched or flattened themselves. Frogs jumped away. Chicks ran, crouched or hopped. Restrained kittens struggled and moved their heads. Rhesus monkeys leapt to the back of their cage and sometimes gave an alarm call. When the image was made to reduce in size rather than expand, the behaviours were not observed. In 1967 Hayes and Saiff tested turtles. Guess what they did. Equivalent findings for human infants are reported in the next section. The specification of time to contact, let us be clear, is not a solution. As ever the solution is action, action tailored to the conditions, that is, to the affordances/constraints of the organism/environment system. Hence the head retraction, blinking, jumping, etc.

Because these reactions are reliably observed in the young of many species, there is strong evidence that at least some, fairly undifferentiated information is gained through interactions selected over evolutionary time. This is particularly the case when we consider the complexity of learning that is otherwise entailed. We would have to assume that for all these species the individual animals had learned the rule for transforming a geometric change in one variable (size of retinal image) with a constant rate of change of another (distance away), or rate of increase of distance apart of elements on a surface, and had learned what sorts of actions were adaptive and that they had learned that the perceptual observation had to lead to the adaptive response.

When gannets are about to enter, that is, collide with, the surface of water they are diving into, they retract their wings just prior to collision (Lee and Reddish, 1981), another example of response to looming, this time to a surface rather than an object (or animal). As in many cases, it may be that a learned element of recalibration of an initial species-typical calibration is used to fit action to the individual features of its body, as with the owl (particularly likely here as it is not just differences between gannets, but between waves that matters). Such is the case with bats.

How bats learn to avoid obstacles

Bats do not see well but detect structures and events by echolocation, sending high-frequency sound waves out which rebound from anything solid, like a wall or a fly. There is an invariant relation between the characteristics of the echoes and the form they rebounded from, thus constituting a possible source of information. Lee *et al.* (1992) showed that bats could learn to fly through a small aperture in a tunnel and that they used the ratio of distance to travel over velocity, the tau function, to provide the information to control deceleration as they approached the aperture to be negotiated. Lee *et al.* (1995) even found that bats could use the same tau function to plan turning movements to land upside down, where angular velocity (rate of rotation) was perceived. At least some of this information must have been selected over evolutionary time as the bat would be injured if all its avoidance or landing knowledge had to be provided through selection by learning. In any case, given that it feeds by echolocation, it would starve to death if it had no initial ability. What pertinent invariances are species-typically encountered? The speed of sound through air is a species-typical invariant pertinent to the use of echolocation as a means of prediction of distance or time to contact. Objects from which sound would reflect back are typically encountered and the ability to send and receive the sounds. Invariances which would be sufficient to give the information are thus available, if the relevant system has developed. That bats survive indicates both that there are primal, undifferentiated interactions involved and that these have been supplemented by learning such that the variety of obstacles, landing points and prey can all be adequately responded to.

Pigeons, people and humming birds

The same principles explain how a pigeon lands 'softly' on a perch, how 'braking' is controlled by keeping rate of change of tau constant, and foot extension initiated at the right point of deceleration and how humming birds 'dock' at a feeder tube (Lee, Reddish and Rand, 1991) using tau. Humans watching a computer simulation showing cars 'looming' can, without being aware of any of their own calculations, tell whether the result will be a hard collision or a soft one (Kim, Turvey and Carello, 1993) and drivers needing to stop before a collision do so by keeping tau at a certain level. Parachutists use it to get a soft landing (Sidaway, McNitt-Gray and Davis, 1989), somersaulters to land on their feet (Lee, Young and Rewt, 1992) and cricketers to time the hitting of a dropping ball (Lee *et al.*, 1983). A generic solution form works because the problem form is generic and the animals share some generic external (like rate of change of image) and internal (like having perceptual systems, skeletons) invariances.

Vervet monkey communication

In a rather different sort of finding, we encounter the initially undifferentiated production of an alarm call, which becomes refined in terms of a narrowing of input to which the call is given. Byrne (1995) describes how vervet monkeys come to give and react appropriately to different social alarm calls which warn group members of specific predators, leopards, eagles, pythons, small cats, baboons, humans (Struhsaker, 1967). There is a developmental progression in production of calls in relation to predator presence. Initially young vervet monkeys give the eagle alarm calls to almost anything flying, including a large leaf. It is difficult to see how they would have learned to make such a call as what they have been hearing is the specific and varied calls for all the predators mentioned, so it would appear be a generic response to an undifferentiated, species-typical input, 'flying-type things'. But this response becomes more differentiated. Later it is restricted to the appearance of large, broad-winged birds, then finally for just the two species of hawk-eagles which are serious predators of the vervets (Seyfarth and Cheney, 1986). That is to say, experience leads to a restriction on the range of input to which the response is given, it leads to a more differentiated response to environmental contingencies.

Changing form of locomotion after metamorphosis

Here we consider two examples of how sensitivity to context is organized in a systematic fashion. Animals which undergo metamorphosis have a pretty obvious problem in matching their activity to the environmental conditions, given that the affordances of their body are transformed so radically. They need to 'know' of their own bodily changes, to 'know' of environmental conditions, and to couple the two sorts of change together. Bullfrogs are tadpoles for two years, in which time they locomote via tail oscillations. When they turn into a frog they need to produce a form of locomotion suitable to a terrestrial, air-breathing carnivore. Stehouwer and Farel (1984) placed metamorphic frogs in three conditions: deep water, a slippery wet surface and a dry, rough surface. Accelerated locomotor patterns in the use of hind-limb stepping occurred in the latter two conditions, but not in deep water. There is a direct coupling between two different sorts of species-typical, invariant input (lack of resistance in water, resistance if touching a solid), and two different sorts of species-typical invariant output (not stepping, or stepping).

Weaning in rats

Thelen and Smith (1994) provide another example of behaviour which has undifferentiated, unlearned elements, but which is sensitive to context in quite complex ways, the weaning of rat pups. We can assume that the initial suckling is primal, being species-typical, unlearned and obviously adaptive. In the first two weeks of life nutrition is by suckling alone. There is then a significant shift in mode of feeding between 21 and 24 days, and by 28 days of age the rats eat and drink independently. The process might appear on the surface to be governed by an 'internal genetic programme', based upon maturational criteria. However, Hall and Bryan (1980) showed that newborns would ingest liquid or semisolid food from the test chamber floor, but only if the ambient temperature was high. Pfister, Cramer and Blass (1986) provided nursing mothers and their litters to rat pups and found they would continue suckling up to 70 days of age, but only if the younger littermates attached to the teat first.

Michel and Moore (1995, p. 317) review a number of other related studies which together demonstrate that 'the underlying regulation of behaviour can undergo marked reorganisation, even when the superficial aspects of the behaviour appear similar'. That is, changes in certain external factors were sufficient to act as control parameters, shifting the 'stable' behavioural activity from one state to another. Again it appears that an explanation of the behaviour is better achieved by seeing it as the emergent property of a variety of internal and external factors in a dynamic system in which developmental outcomes are always contingent upon the context.

The role of experience in 'primal' interactions

One of the factors which has been recognized for a long time to be relevant to early behaviour has been the occurrence of particular events which seem to play significant parts in the process of early development. In animal behaviour 'imprinting', for instance, depended upon the sight of 'mother' a 'releaser' of the appropriate 'innate' behaviour, which was 'a fixed action pattern'. Clearly the systems view is at odds with this completely 'nature-centred' explanation. However, this does not imply that early environmental experience does not have a formative role in development. Masataka (1994) found that squirrel monkeys' 'innate' fear of snakes could arise from experience with live insects, and Wallman (1979) showed that chicks' perception of mealworms as food depended upon having seen their own toes move (both reported in Gottlieb, 1997). Here I consider a small sample of research which indicates the role of early, undifferentiated, species-typical interactions.

Duckling calls

Wood ducklings normally show a preference for their mother's call. Gottlieb (1997) describes how he found that the call had clear prosodic features, its frequency reducing over all the latter part of the call in a regular, i.e. invariant way. Normally, simply 'picking out' that invariance seemed to be enough for the newly hatched infant wood duckling to discriminate and follow mother, not another (non-wood duck) call. However, it turned out that ducklings did not prefer the mother's call if they had been isolated from other unhatched ducklings *whilst in the egg*. Pretty amazingly, it was shown that the preference only occurred if the wood ducklings had previously heard the alarm call of their siblings whilst still in the egg, and that it was a specific aspect of that call that was critical. Even though the call seems very unlike the adult mother's call, one aspect was the same, a fall in tone towards the end of the call, a frequency reduction. Thus, the apparently 'innate' behaviour of following 'mother' was actually dependent upon hearing specific sounds produced (obviously they produce sounds and these are audible), and hearing them from another duckling, not their own call, as had been believed for some time.

Mallard ducklings, however, only needed to hear their own call while in the egg for the preference to develop, but in both cases the effect of the auditory experience was to reduce the range of frequency of input to which the duckling was sensitive, so that after hearing the sibling calls, or their own for mallards, they were only responsive to calls of certain invariant patterns (descending) whilst before they heard the calls they were also responsive to ascending patterns. Experience was thus narrowing the developmental pathway by narrowing the range of inputs to which they were sensitive. The developmental significance is that the experience protects the duckling from developing a preference for the (non-mallard) maternal call of another species.

Gottlieb later found that if vocal mallard ducklings were reared socially (near other duck eggs) but heard chicken maternal calls in the egg, they preferred the chicken call after hatching, while those isolated and hearing the chicken call in the egg did not later produce the chicken call preference. That means social rearing was sufficient for the hearing of an atypical call to be regraded as typical, and it being preferred. One input was species-typical (sounds of siblings calling) one was not (sound of chicken not mallard). The developmental consequence was atypical as the social factor over-rode the auditory invariance factor. In these and many other cases we are thus seeing that the behaviour of neonates is a function of their experience in the embryo and that interactions soon after birth cannot be taken to be independent of earlier experience. Undifferentiated, generic experiences are not only affecting ordinary learned behaviour, but those we have previously been led to believe were 'innate'. The same may be true for human infants.

Seeing and hearing mother bird: the need for intermodal experience

Identifying the effective species-typical input for maternal preference was studied by Sleigh, Columbus and Lickliter (1998). They examined the conditions for preferential attention to the mothers of bobwhite quail chicks. In these experiments it was found that in the first 72 hours after birth, bobwhite quail chicks which were exposed to species-typical maternal auditory input (heard mother's call) but not simultaneously to species-typical maternal visual input (saw 'mum'), or vice versa (whether there was a gap between the presentations or not), did not develop a preference for the sight and sound of 'mother' over the sight of a scaled quail hen (not the same species) apparently emitting the bobwhite call. However, for the group of chicks who received concurrent maternal auditory and visual input, a significant preference was shown when they later encountered the concurrent auditory/visual maternal input. Even when chicks were continually exposed to the sight of 'mother', the lack of concurrent sound of the mother resulted in no preference being shown for the multimodal 'mother'. Thus, the prior, intermodal experience of intersensory integration of audio and visual input seems to be essential for the 'normal' developmental route of preference for mother. As such intermodal experience is species-typical, the generic interaction usually occurs, and thus the adaptive preference ensues. This research indicates something of the complexity which may be encountered in identifying the specific conditions even for primal interactions.

In this section I have given evidence of just a few of the interactions by which invariances of only species-typical differentiation, or more usually a systematic combination of relatively undifferentiated information with the more finely-tuned differentiation of action and perception afforded by plastic interactions come to be utilized. The latter system is found in many species and many sorts of problems. Every instance demonstrates the impossibility of a dichotomy existing between what has been selected over evolutionary time and what is selected in ontogenetic time, between primal and plastic interactions. On the contrary, as systems of undifferentiated interactions are often based upon invariants which have been selected over great periods of time and space, while differentiated ones have not, it is precisely the integration of the two sorts of systems which has been selected. Whether it be birds, bees, ants, bats, rats, monkeys, frogs, turtles, etc., the message appears to be the same, that development typically involves nested systems by which increasing differentiation, coupling of the organism and environment, occurs.

Coupled primal and plastic interactions in humans

Generic mechanisms of the sort I have described should be found in humans simply because they face many of the same survival problems as other species and because it would be anti-biological to assume a total discontinuity between the forms of organized adaptation that non-human and human animals show. Together with the comparative evidence, we will be able to conclude that across species and problems there exists a generic mechanism involving interactions involving broad extensions of invariance and producing undifferentiated information which 'directs' more differentiated interactions in adaptive ways, as discussed earlier in the chapter. The evidence again demonstrates the intimate causal relations between what was termed 'nature' and 'nurture' and classed as alternative forms of cause.

Reaching

Many experimenters have produced evidence that newborn infants can, with support which renders the relative weakness of their muscles less relevant, extend their arms towards visual targets (Amiel-Tison and Grenier, 1980; de Schonen, 1980; Aitken, 1981; Fontaine, 1984), as these photographs (Figure 23) from Amiel-Tison and Grenier (1980) clearly show.

This does not imply knowledge of objects in any differentiated sense, but does imply that there is some reaching extension to some relatively undifferentiated property of objects (but not as undifferentiated as before the considerable experience of similar acts in the womb). It is typical for the species and it is exploratory action of some sort, constituting a relatively undifferentiated search of a task-space (reaching towards something) constrained by the perceptual, cognitive and motor limitations of the infant. Further, this search leads to the accumulation of information required for self-organization of the earliest 'reaching' into a slightly more sophisticated form, when exploration, action, perception, cognition all become slightly more differentiated. One such self-organization takes the form of a change

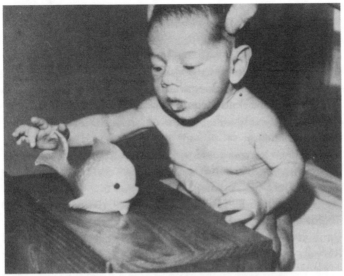

(a)

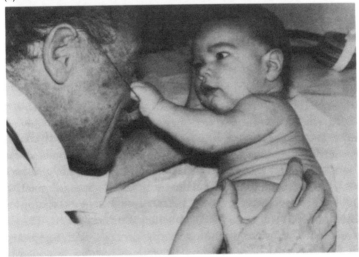

(b)

Figure 23 When the newborn does not have to worry about the weight of his or her head, very skilled behaviour will be demonstrated

a   17 days old.
b   Two months old.

Source: Amiel-Tison and Grenier (1980), p. 16.

from reaching without grasping to reaching with grasping (Wimmers *et al.*, 1998). Other workers also detail the changes by which a more precise coupling of action to objects is afforded through practice (Hofsten, 1986; Goldfield, 1995, Chapter 11; Siddiqui, 1995; Butterworth, Verweij and Hopkins, 1997). The earliest, undifferentiated exploratory activity leads eventually to undifferentiated knowledge, but sufficient for more differentiated exploration to take place, etc.

Looming

Bower, Broughton and Moore (1970) observed a whole variety of avoidance behaviours in human infants, including head retraction, eye widening, interposition of hands between face and object and blinking, all this at a few days of age, and shown for a 10-day old infant, in Figure 24 (Bower, 1989).

These results are supported by the studies of Ball and Tronick (1971) and Yonas *et al.* (1979). Nanez and Yonas (1994) presented four- to eight-week-old infants with textured light areas that expanded or contracted radially from the centre of a screen. They arranged that the elements, e.g. dots of the array, increased in distance apart over time, or that a central part of the elements did not. If infants could utilize the dynamic invariances they should 'decide' that in the first case an object was looming towards them, while in the second case they were merely approaching an aperture. The infants produced greater blinking and backward head movement to expansion for the 'object approaching' condition, but not for the 'gap approaching' condition. They thus not only picked up dynamic changes in indications of relative motion, but were clearly aware of the very different affordances that the looming of an object or an aperture specify.

Intermodality

I have discussed intermodality briefly, but it is important enough to warrant further consideration. The aim is both to show that the evidence for it is strong and that the production of intermodal knowledge follows the principle that

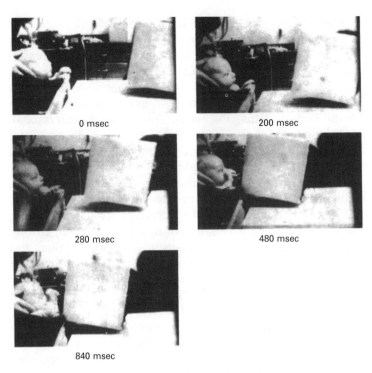

0 msec

200 msec

280 msec

480 msec

840 msec

Figure 24 Defensive behaviour of a 10-day-old infant to a looming object
Source: Bower (1989), p. 16, from Bower (1971).

undifferentiated knowledge produces information which affords more differentiated knowledge to develop. The ecological position holds that states and events are perceived through their dynamic properties. This means they are independent of mode, and thus implies that intermodality should be observed. If true, we should find that the extraction of invariance from one modality immediately provides information to other modes, for instance, that touching something gives information about what it looks like, and vice versa, without learning. In addition, we should find that exploration of known but relatively undifferentiated intermodal links should lead to more differentiated intermodal knowledge. A growing body of evidence supports these hypotheses.

Wertheimer (1961) presented sounds randomly to the left or right of his newborn infant and observed a tendency for the eyes to turn towards the sound. To see and hear concurrently is species-typical, and the outcome of the interaction between the inputs and the neonate is adaptive action in that it tends to afford extra information, visual, about the source of the sound. Thus, the initial interaction is intermodal, undifferentiated, but affords more differentiated intermodal linking to occur. Muir (1982) also observed that two-day-old infants would turn in the right direction to sound and that there was a relation between the amount of turn and the deviation of the source of the sound from the midline. Muir and Field (1979) found that babies turned more to a sounding rattle than an otherwise identical, silent one, suggesting again an unlearned link between vision and audition, and similarly, Castillo and Butterworth (1981) observed that neonates preferred a sound that had an obvious source. Lewkowicz and Turkewitz (1980) found that brightness and loudness summated in their effects on neonate arousal and suggest with a later experiment with colleagues that it is the intensity of stimulation that matters and that it is irrelevant from which modality the stimulations are received (Turkewitz, Gardner and Lewkowicz, 1984).

Hofsten (1982) found that the accuracy of reaching movements in five-day-old infants shown a brightly coloured spherical tuft moving across their visual field was greater when they were visually tracking the image then when they were not: the information from one input, visual, thus informing information from proprioception. Kuhl and Meltzoff (1982, 1988) found that infants of just 18 to 20 weeks preferred to look at a moving face where the movement matched the sound of a voice producing different vowel sounds. The experiment was replicated with the same and later different vowel sounds and shapes in two more experiments in 1984 (reported by Kuhl in Brauth, Hall and Dooling, 1991). Rochat and Morgan (1995) showed that three-, four-, and five-month-old infants preferred to explore by looking (visual mode) at and moving their own legs (getting kinesthetic feedback) when images of the legs were altered in the right–left, or left–right orientations. They did not preferentially attend to an 'up/down' spatial distortion compared with the 'real' image. The looking preference and the extra movement imply that

> Young infants appear to be attuned to certain aspects of invariant perceptual information (directionality of movement) used to calibrate intermodal space. Without such attunement, infants would not show the phenomenon reported here. The detection of an inversion presupposes that infants perceive changes in the spatial regularities associated with the vision and proprioception of their own legs in motion. (Rochat and Morgan, 1995, p. 635)

That is, if there were no intermodality, there is no reason to account for the increased looking and activity. As with the other experiments, the initial, unlearned, undifferentiated intermodal knowledge ensures exploration of intermodal events in more detail, so more differentiated intermodal knowledge develops. The evidence for primal, undifferentiated intermodality and its use in producing more differentiated intermodal knowledge seems strong.

Neonatal imitation

There has been considerable discussion of data indicating one form of intermodality, neonatal imitation of soundless movements. This is not surprising as its existence would imply a revolution in our view of how knowledge becomes available to infants. Meltzoff and Moore (1977, 1983a) observed that neonates as young as 42 minutes could imitate the actions of other people, specifically, tongue protrusion, mouth opening and lip pursing.

The photographs in Figure 25 are famous examples of the reproduction of actions. Vintner (1986) observed imitation of facial gestures when the dynamic movement of mouth opening and tongue protrusion were shown, and that no such imitation was found in response to a static state. Legerstee (1991) even found that dynamic movements were not enough on their own as it had to be facial gestures produced by real people rather than by objects simulating the gestures. The

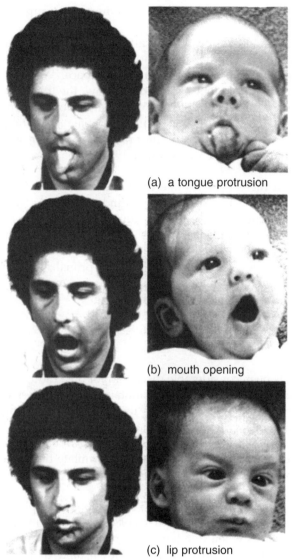

(a) a tongue protrusion

(b) mouth opening

(c) lip protrusion

Figure 25 Sample photographs taken from our videotape recordings of neonates imitating:

Source: Meltzoff (1981), from Butterworth (1981), p. 98.

movement clearly needs special qualities to be recognized as such. Abravanel and Sigafoos (1984) noted that the phenomenon seemed to disappear after four to six weeks of age, as happens with many neonatal behaviours, but Meltzoff and Moore (1992) claim it continues to three months and comes to include imitation of static facial expressions (mouth openings and tongue protruded) at six weeks. Kugiumutzakis (1993) found that they were more likely to be produced in a natural, affective interactive sequence than in a fixed, context-insensitive format and further they required effort to produce.

Imitation of sounds

In Kuhl's experiments on intermodality mentioned earlier, it was observed that when the pitch contour of the infant's vocalizations in the first experimental set-up was compared with the prosodic invariances of the female's just-produced speech, the infant produced 'an almost perfect match to the adult female's rise–fall pattern of intonation'. The infants were thus able to accurately imitate sequences of sounds, involving variation in rise–fall patterns over time. This imitative ability extended to making a good enough imitation of the sounds for different vowels that an observer could spot the difference. There have been reported failures to observe neonatal imitation, but it is now becoming accepted that what was originally regarded as highly improbable is a natural human competence. Butterworth and Harris (1994) report that it has now been observed in cultures as diverse as North America, Switzerland, Sweden and a nomadic tribe in Nepal (Reissland, 1988).

How imitation occurs

It is notable that the infant does not perform any imitation of acts it does not normally produce spontaneously (Maratos, 1998). This fits well with the explanation of Meltzoff (1985, p. 15) that 'neonates can . . . apprehend the equivalence between body transformations that they see and body transformations of their own that they feel themselves make'. That is, as the infant has moved a good deal before birth, it has a record of the movements it has made, which include some facial movements and thus these, like sucking the thumb, tongue protrusion, etc., undifferentiated, 'biological' movements, can be reactivated. When the infant sees a moving face they perceive the same dynamic record as their own movement produced, and thereby recognize, prefer it and often reproduce it. An alternative and related explanation is offered by Bushnell (1998) who suggests that infant haptic (by touch) exploration of its own face could also give an amodal record. Either way, prenatal motor action may afford imitation after seeing an act. Both explanations account for the data and are consistent with the ecological emphasis on dynamic information as being informative for the infant before static information.

At first the imitative responses occur only after a long latency, repeated demonstrations, and are rapid, of small amplitude and duration. That is, they are relatively undifferentiated. This is predicted by my argument that they are undifferentiated interactions of great extension, being typical for the species. However, my argument has to be that these initial imitations constitute exploration of the task space which will lead to later imitation being more differentiated. Maratos (1998) tells us that at 10 months the imitative reactions were immediate, given once only, and very accurate, and the infant often looked amused, all evidence of greater differentiation. One example of the change from approximate to accurate imitation is shown in the sequence here (Figure 26).

It seems we can conclude that generic, undifferentiated, amodal information arising from one's own and others' movements is used to produce a re-presentation of acts embodying roughly the same information, and that exploration of such intermodal equivalence leads to further reorganization as the intermodal links become more differentiated.

Knowledge of other minds?

Neonatal imitation must have an adaptive function. Meltzoff and Gopnick (1993) have argued that it serves to make the

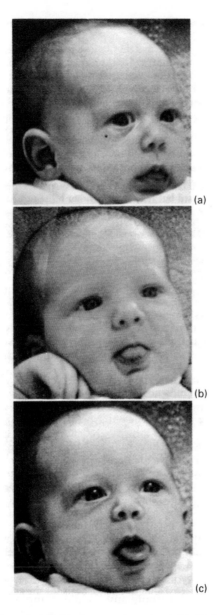

Figure 26 Three levels of accuracy in neonatal imitation of an adult tongue protrusion gesture

Source: Meltzoff (1981), from Butterworth (1981), p. 100.

infant aware that adults are like themselves. They claim that the baby knows that the behaviour of the adult is related to the mental state of the adult. These are strong claims, understandable given the remarkable complexity and sociability of the human infant. However, I assert that the only knowledge involved is about one's own and others' movements, not others' minds. But if I do not accept their explanation of the function of neonatal imitation I am going to have to give a better one myself. Here goes. Imitation leads to increased attention and reactivity from other humans; it is a *provocative* act, typically provoking a positive reaction. No conscious awareness is implied, no knowledge of other minds, or even other people. But as it leads to reactions and increased attention the infant comes to be in a dyadic situation whereby it can learn about other people, about communication, and, eventually, about other minds. The imitation by the infant is a means not of ensuring preferential attention by the infant to the mother but by the mother to the infant. But adults imitate as well, provoking attention by the infant. Both components in the dyad are acting to maximize attention to each other, so the interactive dyadic system can afford maximum opportunities for more differentiated exploration. As a result the infant learns about the producer of the initial acts, and about the relations between them and itself, about the social regulation of interaction. The infant thus *seems* to know a great deal about other people because they *do* know a lot, because they have spent a good deal of time *concentrating* on this subject matter.

This view has applications to other areas where precocious ability needs explanation. I am thinking of 'biological motion'. It could be that it is differentiated from other forms of motion without learning. However, it could be that the amount of attention humans are getting anyway, as a result of the operation of the imitation and 'motherese' (reviewed later) interactions, means that a lot is learned quickly about them, including the biological nature of their movement. As in many of the cases we have looked at, we can now see that there is no reason, no need to attribute any 'innate' complex ability. What is instead required is a recognition of the need for mechanisms to channel attention and allow exploration of initially undifferentiated task spaces.

Intermodality and self-recognition

If the argument that infants perceive the amodal, dynamic features of perceptual input is correct, then when infants are naturally (species-typically) smiling, grimacing, frowning, generally moving their faces, they should be receiving dynamic feedback in the form of kinesthetic feedback even when they do not, as is usual, see their own faces as they move them. In this case they should be able to differentiate between their own faces and those of others, even though their experience of seeing self is very limited, and no conscious awareness of self has developed. Legerstee, Anderson and Schaffer (1998) investigated the recognition of faces and voices by presenting five- and eight-month-old infants with static or moving video-tapes showing their own faces, those of peers and those of (sometimes animated) dolls, and ones displaying their own voice, or of peers or non-social sounds. If infants recognize their own face or voice, they should attend to it less as it would be a non-novel stimulus. In addition, if they can differentiate between social and non-social inputs, they should produce more social acts, smiling and vocalization in response to social stimuli. Such hypotheses were confirmed. The studies thus show the complex dynamic information-processing ability of even five-month-old infants and strongly suggests the use of intermodal equivalence. It also shows they differentiate between social and other inputs and between themselves and others, helping in the identification of what is especially human and social about people, including oneself.

Smiling

Wolff (1959, 1963), Emde and Koenig (1969), Emde, Gaensbauer and Harmon (1976) observed that the first human smiles did not appear to require external input, the control parameter being internal, contextual factors, possibly by-prod-ucts of transitions between sleeping and waking. By five weeks smiling did occur to the human voice and by six weeks to a species-typical face, along with eye-contact. That blind babies also smile shows that the species-typical input does not have to be visual. But smiles, like imitative acts, are provocative, most commonly leading to a more enthusiastic input from the 'other'. To have such effects is adaptive because it ensures attention is maintained and early learning about social interaction is maximized. These changes all involve an increase in differentiation of smiling, and the regular sequence suggests that the earlier experience is pertinent to the later. It is not hard to see that the same situation is found with crying.

Turn-taking through burst-pause sucking

Turn-taking is recognized as a basic communicative skill, so early exposure to the alternate acts that define turn-taking would be adaptive. The adult would need to act as the control parameter in these exchanges, but there is a need for acts by the infant which stop so the adult can 'take a turn' and then stop when the infant acts again. Kaye (1977, 1982) observed that all human infants pause in their breast-sucking activity, even though no feeding or breathing requirements are involved and no other primates pause. When they stop, mothers were more likely to 'jiggle', stroke and talk to the infants. When sucking restarted the jiggling stopped. That is, the infant pause and burst pattern was indeed utilized by 'mother' as an opportunity to take a turn and to 'offer' turns, functioning as a source of information to the infants of species which could utilize it. At first mother only jiggles during her turn, but later 'offers' cooing, smiling, frowning, etc. to fill the gaps when when the infant stops. The mother thus alters the complexity, the differentiation of her input as the infant becomes more capable of dealing with it, with the result that the interactive system itself develops. Once again, development is characterized by increasing differentiation, and again we can identify how this arises.

Using line of gaze as information for joint attention to objects

Adults transmit information directly about the world to children, but they are also indirect sources in offering to the infant knowledge of their own interests and foci of attention, shown by, among other means, the focus of their own visual attention. For children to use line of gaze of adults as information for joint attention to objects would be adaptive in three ways. First, because adults know more, they are more likely to be viewing states or events of significance. Secondly, it would create joint attention, a condition for communication. Thirdly, in developing this skill the infant is learning that the act of another is about something other than the act, so they are being helped to learn that humans can refer, another necessary condition of developing communication. Even so, for two-month-olds to sometimes change their direction of gaze, contingent upon the direction of gaze of the adult, was an important and surprising finding (Scaife and Bruner, 1975). Butterworth (1991, p. 103) describes a series of studies carried out to throw light on the processes involved in the development of the capacity to use social information to gain joint attention. He concludes:

> The general claim from these studies is that following the gaze of another, following a point, and producing a point are all processes of shared attention that are species-specific social–communicative adaptations that emerge in infancy and provide the basis for establishing the beginnings of symbolic communication.

In all the cases Butterworth describes, progress is exactly as we would expect, gradual, moving from inexpert and undifferentiated action to more differentiated, expert involvement. They all involve generic, species-typical actions and interactions by which information about interaction is developed which itself leads to the reorganization of the infant's role in social–communicative exchanges. All such adaptations involve the notion of shared attention, of 'topic', the subject of the shared attention, turn-taking and responding to or initiating reference. All these are, as Butterworth says, the prerequisite, basic skills without which symbolic communication could not be built. In fact he argues now (in Simion and Butterworth, 1998), that as pointing can serve to link a visual referent to the concurrent sound stream, it, in a sense, 'authorises visual objects to take on auditory qualities and this is an early means for the infant to learn that objects have names. Pointing is special; it is the royal road to language'. This does not imply that the infant's use of gaze or pointing involves intersubjectivity, but suggests it is a condition of it evolving.

As in the other cases I have described, the initial actions are not differentiated or very specific to the ecology, not coupled tightly, but the exploration that takes place, the attempting to, for instance, point, results in progress to a new, more complex level of coupling of task demands and organismic abilities.

'Motherese'

The use of 'motherese', or infant-directed speech, is an area where evidence of the integration of interactions of different extension in the developmental process is strong. Caregivers do not just look at, feed and cuddle babies. Despite everyone knowing that babies do not speak or understand speech, it is species-typical for caregivers to talk to infants. There must be a reason. One aspect of this speech, its prosodic features, has been studied in sufficient detail that we can reach some pretty firm conclusions about its functions. Patricia Kuhl (in Brauth, Hall and Dooling, 1991, p. 75) writes:

> when given a choice among sounds, young infants prefer to listen to 'Motherese', a highly melodic speech signal that adults use when addressing infants ... Moreover, the prosodic features of 'motherese', its higher pitch ... and expanded intonation contours, appear to be universal across language ... We do not know what makes mothers (fathers too) speak to their infants in this way, but we do know that mothers in every language we have examined thus far produce this kind of speech and that babies demonstrate a preference for it.

We cannot assume that prenatal learning has not been important in this area as we know the foetus has had extensive auditory and motor experience in the womb. Thus my claim is not that the neonate has an unlearned preference for 'motherese', but that earlier, non-obvious prenatal experience has been part of a developmental system in which the still relatively undifferentiated, post-natal input of 'motherese' leads to preferential attention. What we can be confident of is that the preference is adaptive, as it is (besides the face), a rich source of interactive potential. In fact given the evidence on intermodality we could even regard it simply as one aspect of a general preferential orientation to the main source of care, sustenance and education, as the infant attends to a source of information, not to sound or touch or vision.

The orientation could be due to the recognition of mother's voice, newborns having been shown to demonstrate a preference for their mother's voice over that of another woman (DeCasper and Fifer, 1980). But as such speech the baby heard before birth would probably not have been motherese we would expect non-motherese to be preferred. However, Cooper and Aslin (1990) did find a listening preference for infant-directed speech at birth and at one month and, crucially, the preference did not develop gradually with experience, suggesting that learning of it was not involved (or had already occurred). Mehler *et al.* (1986) tested the ability of four-day-old infants to distinguish between French and Russian input from the same speaker, having already found that 12-hour old infants preferred speech to non-speech. The infants could distinguish different prosodic patterns by four days' experience. Prosodic features are not just detected, differences between them are picked out by four days.

'Motherese' in sign language

If it is the exaggeration of tone of voice, loudness change, frequency extremes and speed variation that characterize the prosodic, dynamic invariances that make 'motherese' preferable, then if the argument for intermodality is valid, non-vocal means of infant-directed communication such as sign language to infants should display the same characteristics and have the same effect. We should also expect a similarity on evolutionary grounds as if motherese is a mechanism which aids scaffolding through the increased attention resulting from its production, then it should have evolved when scaffolding did, almost certainly long before language did. Masataka (1992), and others, found that mothers did indeed sign slower, repeat signs, and exaggerate them. In a later experiment Masataka (1996) played videotapes of deaf mothers communicating in Japanese Sign Language with deaf infants or with adults, to deaf six-month-old infants. The infants showed stronger attentional and affective responsiveness to the 'motherese' form of signing, clear evidence for signed motherese and a preference for it. Most surprising, Masataka (1998) showed such tapes to hearing infants who had never seen signing before. They also preferred, on their first ever exposure to this 'version' of the dynamic invariances, the greater sweeps of peak visual movement displayed in signed motherese than the adult-directed signing. This is strong evidence for an amodal preference for motherese.

Differential effects of different prosodic invariances

Later research on 'motherese' shows that the infant reacts differentially to different forms of motherese. Specifically, they are soothed when they hear low and falling pitch contours (Papousek, Papousek and Bornstein, 1985); they are engaged and likely to respond to rising pitch contours (Ferrier, 1985); maintenance of attention is accomplished with bell-shaped contours (Stern, Spieker and MacKain, 1982) and prohibitions were expressed successfully through signals with an abrupt rise time (Kearsley, 1973). Fernald confirmed these results (1992, 1993), showing that the communicative function was expressed in roughly the same way irrespective of the spoken language involved, and that infants responded in a consistent fashion. It looks very much as if the early undifferentiated preference for motherese led to exploration which resulted, within the first few months of life, in knowledge of the co-variations between prosodic and affective expressions of others, a more differentiated level of knowledge. The fact that there are some variations between cultures also indicates a learned culture-specific element (Fernald and Morikawa, 1993).

As a matter of interest, if the neonate is designed to hear

prosody, then from a co-evolutionary, ecological perspective, the design of prosody should be coupled to the design of the infant auditory system. The newborn infant has better hearing of high frequencies and we do find that 'motherese' involves a higher pitch range than other speech. In addition, signals should be obvious, repetitive, limited in number and attention-getting. Fernald *et al.* (1989) describe how they are found to have just such characteristics. As we should expect from dyadic (two-person) systems, the acts of each are coupled to the other – mothers adapt as much as babies. Prosody appears to be a significant form of invariance for early attention and communication, and acts to provide relatively undifferentiated but nonetheless significant information. During this period the groundwork for first words will be developing, as more differentiated and co-ordinated receptive and expressive communicative skills emerge. Let us now look to the processes from which symbolic word use emerge.

How language emerges

Adults as sensitively contingent

My first claim is hardly new, being no more than social inter-actionists such as Bruner have told us for years, that the scaffolding offered by the more competent and utilized by the child is an essential part of the process by which many of the underlying skills necessary for language use are developed. In systems terms the components, the individuals comprising the system, explore that system by acting in it, their actions and reactions providing information about the rules by which the interaction operates. The result is self-organization of that system and self-organization of the components, in particular that component called a child. In so doing the child is becoming more coupled to the dyad, capable of more refined communication.

The start of such mind-sharing skills is pretty basic and involves, as usual, undifferentiated forms of action which are not specifically coupled to environmental contingencies. When an infant sucks, burps and swallows in the first eight weeks of life (Crystal, 1987) adults respond in a sensitively contingent way as they interpret the behaviours and respond accordingly. From eight to 20 weeks the infant starts to make cooing noises and the 'mother' correspondingly changes her behaviour by offering softer vocal responses as her 'turn'. Then at 20 to 30 weeks we observe frequent repetition of vowel–consonant sequences, which the mother imitates (Papousek and Papousek, 1977) in turn. At 25–50 weeks babbling is common and by 37 weeks, consonants and vowels are changed one syllable from the next, with some rhythm to the production. The response to coos and grizzles remains one of interpretation as indicators only of physiological state, this being clearly differentiated by the mother from her reactions to more 'syllabic' sounds. It is important to recognize that these basic, undifferentiated interactions are just as important for complex thought and action because they are part of the system, the developmental system, by which increasing differentiation of the organism in relation to the environment, is achieved. Take these away and the later ones may not be possible.

What is suggested is that differentiation is developing in three aspects of interaction. The 'mother' increasingly differentiates her responses. The infant increasingly differentiates his or her responses and the perceptual/cognitive structures of the infant, internal invariances of one component of the system, are themselves becoming more differentiated. Given that the dyad is the knowledge-producing system here, the unit of analysis, this co-variation of differentiation is to be expected, as that increasing differentiation is distributed throughout the system.

But all this is a long way from the use of linguistic symbols. What has to occur before there is any chance of symbolic communication is for the co-variations that describe the interaction to become more complex. I suggest this involves two conditions being met. One is for the communicative functions to become more differentiated through the increasing differentiation of responses to the infant, the other is for all these interactions to themselves be embedded in increasingly complex contexts, routine domestic or play activities.

Infant episodes

There are any number of studies detailing the active involvement of infants just a few months old in simple 'play' routines, games like 'round-and-round-the-garden', 'pat-a-cake', for instance and domestic routines, being fed, changed, put to bed, etc. (Winnicott, 1965; Kaye, 1977; Brazelton, 1979; Trevarthen, 1980; Schaffer, 1984; Hobson, 1993; Nelson, 1996). Routine activities like these are species-typical. The whole event or episode may last just a few seconds or a few minutes, but always consists in fixed sequences of actions, with a clear start, a clear finish, and even clarity to change points in between. It is quite clear that infants come to actively participate and anticipate actions and outcomes in such 'formats'. That they do entails the infants have 'picked-up' the invariances specifying the characteristic features of these episodes.

Older children and adults who have no access to symbolic forms can also participate in a wide variety of episodes. Many such children are classed as having special educational needs of a variety of forms, but they all show the ability to utilize the invariant structure of routine episodes to help 'make sense' of activities which comprise the routine (Snyder-McLean *et al.*, 1984; Souriau, 1990; Richardson, 1991; Goldbart, 1994). Indeed, it is becoming a major feature of pedagogic planning to give meaning, purpose and thereby motivation to such learners by embedding teaching within such routines.

The view that regular events will become coded as scripts with a meaning and will function as a means of making sense of new experiences is important and ubiquitous in psychology, though it goes by a variety of names: 'event theory' and 'general event representations', later 'mental event representations' (Nelson, 1986, 1996), script acquisition (Schank and Abelson, 1977; Abelson, 1981; Mills and Funnell, 1983), 'formats' (Bruner, 1983), 'frames' (Goffman, 1974), 'joint action routines' (Snyder-McLean *et al.*, 1984), 'joint involvement episodes' (Schaffer, 1992), using context-specific knowledge as means of interpreting new events (Inagaki, 1990) and 'activities' (Leont'ev, in Wertsch, 1981). All these views recognize the importance for the child of events being dynamically structured at a level the child can comprehend, that is, extract information from. The 'strong' view of the importance of such episodes is that they are the very building blocks of cognition, the units of meaning to which all future experience is assimilated, so that the initial reaction to any event which is not an existing episode is 'no script, no meaning'. Perhaps participation in episodes is the most common and most important means by which a child gains access to culture. Nelson (1996, pp. 16–17) describes the characteristics of episodic routines and their corresponding mental event representations (MERs):

> events come in packets with boundaries, beginnings and endings . . . Within an event, actions are sequentially organised . . . either by convention or through constraints on causal relations. Causal relations include enabling [affording – my addition) actions . . . as well as direct cause and effect relations. Participants are often specified by role . . . Scripts are typically organised around reaching goals . . . and those actions that are central to the achievement of a goal may be invariant constituents of a script.

Thus, for a child to participate fully in episodes they need to have the capability to pick up, notice, the regularities which mark the start and finish to the whole episode and its parts, the relevant roles, actions and objects and their sequential involvement. The role, for example, of agent is seen to be understood in the clear expectation of the infant that the adult will carry out certain functions and the infant others. The obvious and crucial point for this discussion is that though these capabilities require the extraction of a variety of invariances, none of them involves symbolic invariances. The conclusion is that such formats provide opportunities to learn about action and interaction, to gain some of the knowledge required for linguistic competence.

We need to be clear about the limitations of this form of organism/environment coupling. In order to participate in episodes the members need to be able to identify which 'scene' is being played and to know which 'part' that entails them playing, but they only need to know this as it happens. All thinking and action is tied to and completely limited by the immediate context, to 'here and now' activity. One is what one does. Past episodes or parts of them cannot be referred to and future ones cannot be planned for. One could never carry out an act about another episode. But it is the affordances that derive from this simplicity that I particularly want to emphasize. Exactly as with Elman's (1993) artificial neural network model of sentence processing, with Bernstein's motor structures, with the variety of cases I have looked at, infants can make sense of and take part in these simple events with predictable dynamic structure precisely because they are simple, the demands of the task-space (participation in the simple routine) being limited and thereby coupled to the limitations in the infant's abilities. And, most important, we will be predicting that exploration of such episodes will lead to self-organization and the consequent ability to participate in more complex routines.

Differentiated scaffolding

Much of life is routine, so specific interactions are commonly nested within these routine events. The episode provides topics for joint attention, interest and comprehension, but these conditions must be used skilfully by the participating adults. Let us now see how these skills manifest themselves in the process by which the infant moves from simple anticipation to communicative intention and soon to first words. Lock (1980) has analyzed the process in terms of the sequential development of affordances, predating the efforts of many. This is my version of his analysis. The starting point is the state of the infant, their behaviours expressing distress, hunger, cold, pain, whatever. Lock describes these as implicitly expressing 'whatever this bodily state is, I do not want it'. This affords interpretation and hence action by the adult. Usually the discomfort is removed and the infant feels better. The infant naturally expressed these undifferentiated behaviours but the sensitive feedback from the adult gives information about the interactive system to the child, it affords differentiation, because it involves consistent responses, displays simple contingencies. The infant explores this constrained, undifferentiated system, acting, being reacted to, and reacting to responses and thereby comes to have a slightly more explicit and elaborate idea, namely, 'whatever this bodily state is, I want a different one'. Over time the infant is exposed to behaviour from adults which is contingently sensitive on its own acts (receiving food when hungry, warmth when cold) and simultaneously to the higher-order invariants, 'my action has desirable consequences', and 'I have an effect on the world'. These contingencies afford the infant the opportunity to gain information about what goes with what and to begin to build the idea that 'I want that' has the extra implication 'you do something to get me that'. As the infant, through its search via action, accumulates knowledge of the 'rules', exactly the same as saying it explores the task-space, so reorganization takes place, and the infant starts to play different 'games', act differently. Eventually they cry in order to get attention rather than getting attention because they cry.

To make this inference is to have utilized invariances in a very special way, beyond the capacities of most species. But for humans this process is species-typical and the utilization of the invariances encountered affords communicative agency. They reach, for instance, to indicate that the adult should get something for them, rather than simply as an effort to get it themselves. They act to imply 'you give me cuddle' rather than 'I need something'. As soon as one level of differentiation is reached, the next is implied, afforded and so the process of change continues. What is, becomes not itself, the developmental dialectic, the product of each process affording the next process. Hence we find next (Lock, 1980), that an infant that has learned to cry to get attention and to point to indicate a desired object will put the two preverbal communicative acts together and make a crying noise which gets attention, then a reach/point which indicates what it is they want.

The use of 'words', initially single words, marks a shift towards conventionality in that a word is a convention in itself, but the use is not initially conventional but idiosyncratic. For instance, the word 'shoe' may be used to mean 'that is a shoe', 'take my shoe off', 'my shoe is off', etc. At this point a word is not being used expressly to name something. The differentiation of word meaning is still in its early stages, as in these stages there is no clear distinction between the clarification, the differentiation of motives and intentions of the child and the linguistic means of expressing them. Nor are events analyzed in terms of objects, actions and actors, or agents and patients. They are not yet that differentiated, but they are becoming so, as I mentioned by the very acts of participation, exploration.

Infant play

It is not long before infants show they have escaped the limitations of purely episodic functioning. When still preverbal they become perfectly capable of using communication to refer to states and events present and past, without these being in symbolic, that is, linguistic form. They convey meanings, like agency (I'll do it), possession (mine), denial (not me), recurrence (again), etc. through gestures and vocalizations. Nelson (1996) also describes the pretence with objects, practice and imitation which the 10-month to three-year-old child typically exhibits. We see the re-enactment of episodes in an imaginative, expressive way in games and play, using and building on the scripts developed in routine activities. And all such complex activities are common before language is established. But we do not see such activities when the infant has been deprived of access to normal routine activities. Thus the participation in events seems to be a necessary condition of later using knowledge embedded in episodes to move to play, pretence and reference to the past and future. It is not, however, sufficient, as the lives of higher mammals are filled with reasonably complex domestic and play routines, but participation in them is not sufficient for imagination to emerge. Something else is necessary.

We do not know how this second level of differentiation emerges from the first. Perhaps the following sorts of events may be involved. As the dynamic structure of events is predictable and the sequences involve shared knowledge (all the participants know what follows what and why) then one's acts embody the shared assumptions. When the routine is disrupted some sort of action indicating what had been expected or what should have been where it normally was or what should happen next, is likely to occur. These are references to the past or the future, though they have depended upon their occurrence on prior participation in sequences where actions were tied to the present. Such acts might be the start of the differentiation in reference which leads to portraying events, to 'pretend play', as for instance, the point to where a biscuit tin was (it has gone missing) turns into the carrying of a 'pretend' biscuit tin. The suggestion is thus that a form of invariance arises whose *content* is initially limited to past episodes but where the timing and distribution of such acts becomes *decoupled* from the enactment of those episodes. Life has come to have a past and a future, not just a present. All of this occurs without any need for symbols, but I suggest that it could not have arisen without utilizing the dynamic invariances that specify the routine events.

It has to be part of the task of developmental psychology to make explicit how this arises. And of course exactly the same problem arises in relation to the emergence of the abilities to extract information from symbolic, abstract invariances. We will see when we consider the invariances involved specifically involved in language acquisition that participation in these play and preverbal communicative activities will probably not be sufficient to lead to symbol use, any more than the ability to participate in episodes is, on its own, sufficient for imaginative play to emerge.

The conditions for a form of communication which allows the sharing of all possible thoughts is not the evolution of an infinite number of communicative units, but a system of rules such that there is an infinite number of combinations of what units there are. That is what we get with the emergence of a formal linguistic code, language, releasing communication from its still semi-embedded state within local contexts. As with the change to imaginative play, etc., from participation in simple episodes, the change to the use of linguistic invariances will not be accomplished by practice alone.

Only humans can utilize the interactive affordances on offer

This short account indicates that the adult plays a crucial role in early communicative development. They are a necessary component in a system of interactions by which communicative development proceeds. They organize the context. Further, they are dynamically changing in their contribution to the system, developing their own 'input' so the infant can move through the different implications of its own actions and come to explicate its own motives and meanings. The adult must scaffold skilfully, acting as a sensitive and changing control parameter. But to agree all this is not to change the logical stature of the contribution of the adult from being necessary to being sufficient for communicative or language development in the infant. As we have observed in previous chapters, the infant has to have the internal structures to utilize the external structure in an informative way. If, for instance, an infant could not extract turn-taking invariances, they would not come to take turns, however often instances were displayed. The invariances would not be informative. Equally, however many non-verbal skills could be developed, none are in themselves sufficient to afford linguistic invariances to be informative. So how is the gap between non-symbolic and symbolic communication bridged? The beginnings of an answer are emerging.

The development of true language

Primal perception of speech contrasts

Several studies reviewed by Jusczyk (1997) report a preferential attention by infants to speech sounds over non-speech sounds, but more than this, investigators have shown that infants pick up, differentiate between, nearly all the sorts of speech sounds that humans make, irrespective of whether they had heard them before (Eilers *et al.*, 1982). Trehub (1976), for instance, investigated the responsiveness of English Canadian one- to four-month-old infants to differences in vowel sounds they had never previously encountered, found in Polish, French and Czech. They discriminated all of them. Polka and Werker (1994) found English-exposed infants sensitive to a German vowel contrast not found in English. With other reports, Jusczyk (1997) concludes that for at least some speech contrasts, infants do not require prior experience to discriminate them. It is also known that there is a decline in sensitivity to both vowel and consonant distinctions which are not encountered in the native language – use it or lose it. This appears to be the converse of the mechanisms observed in ducklings I described earlier. There, lack of experience led to inputs not being narrowed. Here, experience leads to inputs being narrowed, as infants can detect all speech sounds initially, but lose sensitivity when it is not required. In both cases it is adaptive, the perceptual abilities being reorganized to fit the ecological priorities.

From sounds to words: relations between what can be directly perceived and what cannot

Jusczyk (1997) demonstrates that up to about seven months of age the infant has the ability to detect prosodic (pitch and rhythm) features, but is not able to extract more complex linguistic forms, similar to Elman's (1993) model. That is, infants simply do not perceive grammatical relations, or semantic ones. They do not exist at the time that prosodic features do, so all attention is focused on what phenomenally exists, the prosody. The comparative simplicity of these means that any information that may reside in the pattern of pitch and rhythm can eventually be extracted. This is crucial, because it is another clear instance of undifferentiated interactions functioning to reduce the complexity of input so the task-space is not too complex when the psychological tools are still unrefined. The infant can concentrate on exploring the dynamics of prosody.

Now Jusczyk's argument reaches what I consider to be a critical point. He tells us that there is some degree of co-variation of prosodic features the infant can pick up with word beginnings and/or endings, so that when the infant picks out the prosodic features they would be 'accidentally' be picking out words and could thus start to learn about some of the invariances in word use. This is the bridge between non-linguistic and linguistic invariances, and there had to be one. Again, simple differentiation gives access to opportunities to

develop more complex differentiation. The matter is complicated because it is not that the species-typical preference for
prosodic features like stresses and contrasts implies that the
same prosodic features carry the same information in all
languages. They don't. For instance, in the English language
two-syllable words usually start with a strong (emphasized)
syllable. What this implies is that if English-learning infants
can detect the prosodic feature of emphasis (as in 'table',
'rhubarb', but not 'employ'), then they would effectively have
a means (albeit a very approximate, undifferentiated one) of
dividing up the sound stream into words. In other languages
different rules are encountered, but there are always rules so,
so long as the infant attends to prosodic features they will start
to pick up the co-variances between prosodic and linguistic
invariances that exist in 'their' language. They can then focus
on the differences that make a difference and not on others.
The contrast between *ba* and *da* in English is relevant, for
instance, and so continues to be perceived well, while sensitivity to contrasts that are initially differentiated but do not occur
in the native language declines as their non-occurrence leads to
a lack of focus on them: the infants' abilities are becoming
better coupled to the contexts it inhabits, better connected to
the inputs it receives. Once again, development is seen to be
context-sensitive.

Jusczyk (1997) reviews a number of studies which show that
between six and 12 months infants do become able to use more
and more different sources of information to indicate word
boundaries, to pick out words. An initial, basic, relatively
undifferentiated form of word segmentation occurs, and this
affords attention to 'words' more often than before and thus
produces more information about words, e.g. about the rules
governing the grouping of the pieces which together comprise
the whole word.

For instance, in all sound-based languages there are rules,
i.e. invariances exist, which specify which units of sound
(phonemes) are allowed to be joined together (phonotactics)
and for specifying the variations in phoneme production
according to the context the phoneme is in (e.g. in '*pot*' and
'*spot*' the sound of the '*p*' is slightly different) (the variations
are called allophones). Once some of the contingent variations

in use based only upon prosody have been extracted, so some basics of the structure of language become clearer, different and extra invariances become affordable, and attention to them gives new and extra information. In other words, it is the same process we keep finding, the successive development of affordances through the exploration of simple, undifferentiated task spaces, the result of which in this case is the development of skills in word segmentation, skills which are themselves necessary conditions for the rest of language acquisition.

Another area of research in the development of language concerns whether the ability to attend to and pick out prosodic features of speech could give information about syntactical (grammatical) structure, e.g. clauses and phrases. This phenomenon is known as 'prosodic bootstrapping'. Jusczyk (1997) points out the conditions for this to occur. There must be acoustic correlates of syntactic organization (so the infant has relevant input to attend to), the infant must also be able to pick these out from the stream of sound, and finally they must be able to actually use this information to syntactically organize the input. He shows that they can make use of the information. The end-result is that the infant has available information both about how units of language as large as clauses and later phrases are grouped and about the units, the single words that the larger elements are composed of. It appears that learning language depends upon utilizing a combination of such invariances. Further, it appears again that learning some simple rules by only being able to detect certain invariances, itself affords the learning of later, more complex invariances.

In other words, the developmental system is designed to 'release' information into task-spaces which matches the ability of the child to utilize it. The developing infant can thus only respond to certain aspects of the environment (forms of invariance), but participation in these affords learning which enables access to other aspects, other forms (of invariance). Exploration of one world creates the conditions for them coming to inhabit a different one.

Discussion points

1 Describe cases which demonstrate how the developmental system includes mechanisms to couple action to contingent environmental conditions.

2 Describe some of the factors necessary for early 'reaching' and how their interaction leads to development.

3 Why is evidence for intermodal knowledge support for a dynamic systems view? How is neonatal imitation explained using 'intermodality'?

4 How does the organization of routine events aid development?

5 How do other people enable the infant to come to elaborate its own intentions?

6 Why do some primates use tools, when their attempts are so unsuccessful they should extinguish? Do they 'ape' adults?

Chapter 8

The origins of knowledge

As we have seen, there is a significant difference between the traditional and the ecological systems view of the mechanisms by which knowledge arises. In this first section I review the different positions, and analyze a modern version of the traditional view, Jean Mandler's (1988, 1992, 1997), to show how easy it is for a mixed, in fact, contradictory paradigm to be used, as she herself describes processes which are consistent with those of dynamic theorists, yet retains traditional dichotomies. I try to show just why she is bound to take the position she does, given certain traditional assumptions she makes and to once again emphasize where the differences are significant and incommensurable (cannot be evaluated within the same paradigm). In the second section I consider the origins of knowledge from a dynamic ecological perspective to show that the same developmental principles underpin the means by which knowledge of the physical and social worlds emerges, but that knowledge of the social world does require the utilisation of different sorts of invariances than are sufficient to understand the physical world. Finally I look back over the route we have taken. First, a review of the alternatives.

The origins of knowledge: percepts or concepts?

The primacy of concepts

The traditional cognitivist position argues that when perceptual data enters the mind it has no meaning and involves no categories. Valid knowledge is only to be found in the final, relatively static concepts, representations, abstracted from analysis of perceptual data. The concept of a dog, for instance, develops through exposure to and experience of a multitude of different dogs, with a variety of different perceptual characteristics, but all necessarily sharing that essential 'dogginess'. The concept specifies these critical features and is thus disembedded from the variety of (confusing) contexts in which individual dog encounters have been embedded. These concepts then function as criteria and means of judgement of individual perceptual inputs. As a result, there is a one-way connection between perceptual data and concepts: the concepts change perceptual data into something valid and reliable (knowledge), but the perceptual data does not inform the concepts. Intelligent action also requires other concepts, of course, but the same logic applies to them. Perception provides data, cognition provides concepts, two distinct processes. It follows that there can be no complex, intelligent action without a representational system, a body of concepts.

On this view it is not an empirical matter whether concepts are prior to intelligent action, it is the condition of it arising. Thus the view implies that perception and cognition are not closely coupled, what with one as just a simple source of imperfect data and the other a result of analysis, and nor are action and cognition, as action is simply any form in which output is coded. Mental structures are separate and dominant in psychology. It is a case of mind over matter. Some version of this view was held by Piaget, of course, but also by Vygotsky, Bruner and others. A large body of evidence is consistent with the position. Experiments attest to the fact that even young children are capable of 'seeing beyond' simple perceptual similarities to classify instead in terms of what things are really like. For instance, Mandler, Bauer and McDonagh (1991) found that 18-month-olds distinguished clearly between animals and vehicles, even though the perceptual dissimilarity of elephants, birds and fish, for instance, is argued to preclude the formation of a category on grounds of perceptual categorization. That correct categorization did occur, shows, we are urged to believe, that there is a separate non-perceptual process which produces conceptual meaning.

Many experiments involve apparently impossible events occurring, as when single objects appear to become two without intervention, or the law of gravity fails to operate. In one, Baillargeon (1986) gave six- and eight-month-old infants experience of the following episodes. They see an inclined plane with a track at the end and a screen hiding part of the track. The screen is then lifted to show the rest of the track and is then replaced. Thirdly, a cart rolls down the incline, behind the screen and then emerges and rolls out of sight. This was the habituating event. The events are then repeated up to the screen lift. One of two alternatives then followed. Either the screen lift reveals a box behind the track and the rest of the episode is identical, or the screen is lifted and reveals a box *on* the track, the rest of the episode being identical, so that an impossible cart-through-box event occurs. It was this third event which generated more looking than the second, possible scenario, leading Baillargeon to conclude that the infants were surprised because they had abstract knowledge of the properties of objects like permanence, maintenance of trajectory without other agency and their obstructive quality (for other, moving objects). In general, the surprise that infants show is taken as evidence that they must have known such appearances were not real, as there must have been a mismatch between their conceptual knowledge and the perceptual data available, thus proving they had the requisite conceptual knowledge. All such evidence is taken to show the existence and use of concepts and to demonstrate a basic separation, a lack of coupling, between perception and cognition.

Mandler is explicit in separating her view from one in which perceptual information is central, as it is in dynamic systems theory (1993, p. 146):

> perceptual categories are patterns that by themselves do not have meaning ... perceptual analysis ... redescribes perceptual information into a conceptual format ... These [primitive – my addition] concepts are not the same as perceptual categories, which have to do with what things look like rather than what they are.

The sorts of early concepts made available by this process are animacy, inanimacy, causality, agency, containment. For instance, 'animacy' can develop, Mandler considers, if the infant can differentiate between animate and mechanical (biological and non-biological) motion and can, in addition, extract the information that the 'animated' parts of the world can start to move in a non-mechanical (biological) way without being externally pushed. This latter act gives an image-scheme of 'self-motion', in contrast to perceptual analysis of objects which reveals to the infant that they move in a mechanical way but only if caused to by something else. She also outlines evidence for the conditions for the development of other areas of cognition and of language. Mandler's work is important because it is a rare attempt to be more specific about the initial processes by which knowledge arises.

The dynamic systems response: stability versus sensitivity

On the other hand stand the dynamic systems theorists and ecological psychologists who claim that concepts, schemas, representations (whatever term is used for mental functions which are supposedly distinct and isolated from perception once built), are totally dependent upon perception in that perceptual data are not only the building blocks of concepts in the first place, but also the over-riding test of their veridicality at all stages of their existence. Moreover, complex action is carried out with reference to the on-going monitoring of environmental conditions, i.e. perceptual input is appraised to test the outcomes are as desired and the conditions as previously tested.

The dynamic systems position implies, of course, that some information must be inherent in perceptual data, not requiring any extra form of validation for it to gain the status of knowledge. It implies some version of direct perception. As with the cognitivists, it is not difficult to find data which confirms this view. Quinn and Eimas (1996), for instance, describe how three- to four-month old infants formed a categorical representation for domestic cats that included familiar and novel cats, but excluded birds, horses, tigers, dogs, lions, and for horses that excluded cats, giraffes and zebras. The infants were thus categorizing at a basic level. They could also form a category that included many species of animals but excluded furniture, birds and fish. This is classification at a super-ordinate level, or approaching it. Quinn and Eimas ask how this could be achieved and hypothesize that the supposedly unlearned orientation to faces (Johnson and Morton, 1991), discussed earlier, might be involved, as follows. Animals have faces (like humans) while birds and fish do not to any serious extent. Attention to faces might have enabled the learning of differences in facial types, e.g. for differences between cats and dogs to be perceptually differentiated. This would imply that no conceptual analysis, no analysis of percepts, was necessary. What is implied is that invariances in the structure of perceptual data can, if utilized, itself specify a category by a process of 'contingency abstraction', a suggestion previously proposed by Richardson and Bhavnani (1984). Quinn and Eimas made only faces visible and found that the infants could use the difference between internal features (position and relation of nose, eyes, etc.) or external features (contour of the head region) to form a categorical representation for cats that excludes dogs. The obvious question arises as to whether Mandler's students could also have differentiated between elephants, birds and fish as one category and vehicles as another on the same basis, 'things with faces or eyes' and 'things without them'. Clearly this explanation offered depends upon fairly differentiated perceptions but there is no reason in principle why generic information could not be sufficient to solve certain classification problems, as for instance, biological motion is a pretty generic property.

But given that both 'sides' can find empirical evidence, I return to an analysis of the assumptions underlying the 'cognitive' position, to evaluate them in terms of their internal logic as well as their relation to empirical data. In this I follow Jones and Smith (1993) and Smith and Jones (1993), established dynamic systems theorists, who also believed that the differences between them and cognitivists like Mandler stem from different basic assumptions. Referring to exchanges of opinions between them, Smith and Jones (1993, p. 81) state:

Although the article and the commentaries are all about the role of perception in children's concepts, the sub text concerns the validity of our most fundamental assumptions about cognition.

Varying assumptions

These different assumptions must be clear so they can be evaluated. I can identify three. On the traditional view we have the clear distinction between perception and cognition, the two playing completely different roles in the formation of knowledge. Concepts are also to be seen as totally separate from behaviour, output, as that is no more than the manner of presentation of results. Hence Mandler, like all traditional cognitivists, assumes dichotomies between cognition and perception and between cognition and action and in this tripartite division cognition is king. But we have seen that adaptive behaviour can only ever be a function of the self-organizing properties of the whole internal and external context, so there could not possibly be privilege accorded to any one component or type of component, *not even* to a schema, a concept, a plan. Remember the cases of escape from prey down a burrow in Chapter 3. The prey could not possibly have escaped without some cognitive activity, it is an essential feature of all adaptive, intelligent action. But neither could it have escaped without some perceptual or motor powers. More to the point, it was the total pattern of abilities, in relation to those of the predator and the physical geography, which determined what would be 'intelligent', not any single item or aspect. Movement, perception and cognition are necessarily aspects of a single phenomenon, not three dichotomous psychological units.

Secondly, there is the direct opposition concerning the extent to which perceptual processes continue to be involved in complex psychological processes (whether we call these conceptual or not). Smith and Jones (1993, p. 185) explain their position: 'In our view, what is smart about all of human cognition is its continuous exquisite adaptiveness to the particulars of real-time external (and also internal) events'. That is, cognition is 'smart' only because it takes advantage of feedback from perceptual input at all points. Given this, 'Intelligent variability in cognition also forces us to confront the real issue: namely, do cognitive structures like concepts actually exist?' (Smith and Jones, 1993, p. 182).

So on the dynamic systems view the continued use of perceptual information is critical in affording action which is sensitive to variations in conditions, contexts encountered, that is, critical to complex behaviour, while on the traditional view the whole point of concepts is to allow action which is determined independently of contextual variations, i.e. is disembedded. If skilled action does need such a close coupling, there should be a body of evidence demonstrating that the context in which humans operate is significantly affected by, integrated with, the contexts in which it occurs, evidence effectively contradicting the computational metaphor. If one thing is certain in psychology, it is that ever since the publication of Donaldson's *Children's Minds* (1978), a vast body of research has proved beyond a shadow of doubt that context *is* critical, that what we learn is intimately related to the conditions in which we learn it. It has indeed been one of the centres of attention for research for 20 years, and there is now an acceptance that thinking is intimately related to contexts, that cognition is perhaps necessarily and always situated.

An example from locomotion

Adolph (1997) showed this as well as anyone in a series of experiments in which the two main variables were the locomotor ability of the child (they could either crawl or walk) and the angle of slope they were asked to go up or down. When infants first crawl they show no awareness of the 'affordance' of falling. After experience they gradually come to show reluctance according to the steepness of the slope. As these crawlers became walkers they were presented with the 'same' task. Now if the knowledge gained in the earlier experiences on the slopes is of a general, context-free sort (i.e. the generalized essence that slopes can be difficult and dangerous to traverse has been grasped, a set of rules) then the behaviour of the same children, now walkers, on the same slopes should show the same reluctance. No such inhibitions were shown by the majority of the infants.

During the whole series of experiments the infants were seen to have displayed a variety of methods of collecting information about whether a given method of getting up or down would be safe for a given slope. They might just glance. Sometimes they chose a long look, sometimes also touching the brink, and sometimes actually trying out the method. The exploratory movements must afford knowledge of the safety or otherwise of particular steps or mode of crawling. It appears that information gained by looking and touching did generalize to new surfaces and levels of skill. However, transfer to a new posture, being upright, creates a new task-space, to keep a vertical body in balance whilst locomoting. The old information cannot solve this task and anyway, new means of exploring, by moving, as ever, are themselves subject to danger, 'I cannot find out if this is dangerous as to do so might be dangerous'. Adolph offers the analogy of changing from driving one's own car to another – easy transfer – and changing to the cab of a tractor-trailer, where we would be most uncertain, and rightly so, of our ability to drive competently. It is critical to understand that the changes in the children's ability to move around, from crawling to walking, required new forms of exploration to establish what was safe. Sensitivity to context includes sensitivity to changes in one's own abilities, as they are part of the causal flux.

These experiments show that the behaviour of the children was a function of their perceptual exploration, their motor capabilities and their cognitive levels, not one or the other. And they also show that the context was critical in affecting outcomes. The essence here is plasticity, not stability. And it is a strength, not a weakness.

Forgetting context

I referred earlier to experiments involving apparently impossible events. The interpretation given by the cognitivists is that the surprise implies a mismatch between their conceptual knowledge and the perceptual data available, thus proving they had the requisite conceptual knowledge. As Thelen and Smith point out, surprise is likely because the expectation that the habituation event would recur was not met. The 'impossible' event follows instances of 'possible' events to which the subjects had become accustomed, having extracted the invariances in the regularity. In this situation infants, indeed, adults, will be surprised when their expectations are not met. So when the conclusion was reached that the surprise children showed when observing 'impossible' events was evidence of an underlying belief system about matters of conservation, laws of motion, etc., we can see that this is a wholly unjustified leap of mental attribution. Such an attribution could be made only by a viewer who ignored the perceptual context and focused only on a preformed essence. The child is surprised at seeing something that is different to what has been observed frequently. They are surprised and so look, would you believe, surprised. Surprise does not imply comprehension, only anticipation. This may be akin to Donaldson's (1978) famous analysis: it is a dangerous thing to make assumptions about the contextual factors the child is utilizing. The conclusions reached may tell us more about the egocentricity of the observer than the child.

Even on purely logical grounds we can show that Mandler's assumptions of the properties of perceptual versus cognitive processes based upon her dichotomy between thinking and perception is not so much based upon evidence as used as evidence to specify what can count as perception, a circular position. Mandler defines perceptual categories as being 'to do with what things look like *rather than* [my emphasis] what they are', thus ensuring both that nothing complex *could* be involved in perception and that perception is seen as totally separate from cognition, because cognition can be complex. This is not a position based upon evidence, but an assumption which constrains what could count as evidence. If you disallow anything complex or transformative in the involvement of perception, then of course you have to argue that super-ordinate categories (like animals) are not possible by perception. It is tautological.

Mandler (1997, p. 173) then writes, as if she is describing empirical evidence, that 'Perceptual analysis . . . involves the active recoding of . . . incoming perceptual information into meanings that form the basis of accessible concepts'. Meaning is formed only after attentive analysis of something simple.

But of course she claims this. So long as one is committed to the dichotomous position that perception is to do with what things look like *rather than* (hence a dichotomy) what they are, then one cannot say that perception can be meaningful, because that would imply it was not just about what things look like. She would be contradicting herself. The process of perceptual analysis has to be posited to fill the gap that would otherwise exist between a simple percept and a complex meaning, between appearance and reality. As information does not arise from interaction itself, according to her, another process must be posited, so she gives 'it' a name – attentive analysis. This is nearly saying that one attends to, perceives, the percept, in order to begin to build the concept. The process continues, as we then need someone or something to look at and compare the perceptual data with the conceptual templates to decide which category the input should be assigned to. Finally we then need another 'looker', or the same one with a different hat on, to look at the results of the categorization process and decide what to do about it. Without interaction of components we are left with static processes of attending – I stare therefore I learn. It is a contemplative, static, mentalistic theory. It all follows from not believing that it is interactions, and only interactions, which produce information. It is thus no accident that preformed entities are required to explain complex behaviour and that before they are formed no complex action is possible. If interaction cannot produce it, the complexity must already exist. That is why 'representations' have to be logically essential explanatory items for cognitivists, not empirically valid ones.

But we are not obliged to make the same preformationist assumptions and thus not required to be dragged into the preformationist logic. Similarly with regard to thinking and action, the implication of the traditional position is that first the brain makes a decision about what is out there, then it separately makes a decision about what to do about it. Though this decoupling becomes possible in advanced activity, developmentally the two must be integrated, as it is only in action that selection is ultimately tested. Recall the case of orientation to the face. 'Knowing' there is a face out there somewhere is of no value on its own. When the orientation affords continued perception we have knowledge, not before. The same is even more obvious in the case of predator avoidance, as opposed to predator recognition.

The mistake, and I believe it is a critical one in psychology, is to have forgotten the *developmental* aspect to internal organization. As I discuss later, we do end up with something akin to disembedded concepts, because we do end up being able to decouple action from thinking, but the large mistake is to thereby conclude that cognition is decoupled from action in its development, because it is not and cannot be. Successful thinking is like successful adaptation, it is only tested in action.

Representations thus do not have superpower status in our model. In fact the logical position of 'concepts' and 'representations' in dynamic systems theory is the exact converse of that of cognitivism. Rather than being preconditions of intelligent action, they are, if the terms are useful at all, the names for the results of it, and must be. Action takes place, the organism benefits or suffers from it. As a consequence change in action is directly linked to outcome, just as it is in evolutionary selection, and behaviours 'settle out' of the complex of interactions. Nor do symbols, representations ever attain the full, static, fixed nature attributed by cognitivists. They appear to at times but as I repeat, such stability is only half the story, instability, change, development is the other, as input changes can lead to reorganization of the system.

I have already discussed the third assumption of the traditional position, namely, that perceptual data is inherently unreliable and thus that no certain knowledge is available without the validation provided by a separate, conceptual process. Mandler's version is that her perceptual analysis reveals new conceptual information. But if the information is not in the input, we are bound to wonder how can it suddenly appear simply by analysis of the content of that input, whether this process be called redescription, analysis, transformation, or perception. The answer must be that there is an external (cognitive) source of validation, separate from the perceptual input. And this leads to the critical question as to how that source was originally validated, and if we get an answer to that question, then how was the source that was used to validate the previous source derived . . . etc., in an infinite regression.

The conclusion has to be that some perceptual knowledge (however basic, undifferentiated) *must* be valid. Extra information is revealed over developmental time, through interaction and self-organization, so each time new invariances are capable of extraction. These are then new perceptual categories which are used to see the world in yet another light.

The three differences, in the causal privilege of concepts, the ever-embedded nature of thinking, including the embeddedness of perception and cognition in action, and the inability to validate conceptual knowledge without an argument from infinite regress, are closely related. The traditional position on these issues implies that complex behaviour could not exist without complex concepts and that it specifically could not arise from simple actions in simple contexts with simple perceptions. On the other hand, dynamic systems theorists should argue that this is the only way intelligent action can develop. What we need is a real, behaving example which shows how, from simple action and simple perception in simple contexts, with no in-built complexity, complex action and apparently complex cognition can emerge. Hopefully you will yourself put forward the case of Mataric's robot, as a perfect example proving it can and does happen.

What is common and what is different in the views

Many of the claims that Mandler makes about the processes going on are almost dynamic systems claims, but her commitment to dichotomies pulls her back from accepting that her anti-systemic assumptions need changing and makes her revert to the old dichotomies. We end up with an odd mixture, much of which we can agree with. For instance, she argues that information used to form concepts is perceptual. Apart from the word used to describe the result, 'concept' or 'attractor', there is no disagreement. She attaches importance to movement (see Mandler, 1993), as evidenced by the need for paths of movements to be parts of the process as, of course, do dynamic theorists. She tells us (1992, pp. 274–5) that 'Perceptual analysis . . . involves attentive analysis of what is being perceived . . . it takes place on-line' and (p. 279) that '[image-schemas] do not require other symbols or another system to interpret them . . . they are grounded directly in the perceptual world of the infant'. We can agree with all this. We can share in common with Mandler the view that mental activity carried out with respect to external data which has characteristic qualities (e.g. biological motion) reveals the information for the members of species that have the relevant mental apparatus. This is precisely what Gibson claimed. If Mandler is claiming that the perceptual data gets meaning when it is fully processed, we agree. If she feels that it is important to separate invariance from information, we agree. Mandler argues that there is something in the spatial structure of objects and their movements that can be 'abstracted'. Indeed, ecological psychologists want to emphasize the coupling of organism and environment and so focus on this external structure, higher-order invariances which implies the environment is complex (as it contains the invariances) and perceptual systems are complex (because they can pick them up).

But it is when she refers to 'essences' that her claims turn to dust, as the form of explanation becomes preformationist. Here there is no common ground. Mandler was bound to have to use some such form of explanation because she has to rule out a result of psychological activity being called perceptual if it involves complex processing, given her dichotomy between simple perception and complex concepts. Simply, if the results of the processing are grounded in the perceptual world of the infant, as she herself claims, what is so inadmissible about calling the process perceptual? Perhaps this is the question Mandler needs to answer. Possibly she feels obliged to emphasize the huge difference between a simple datum (invariance), as when an infant hears sounds when someone speaks, and highly complex awareness when they have come to appreciate the linguistic, grammatical, syntactical, pragmatic structure (invariances) inherent in the sound stream. There is nothing wrong with that. But now that we are familiar with the notion of complex, higher-order invariances, it becomes harder and harder to escape the conclusion that such invariances might just specify concepts and categories without the need for any extra 'attentive analysis', any 'abstracter'. As the detection of higher-order invariants itself develops, so our more educated attention affords extra information to become available to 'enrich these initial representations informationally' (Eimas, 1994). This is important so I will elaborate.

Perception affords categorization, initially in terms of very undifferentiated categories, like some frequency 'shapes' in prosody, some light/dark patterns that specify, for instance, 'face-like things', and later more differentiated categories, Joe's face, etc. This developmental process leads to the extraction of ever higher-order invariances and the existence of ever-more differentiated categories. But the crux is that I have not said two things here, but the *same* thing in two different ways: complex categorization occurs when higher-order invariances are utilized.

There could still be disagreement about just how stable or unstable the 'concepts' or 'attractor states' are. It is not, I think useful to focus on either the stability or the instability. The whole power and purpose of the sort of cognitive system I have been proposing lies in its dual abilities to both hold and use relatively stable systems of transformation of input, and to remain sensitive to changes in form of input (context) so new stabilities emerge through change. If they had no resistance to variation in conditions they would not be useful. If they were totally impervious to contextual-type effects, they would be equally useless. Attractors, the products of interaction, display sensitivity to context and resistance to disturbance. This dual character is suggestive of a dialectical relation. Maybe this matters more than the label.

Uncoupling of representations and action: thinking as mental play

There is at least one difficulty with the dynamic systems position, pointed out by Clark (1997a). He correctly reminds us that humans are capable of considering options, imagining possibilities, even thinking them through, without action, and that this requires representations. The point is that this consideration can be carried out 'off-line'. Here a representation not only stands *for* something outside, but also stands *in* so that manipulations can be carried out with the internal representation. This is plainly the case. It looks as if representations can play the 'disembedded' role that traditional psychology claims, bring able to direct intelligent thinking, without having to be coupled to perception.

It would be a mistake not to accept this important role for representations. But as Clark himself points out, there does not have to be a dichotomy between advanced thinking as activity always coupled to real time or as not coupled to real time. I think the central issue is one of coupling. To refer to anything ever involves some element of uncoupling in so far as the word or sign or gesture is not what is referred to: the referent may have ceased to exist, may not yet exist, may never exist. After an extended period of development children have a whole bank of such signs, coupled to each other via the coupling of their referents in the 'real world'. At this point and not before they can come to play with the contents of the bank in the knowledge that because there is a connection between the symbols and their referents, their play with concepts, their 'play on words', can have some relevance to the real world.

When animals play, they are involved in action, but the relation between the activity and its original function has been uncoupled. Instead of serving to catch prey, defend a territory, etc. the activity becomes a means of developing and testing the skills which will be necessary for survival later. The 'bank' of activities can be used in play. I suggest that we may see mental representations which stand in for states and events and can be played with to serve other functions than they were originally selected for (part of the guidance system for action), as the equivalent of the playful acts of pseudo-aggression in animal play. I suggest that when we consider the consequences of actions we are indulging in the equivalent of play, participating in the activity without having to bear the consequences of wrong decisions, as many species do. It is just that we have a little more to play with. Thus, mental representations are important both because they consist in complex higher-order invariances, and because we have evolved the capability of playing with them so that we can gain the knowledge that playing with them gives without the danger.

However, this does not change the fact that the attractors

which relate to higher-order invariances, or concepts, whatever they are best called, can only have developed in the first place from actions which were coupled, were based in material contexts with material outcomes. The developmental basis of uncoupled thinking is coupled thinking and action. Thus we can accept both that representations can be uncoupled from action and that they derive from and are always and only tested in the real world of material action. We come to be able to intentionally uncouple action from perception once we have developed complex mental representations. In fact when we cannot, or when uncoupling is not under intentional control, we are considered unfit to live without care.

As to uncoupling, we have to accept that we are capable of working in at least three ways. We can and do consider options, imagine, whatever. So thinking can be uncoupled from action. We can and do take account of changes in circumstances, show the 'continuous exquisite adaptiveness to the particulars of real-time external (and also internal) events' referred to earlier. So we are not bound by the inner representations, irrespective of context and we can couple action to perception, however complex our representations. And we can use representations which are not based in present action to guide action, as in basing our route on a remembered map. The difficulty remains of explaining how uncoupling occurs. I am just trying to reframe the questions.

Knowledge of the physical and social worlds: same or different?

A short interpretation of Piaget's and Vygotsky's positions from a dynamic, ecological perspective will serve to introduce this section and to show that the same developmental principles underpin the means by which knowledge of the physical and social worlds emerges. This does not imply, however, that they depend upon the utilization of the same sort of invariances. I shall try to demonstrate that they do not.

I should make clear that when I refer to 'the physical world' in this chapter I am referring to anything not human, even if its nature is dependent upon humans. Thus, cultural artifacts are included when I use the term 'physical' even though their meaning and function is at least partly socially determined. Similarly, when I use the term 'social' I do not imply that all social states and events do not have a material basis: they all do. For instance, greetings are social events but they require physical movements. This means, of course, that in some senses there is no distinction between what is social and what is not, as Ingold (1996) has made clear. I know. Nevertheless, I think I can show that there is an area of knowledge that must be seen as specifically social.

Two forms of invariance

Let me then start by trying to map the central terms, 'invariance', 'information', 'affordance', and the 'pick-up' of information through exploratory action, on to the two theories. As a Marxist, Vygotsky believed that the laws of dialectical materialism underpinned all the relations between the individual and the collective, from the familial to the level of socioeconomic system. He believed that apart from the preverbal level, the 'natural', biological line of development, which he regarded as extremely basic (in this he showed that biology and culture were, for him, a dichotomy), all development consisted in the appropriation of cultural tools, the psychological mechanisms and skills which were the result of human 'progress'. This was his 'cultural' line of development. 'Culture', as I stated earlier, is to be regarded as that set of relatively invariant forms of economic and social organization, communication, and associated knowledge (which includes skills and 'tools'), attitudes and values which underpin a 'way of life'. It thus applies to all the levels of organization, all the sorts of invariances which structure a society and individuals.

At the macro-level there are invariances in the relations between socioeconomic forms, capital, wage labour. Within these we find invariances according to class, to gender, to age. At an intermediate level Goffman's 'frames' involve invariances. At a lower level still, there are complexes of invariances underpinning specific social relations, such as mother–infant interaction. Vygotsky recognized that all such invariant relations were embodied in, expressed through, social interactions of one sort or another and, most important, he recognized that the means by which they informed individual development was through the child's involvement in those interactions. That is, when children participated in such interactions they were capable of detecting, 'picking-up' the information, extracting it from the invariant structure. The process by which the intermental becomes the intramental, social interaction, is the process by which invariance becomes information.

These invariances can exist in the form of explicit rules, like the laws of a nation, but most are not. Instead they are unconsciously expressed and unconsciously learned. Yet without our perceptual abilities to pick up the meaning in the dynamic structure, internalization would not be a possibility, there could be no 'culture'. Sinha (1988) calls them canonical rules and suggests (p. 38) that 'they provide a fundamental basis for the intelligibility of social behaviour'. They do, but only because they are rule-governed, which provides the external invariant aspect, and intelligible, which means they are transformed into affordances, information for social development. Gibson's terminology seems to sit comfortably with the Vygotskean view.

This seems a far cry from the thinking of Piaget. The sorts of invariances that mattered for him were independent of culture, being the supposedly universal invariants underlying logico–mathematical structure and the laws of physics and of logic. Thus we read about conservation, a property of the physical world, or transitivity, a law of logic. In this sense the interests of Piaget and Vygotsky seem worlds apart. But Piaget's schemas are the internal representations of the invariant relations which exist between the acts of the child and the effects on the environment or the acts of parts of the environment and their effects on other parts. Thus Piaget, exactly like Vygotsky, recognized that it was in and through the participation of children in interactions that they became capable of detecting the invariances in the relations between the interactants. In fact, if they could not, the key process of the development of schemas, of operations, a process of internalization of external relations, just as in Vygotsky's general, genetic law, could not take place. For both, information was picked-up only through interaction and the result was internalizations of the invariances in the interactions. For both we develop only because the invariances exist, because we explore them and because we have highly evolved capabilities to pick-up, to utilize the invariances.

Thus the products of development these two psychologists focused on may have been very different but the processes by which they arise were identical. Both were convinced that knowledge was produced only through active, dynamic engagement with the environment. Both recognized that as the structures of the mind developed, the effective structure of the environment was concomitantly transformed. They effectively believed that interaction afforded the information, even if there were no such word till Gibson invented it. They did not define the environment in the same way because they had different assumptions about what constituted knowledge, but they accorded it the same function in the causal processes of development.

A consideration of the evolution of forms of invariance extraction provides a means of seeing the different origins of knowledge the theories describe. Reed (1991, p. 136) writes that

> Selection pressures for the evolution of mechanisms underlying basic cognitive processes – the awareness of the affordances of objects, places and events within one's surroundings – are surely widespread among all higher animals, who routinely cope with considerable environmental variability.

In other words, vast numbers of species have evolved the cognitive skills which afford adaptive coupling to their physical environment, the Piagetian view, skills in the extraction of co-variations, that is. But in addition, as Reed (pp. 136–7) continues:

> When one's own abilities to obtain environmental resources are regularly affected by the behaviour of conspecifics, then one is faced with a constant challenge to adapt one's own actions to intricate, often-changing contingencies . . . our hominid ancestors . . . relatively social and

intelligent creatures thus adapted to the challenges of marginal and changing sub-habitats as individuals in groups, not as one or the other. Both individual and group success were facilitated by social and cognitive adaptations. Eventually it became impossible for hominid individuals to survive alone for any length of time, and it also became impossible for hominid groups to survive without a diversity of cognitive and behavioural skills among its members.

Such skills were based in social interaction and the utilization of social invariances as social affordances. Here is Vygotsky's side of development. Both forms of information production exist. Both involve interaction and information production and Gibson's framework sits easily with both.

Reed is clearly making a distinction here between two sources of knowledge. Gibson was himself of the opinion that the nature of knowledge of the physical world was direct, while knowledge arising from social interaction could not be, because it always involved representation and thus mediation between the knower and what is known. Personal, active exploration gave direct knowledge, but the information that other people could provide in the form of representations of that environment had to be regarded as mediated as it was about the world rather than being the world. Other ecological psychologists have used the same distinction:

> perception is not the only way to gain knowledge. For knowledge is a social matter, and in the case of human beings much of our knowledge is gained indirectly from other people. Furthermore, many of our activities involve the use of symbols and other socially determined sources of meaning. (Still and Costall, 1991, p. 172)

Still and Costall are perfectly aware of the interpenetration of the physical and the social: I am not criticizing their theoretical position. However, in a world where psychology is still dominated by dichotomies, their statement might be taken to imply that perception is one route to knowledge while social knowledge requires another route. I want to make two points.

In the first place the words suggest it is at least possible that some of our activities are not socially mediated. And that implies a dichotomy, between socially determined sources of meaning and other sources. This is not feasible because we are incapable of taking off our cultural heads which inform the utility and meaning of the physical. That it is not feasible also follows directly from Gibson's own statements. He wrote (1979, p. 143) that

> The notion of invariants that are related at one extreme to the motives and needs of an observer and at the other extreme to the substances and surfaces of a world provides a new approach to psychology [143 and (p. 140)] 'There is an easier way of explaining why the value of things seem to be perceived immediately and directly. It is because the affordances of things for an observer are specified in stimulus information. They seem to be perceived directly because they are perceived directly.

So, affordances are directly perceived, and affordances depend upon motives, needs, values. But motives, needs and values are never independent of culture, they are culturally constrained, mediated, and thus so are affordances, which are supposedly directly perceived. There is just one class of percepts, of affordances, to which this argument does not apply. It has to be the products of generic interactions, because these are species-typical, or even organism-typical, not culture-specific. But apart from this special case the argument for a clear distinction between perception and social information on the basis that one is direct and one is not does not appear to be valid.

However, I shall argue that there is a clear distinction, but it requires a different argument to validate it. The distinction is, once again, at the generic level. And the argument starts, once again, in prehistory. Remember, being social is not a feature of humanity which got added on at a later stage of human phylogeny than others. As long as human-like creatures have existed, they have lived as a social species, social invariances being just as intrinsic a part of the ancestral environment as physical invariances and so there is just as much reason to expect the evolution of undifferentiated, generic perception of social affordances for various activities requiring mind-sharing as for undifferentiated, generic perception of the non-human world. In both cases the process of development leads to increasing differentiation, of perception, cognition and action. Thus, perception is central, and more to the point, *equally central*, to the development of both sorts of knowledge.

It is also the same in that not only do all physical objects have a physical form, so do all social objects and events. Try smiling without moving your lips. As Gibson (1966, p. 26) wrote: 'No symbol exists except as it is realised in sound, projected light, mechanical contact, or the like'. Thus the invariances utilized in the production of the two sorts of information are of the same physical form.

But when I consider the development of information about people, i.e. social knowledge, we will see that though social and physical invariances are physical, social information requires interactions involving different sorts of internal structures than those producing knowledge of the physical world. As I have already pointed out, only a tiny proportion of invariances that exist can be informative for any individual organism, because the required internal structures are usually not in place, either because the species it is a member of is not designed that way, as in goats not using sonar, or because individual development has not yet reached that point, as in the human infant not initially being able to transform grammatical features. Which means that we need to clearly differentiate between the physical, material aspects of invariances and the psychological, the 'meaningful-for-the-observer' aspects, which determines their utilization in affording adaptive action. When a social act occurs the physical dimensions describe the invariances, but do not describe the information produced. Infants learn how objects react, look, feel, taste, and they learn this for the physical aspects of people, but they also learn how humans reply, amuse, deceive, share. Most generally, they will learn that people have intentions, motives, feelings, and that includes themselves. If they did not have special capacities which enabled them to appropriate the invariances in social acts, they would not, could not, appreciate the social nature of the events involved. They would perceive the physical acts, but not the social affordances.

When a profoundly autistic child observes the same material world, the same invariances, conventions of greeting, for instance, expressed in arm extensions, hand clasps, moving clasped hands up and down, release of clasp, they see the physical movements, they 'pick them up', but they do not appreciate in the same way the social character of 'greeting' that underpins, gives meaning to the physical acts. It is precisely the lack of ability to do so which is one of the characteristics of the condition, the limited ability to utilize social invariances. Similarly, autistic persons have only a limited ability to know how others feel or think, because, though the social invariances had been presented in childhood, they would not have been fully picked-up, would not have been as informative. External social invariances can be transformed into anything socially meaningful only if the relevant, internal developmental changes have taken place. Thus, perception still matters, but it must be specifically social perception that provides this sort of knowledge, that gives access to the world of other minds and shared minds. The distinction is thus not between perception and cognition, but between the utilization of social and physical invariances.

Scaffolding as social

If humans did not have the perceptual capability to extract social information in addition to perceiving the physicality of events there would be no such thing as socialization through internalization or negotiation. But it would be a mistake to focus on the abilities of the child alone. As I have described, socialization requires sensitive contingent support, guidance and collaboration on joint enterprises, that is, context-controlled scaffolding, and this depends upon the ability of the scaffolder to extract social information from the invariances specifying the developmental status of the child, the pattern of affordance and constraints the child brings to each situation. Thus it is necessary that both components, adult and child, in the interactive system by which education, development and socialization occur, are capable of extracting invariances related to the mental and social capacities of each other.

Finally, a word about constraints and systems. I have repeatedly suggested that children explore constrained systems and thereby gain knowledge of how to act within that system. We do this for all sorts of systems, including social ones, like marriage, or the 'family'. However strong the constraints they impose, they can be explored. There are huge variations between individuals, genders, classes, races, in the extent to which their life is constrained, but it is in the human spirit to explore even within a limited terrain. If we did not, we would not be human. But in that universality lies uniqueness. We are all the same in that we explore, but we are all different in that the pattern of our searches is unique. We are all the same in having to operate within cultural and other institutional constraints. We are all different in that our response to these is personal, even if the options are themselves limited by institutionalized constraints. The environment is unique to each because it is psychologically transformed by our being in it. A jealous person will 'see' an event one way, a shy, racist, chauvinist will see it another. Someone who is chauvinist in some contexts may be internationalist and even-handed in others. Someone who is is mentally ill one year but not the next has inhabited two worlds. We all live like this, to a greater or lesser extent. We all act differently in different contexts. Invariance has to be a universal and necessary characteristic of development, but just as certainly, particularity and uniqueness are as well.

Fogel (1997) sees this particularity in terms of development as inherently creative and emotional. As we explore what we can do we are exploring situations. As we explore situations we are exploring ourselves. Each time we act we are 'at the juncture between the known and the unknown' (1997, p. 420), as Fogel puts it. And when we do psychology, we explore how humans explore. We educate our attention to others, and thus to ourselves.

Looking back

I want to end with a look back over the main thrusts of the book and to express my hopes for how you may have changed through engagement with it and thus with me. The first main aim was to show that an analysis of the traditional perspective reveals fundamental weaknesses, that the maintenance of dichotomies renders any serious attempt at an interactive explanation of developmental processes impossible. The traditional view has served its purposes but now is the time for psychology to self-organize and move to a more differentiated level of analysis. It is time for change because we know enough to determine a new task space to begin to explore, that defined by a view of developmental psychology as the study of dynamic, ecological systems.

The alternative view I have offered is based upon notions of change far broader than psychology. It describes a world in which development occurs through internal reorganization, self-organization, of the developmental system, which comprises the organism in its environment. It is in and only in the interactions between the organism and the environment that invariance, structure, comes to be utilized. Invariance is transformed into information. The effective environment is transformed. Our actions are transformed. Our heads are changed. This applies to all the contexts we inhabit, which stretch from the biophysical to biochemical, from physiological to psychological to social to sociological to economic. We simultaneously exist within universal, species-typical, culture-specific, individual-specific and every other level of influence, all systems of constraints and affordances. As a consequence, we are simultaneously the product of processes which make us both the same as and different from all other people. In the end, all developmental influences are mediated via our personal characteristics, so however much we identify generic features of the developmental system, it is still an intensely individual experience. No species is capable of adapting in one moment to the complexity. That is why the development system itself evolved. This system organizes the number and quality of problems which exist for the developing infant so there is a coupling between the complexity of the tasks facing the child and its ability to cope with them.

I have tried to offer a new perspective, to make an alternative view accessible. I have made a blatant but honest attempt to change your head, influence your development. I have explored a task-space, where I tried to see how I could change your assumptions about development, to help you cast aside long-held habits. You will now know whether you see development through the same lens or not. If you see it in the same way you did, I have failed. But if the interactions which studying this book involved now affords new insights, a different set of affordances, if you have got a 'new head' on, then I may have succeeded, I may have educated your attention.

Discussion points

1   What are the assumptions underlying the traditional, cognitivist position? Evaluate them.

2   'Representations do exist so the ecological position comes to nothing.' Discuss.

3   What sorts of factors can cause someone to 'miss the point'? Consider what prior conditions might underlie 'syndromes' like autism.

4   From an ecological perspective, discuss the ways in which the views of Piaget and Vygotsky are similar and the ways in which they are different. Did they both make the same mistakes?

General questions

Consider the extent to which the aims of the writer have been achieved:

- Do you now think about development differently?

- Does it involve an appreciation of preformationism and dichotomies?

- Do you think you appreciate systems thinking better than you did?

- Have you been able to appropriate the terminology of ecological and dynamic systems thinking into your own repertoire?

- Do they help you think about development?

- Are you more critical of what you read? If so, in what ways?

- Has your attention been educated?

Glossary

Adaptation (Traditional):   The process of change in organisms through natural selection so they survive better in their standard environmental niche. A change in an organism which aids its survival.

(New):   The process of change between organisms and their environments by which they become mutually organized and by which the survival chances of the organism under consideration improve

    discrete-function: only capable of aiding in the solution of a specific problem area

    content-specific: only capable of dealing with data of a specific form.

Affordance: That relation that exists between an organism and an aspect of its environment by which that aspect of the environment can be utilized; one of the set of possible actions and relations among elements of an organism/environment system.

Ancestral: Existing long enough ago for evolutionary change to have occurred.

Appropriation: The result of an interaction of environmental invariance with organismic structure in which the organism utilizes the invariance in its action and thinking.

Assumption: A basic tenet upon which a system of beliefs and values can be based; a belief or value which is not usually accessible to critique by the holder of it.

Attractor: The relatively stable dynamic state which a system typically takes up for a given set of conditions.

Biochemical: Concerned with chemical change in organisms.

Biology: The study of the structure and functioning of living organisms.

Biological: Pertaining to the structure and functioning of an organism; having phylogenetic origins; having an evolved function; being adaptive; due to genetic change.

Biomechanical: Concerned with the mechanics of an organisms structure and function.

Biophysical: Concerned with the physical aspects of biological processes.

Blueprint: A metaphor to suggest that genes carry detailed information, plans for the production of developmental outcomes.

Built-in: (Traditional): Constructed independently of interactions with the external environment, following a genetic blueprint.

(New): Appears following interactions between species-typical components.

Calibration: The setting of any measuring tool using an external validation, e.g. using sight to determine position of prey and altering internal rule by which auditory information specifies position of the prey.

Categories of thought: Basic units which are used to classify any state or event, e.g. male/female.

Category system: Any means of allocating items differentially
   exclusive: a category of unambiguous classification such that no instance could be classified in one category and also fit in any other
   exhaustive: no item may exist which does not fit into any of the designated categories.

Cognition: Central psychological processes as opposed to those purported to be concerned only with operations at the interface of organism and environment, perception and motoric activity. May refer to all three.

Cognitive: (Traditional): Concerned with the complex decision-making process, as opposed to mere initial processing (perception) or translating into action (motor activity).

(New): Unclear function to the term as no clear distinction is to be seen between cognition and perception; redundant, serving only to maintain traditional dichotomous thinking.

Collective variable: The name for a parameter which has an important influence on the changing behaviour of a system.

Computer; serial processor: An information-processing system which is composed of component processors which function sequentially, the results of one feeding as input to the next.

Computer; parallel processor: An information-processing system in which components simultaneously process data, and can thus be connected to other parts in a more complex manner than in a 'train'.

Computer analogy or metaphor: The assumption that the human mind functions as a serial computer

Concept: General mental category arrived at by analysis of perceptual data, containing the essential features needed to correctly categorize a perceptual item as having membership of the category the concept refers to.

Conditions

  necessary: one without which a given change will not happen, but which may not be sufficient, does not guarantee effect

  sufficient: one which ensures a given change will occur, though it may not be necessary, as other means might also have the same effect.

Connectionism: The study of cognition through the use of parallel processors to simulate human behaviour; the view that neural networks change in their connections to each other according to the pattern of inputs they receive. Invariance in input, a reflection of external structure, leads to a corresponding internal invariance. This internal structure then recognizes the forms of input it has previously encountered and partially responds to approximations of them.

Conspecific: Member of the same species.

Constraint: The limitation on structure or function in virtue of the relation between an organism and an aspect of the environment.

Context (Traditional):   Setting in which action occurs; external environment.

(New):   Any part of the external and internal context which contributes to the interactive causal flux from which developmental outcomes emerge

  external: outside the body

  internal: within the body.

Continuum: Dimension with no discrete categories.

Co-evolution: The process by which changes in both organismic and environmental structures and thereby functions, occur as part of a unified system of interdependent causal change, so that the evolution of each of the parts, whether external or organismic, affects the evolution of the others; if the organism and environment are perceived as a single system it follows that neither evolves except in relation to each other.

Contingent: Not necessarily occurring; empirically possible but not necessary; dependent on.

Control parameter: Parameter whose variation is associated with system reorganization. Always involves a relation between factors, as it is changing relations which control system function.

Coupled: Systematically connected.

Cultural artifact: Any standard product of a culture.

Culture: Any group which has a shared way of life.

Darwinian view: The view that natural selection is the mechanism of evolutionary change.

Development (Traditional): The changes that occur over time to an individual based upon their membership of a particular species and their individual experiences.

(New): The processes by which an organism or species and its effective environment become more differentiated and differentially coupled; non-linear behavioural self-organization emerging from the interactions of sub-systems

    developmental status: the point in the process of development reached at any given moment

    developmental process: the interactions by which change in organisms and their co-evolved environments occur

    developmental product: a structure or function which is the outcome of a developmental interaction.

Dialectic: A form of relation among items which are causally connected whereby changes in one entail changes in the other, so the components form a mutually defined whole and the properties of any unit are in dynamic change; a relation where states will necessarily change and turn into something different; the production of an opposite from change.

Dichotomy: A two-part category system in which membership of one part excludes membership of the other and the two categories together exhaust all possibilities

    biological/social: a dichotomous category based upon the notion that as sources or causes of development are due to nature or nurture, and as social states and events are part of the environment, they are part of nurture, while biological states and events are part of nature

inner/outer: based upon the notion that sources or causes of development, being due to nature or nurture, and given that nurture sources are located in the external environment and nature within the organism, originate either from within the organism or come from without

mind/body: the notion that mental states and events are of a logically distinct character to physical, bodily states and events

nature/nurture: a dichotomous category system in which the two possibilities are the two sources of all developmental change; assumes each makes a separate contribution and the debate concerns the extent of each

ontogenetic/phylogenetic: the view that these two categories refer to two distinct processes, one based upon gene change (resulting in changes to a species), one based upon change not involving genes, during the life of an individual member of a species

organism/environment: the view that each of these categories contributes separately to developmental change in the organism; each existing and being a meaningful category irrespective of the other.

Differentiation: The process by which the quantity and quality of different physical, behavioural or psychological forms emerge through development; name for the increasing complexity in perceived structure of the external environment, the structure of action and the structure of the mind, as all are part of one system.

Distributed cognition: The cognitive processes in action when two or more are jointly working on a task; not contained within one mind; a property of the interaction; shared understanding; a processing system with no central decision-maker, but various sub-systems which can function independently of each other.

Dynamic structure: Changes in movement over time which display order, regularity.

Dynamic systems theories: mathematical theories based upon the analysis of non-linear qualitative change in the energy movements in systems. Applied in psychology on the view that human development be construed as consisting in a system of dynamic, non-linear changes in which a host of internal and external, long-lived and newly created factors interact together and from which unpredictable, context-sensitive outcomes emerge.

Ecological validity: The extent to which findings can be generalized to natural situations; extent to which context in which observation occurs has same properties as those in which organism usually lives.

Environment: The (usually dynamic) structure of the world outside the organism; that part of the external structure with which the organism is in causal contact

   effective: the environment as experienced by an organism or species at any given point in its development

Epistemology: Theory of how knowledge develops, how it is validated; the scope and limits of knowledge.

Evolutionary psychology: The view that evolved psychological adaptations are the source of human behaviour and organization, including culture.

Evolutionary time: Time during which adaptations can evolve; time during which species can change.

Functionally equivalent: Having the same effect; appearing the same; leading to the same response.

Generic forms: Forms found in many diverse species, and in many diverse sorts of organs, maintained despite large variations in conditions or functions.

Gene-pool: An ideal notion, the sum of genes shared by a population, usually a species, assuming no drift or other dynamic factors.

Genes, selfish: A metaphor intended to indicate the power of genes to replicate and maintain themselves at the expense of other genes and irrespective of the body they happen to be part of.

Genetic: Relating to the origins of something, relating to its history, relating to genes.

Genetic epistemology: The study of the origins and development of knowledge; the view that knowledge arises only from the interactions between the organism and its environment, being constructed, not fixed by external or internal determinants.

Genotype: Genome; genes which are taken to contain the blueprint for a given phenotype; the total gene-set for an individual.

Information: Any structure which affects, informs or is part of the set of interacting causal factors for a developmental outcome.

Inheritance: The passing of characteristics from one generation to the next, can be by sexual reproduction, or any other means.

Innate: Unlearned; genetically caused/determined; biologically caused/determined; fixed; independent of learning; independent of experience.

Interaction: The process by which two or more components have a mutual reactivity such that upon meeting each is changed by the other, so new components and/or a new product is created

> **interpersonal:**   the process by which two or more humans have a mutual reactivity such that upon meeting each is changed by the other, so they are (in some measure) different, and the product, the relationship, is also different

> **plastic:**   one involving individual-specific components in which the product is changed internal structure so that adaptive action in respect of specific conditions is afforded; corresponds to learning

> **primal:**   one selected over evolutionary time such that species-typical components (structure within the organism and structures in the environment) interact to produce an adaptive, species-typical product, action coupled to the typical conditions encountered at that moment; the sum of these is the developmental system

Interactionism: The view that the process of development is best explained as the outcome of interactions between organismic and environmental factors.

Interactants: Components of an interaction; can mean the humans in interaction.

Interactive complex: The total set of factors, the complete set of informing states and events involved in the interactions from which developmental changes emerge.

Invariance: Any order, lack of randomness, structure, usually dynamic, which could be utilized in adaptive action;

basic condition of adaptive action as one cannot adapt, couple, to nothing

culture-specific: has existed over the area that the culture has occupied for the time that the culture has existed.

dynamic: invariance in patterns which move in space and time

extension of: the physical area and temporal extent over which an invariance reliably exists

external: invariance in structures or functions outside the body

individual-specific: common only to one individual

internal: invariance in internal bodily structure or function

species-typical: has existed over the area that the species has occupied for the time that the species has existed.

Inter-modality: The equivalence of perceptual inputs, irrespective of the form of energy involved, e.g. electromagnetic, air pressure, or the mode of reception, e.g. visual or auditory system; the process by which information from one perceptual mode directly informs perception in another mode.

Isomorphism: A one-to-one correspondence between two states or events. In psychology, between an external structure and an internal representation of it.

Locomotion: Motor behaviour by means of which an organism transports itself.

Maturation: Biological change not requiring learning or any special experience; based upon a genetic programme.

MER: Mental event representation. Internal representations of invariant external events, invariably routines.

Methodology: The set of accepted procedures by which a form of study is to be carried out; the means by which valid evidence is collected and evaluated; the means by which claims are validated.

Morphogenesis: The process by which the form and structure of an organism develops.

Movement

active: intentional action of an organism

passive: movement not due to the effort of the organism.

Mutuality: The relation whereby two items depend upon each other for their existence and meaning.

Myth: An assumed idea, version, story, theory.

Nativism: The view that the main structures of the mind are innately fixed; the theory that the main causal determination of developmental processes and outcomes lies in genetic blue-prints which produce specific cognitive adaptations as a result of natural selection (evolution). The implications are (a) that environmental influences are a different class of causal factor (part of the other half of a dichotomy), and (b) that this latter class is insignificant compared with the power of evolved char-acteristics.

Natural selection: An analogy for the process by which changes in the structure of species appear to be selected natu-rally as unhelpful changes lead to higher probability of death, which, on a large scale, has the same outcome as if they had been de-selected.

Neo-Darwinian: Development of Darwin's views; often inaccurate as he did not believe all that is attributed to him, e.g. selection as only genetic, as he considered that individually acquired habits could eventually become instinctive and heri-table.

Niche: A specific set of environmental conditions a set of organisms lives with and through and has co-evolved with, adapted to; the opportunities and impediments of a creature's environment; the affordance/constraint system that an organ-ism operates with.

Ontogeny: The history of an individual; the development of an individual.

Paradigm: A widely accepted and used conceptual frame-work upon which criteria for knowing and for evaluating methods of finding out are based; epistemological assump-tions.

Parameter

    control: variables which are of most significance in hold-ing the system in stability, constraining the effects of any other variation on the system, however, they can only do this within certain values of the control parameter; at a crit-ical value or boundary condition they trigger reorganization and a phase-shift occurs – control parameters are thus important both in maintaining stability and in evoking change

order: the single attractor state that a system moves towards; the organized outcome of all the interactions of the factors in a system.

Perception

direct: the act of knowing the functional relation between an external state or event and oneself, rather than perceiving only the physical specification of it; the act of gaining knowledge of the world through exploration, without learning.

Phase-shift: The point at which non-linear change occurs in a dynamic system.

Phenotype: Term from traditional biology use to refer to states or events which are taken to be the end-product of interactions only between a correlated genotype and biochemical interactions

extended: a physical product external to the body of an organism which arises from species-typical action which aids the survival of the producing organism or species

Phylogeny: The evolutionary history of a species; changes in a species during the life-time of the species.

Plan: Preformed set of instructions which will lead to a given outcome without any extra information or interactions being required.

Predispositions: Traditional term used to imply that genetically controlled adaptations have developed which make non-genetic change, learning, easier; a built-in tendency or attribute due to biological factors.

Preformation: The belief (part of a paradigm) that knowledge or other essential nature of something resides within something already formed, and is released, but not created by, interaction.

Primal: Pertaining to the developmental system.

Programme

genetic (Traditional): view in which the influence of genes is taken to be preformed, independent of significant interactions with environmental influences, whether internal (biochemical) or external

(New): in biology, a complex system of interactions between genes and biochemical contexts by which phenotypical effects emerge; in psychology, see traditional view (Chapter 1).

Psychology

> **behavioural:** the view that the focus of psychology should be observable movement, i.e. behaviour, and the relation between environmental observables and behavioural observables. Naturalistic contexts are not assumed to be important
>
> **ecological:** the view that the study of humans is most successfully conducted by focusing upon the relations between humans and the various contexts they personally inhabit and have inhabited, as a species.

Relational: Having a meaning only in terms of the relation between terms or states or events.

Reductionism: The view that explanations of events should be at a level lower than the normal description of them, e.g. explaining behaviour in terms of physiological processes.

Representation: The internal equivalent of external structure, e.g. a representation of a face. The assumption is that the brain has to work with representations, as it can work only with the contents of the brain and cannot connect directly to the external world.

Routines: Events with invariant characteristics.

Scaffolding: The support of an adult in a task; the contribution to task performance of a more competent person on a joint task such that the dyad can carry out the task more successfully than the less competent could alone.

Script: A description of the key elements and order of a routine.

Selection: An analogy intended to convey the notion that changes during development are the result of self-organization of the most efficient outcome.

Self-organization: The changes in a system caused by internal reordering without any imposition of structure from outside the system.

Species-typical: Shorthand for that set of generic structural and functional invariances in physiology and behaviour that a species robustly displays despite variations in local conditions

> **species-typical interactions:** interactions involving species-typical internal and external invariance to produce species-typical products.

STE species-typical environment (Traditional): The relatively stable environment in which the species evolved.

(New): That changing set of external structures and functions which characterize the environment of the species over its phylogeny; the developmentally relevant external environment for the species.

Structures: Anything which has some invariance in its form, whether static, like a tree, or dynamic, like the complex variation in the sun's movement which is nevertheless completely structured.

Systemic: Pertaining to systems; systematic.

Systems: A set of components which are structurally and functionally related so that they produce outcomes whose characteristics depend upon the total pattern of interactions between the component structures and functions. The components thus function as a unit and lead to particular sorts of outcomes.

Tautology: A statement which is necessarily true because it it is actually of the logical form 'x is x', though it can appear not to be as 'x' can take different forms. e.g unique shapes are not repeated – unique implies not repeated, so it reads 'unique implies unique'.

Tetrapod: Vertebrate with four limbs.

Transformation: A set of rules which specify which operations must be carried out on a given input for a given adaptive result to emerge.

Way of life: A complex of means of obtaining resources, including the attitudes and values, knowledge and skills involved, as well as the generic forms of economic and social organization.

References

Abelson, R. P. (1981) Psychological status of the script concept. *American Psychologist*, **36 (7)** (July): 715–29.

Abravanel, E. and Sigafoos, A. O. (1984) Exploring the presence of imitation during early infancy. *Child Development*, **55**: 381–92.

Adolph, K. E. (1997) Learning in the development of infant locomotion. *Monographs of the Society for Research in Child Development*, **251 (3)**: 62.

Ainsworth, M. D. S. (1977) Infant development and mother–infant interaction among Ganda and American families. In Leiderman, P. H., Tulkin, S. R. and Rosenfeld, A. (eds), *Culture and Infancy: Variations in the Human Experience*. New York: Academic Press.

Aitken, S. (1981) Intersensory substitution in the blind child, Ph.D dissertation, University of Edinburgh. Cited in Bower, T.G.R., *The Rational Infant – Learning in Infancy*. New York: Freeman & Co. (1989).

Amiel-Tison, C. and Grenier, A. (1980) *Neurological Evaluation of the Newborn and the Infant*. New York: Masson.

Baillargeon, R. (1986) Representing the existence and the location of hidden objects: object permanence in 6-and 8-month-old infants. *Cognition*, **23**: 21–41.

Baillargeon, R. and DeVos, J. (1991) Object permanence in young infants: further evidence. *Child Development*, **62**: 1227–46.

Baldwin, J. M. (1902) *Development and Evolution*. Basingstoke: Macmillan.

Baldwin, J. M. (1906) *Mental Development in the Child and in the Race*. Basingstoke: Macmillan.

Ball, W. and Tronick, E. (1971) Infant responses to impending collision: optical and real. *Science*, **171**: 818–20.

Barkow, J., Cosmides, L, and Tooby, J. (eds) (1992) *The Adapted Mind: Evolutionary Psychology and The Generation of Culture*. New York: Oxford University Press.

Barnes, P. (ed.) (1995) *Personal, Social and Emotional Development of Children*. Oxford: Blackwell, in association with The Open University.

Bensen, J. B. (1993) Season of birth and onset of locomotion: theoretical and methodological implications. *Infant Behaviour and Development*, **16**: 69–81.

Bernstein, N. A. (1967) *The Coordination and Regulation of Movements*, Oxford: Pergamon Press.

Berthold, P. (1998) Spatiotemporal aspects of avian long-distance migration. In Healy, S. (ed.), *Spatial Representation in Animals*. Oxford: Oxford University Press.

Bingman, V. P. (1998) Spatial representations and homing pigeon navigation. In Healy, S. (ed.), *Spatial Representation in Animals*. Oxford: Oxford University Press: 69–85.

Bower, T. G. R. (1989) *The Rational Infant – Learning in Infancy*. New York: Freeman & Co.

Bower, T. G. R., Broughton, J. M. and Moore, M. K. (1970) Demonstration of intention in the reaching behaviour of neonate humans. *Nature*, **228**: 679–81.

Brauth, S. E., Hall, W. S. and Dooling, R. J. (eds) (1991) *Plasticity of Development*. London: MIT Press.

Brazelton, T. B. (1979) Evidence of communication during neonatal behavioural assessment. In Bullowa, M. (ed.), *Before Speech: The Beginning of Interpersonal Communication*. Cambridge: Cambridge University Press.

Bremner, J. G. (1997) *Infancy*. Oxford: Blackwell.

Bremner, J. G., Slater, A. and Butterworth, G. E. (eds) (1997) *Infant Development: Recent Advances*. Hove: Psychology Press, Erlbaum (UK) Taylor & Francis.

Bronfenbrenner, U. (1989) Ecological systems theories. *Annals of Child Development*, **6**: 187–249.

Brooks, R. A. (1986) A robust layered control system for a mobile robot. *IEEE Journal of Robotics and Automation*, **RA-2**: 14–23.

Brooks, R. A. (1991) Intelligence without representations. *Artificial Intelligence*, **47**: 139–59.

Bruner, J. (1983) *Child's Talk*. Oxford: Oxford University Press.

Bruner, J. and Haste, H. (1987) *Making Sense – The Child's Construction of The World*. London: Methuen.

Bushnell, I. W. R. (1998) The origins of face perception. In Simion, F. and Butterworth, G. (eds), *The Development of Sensory, Motor and Cognitive Capacities in Early Infancy: From Perception to Cognition*. Hove: Psychology Press, Taylor & Francis Group.

Butterworth, G. E (ed.) (1981) *Infancy and Epistemology: An Evaluation of Piaget's Theory*. London: Harvester Wheatsheaf.

Butterworth, G. E. (1991) The ontogeny and phylogeny of joint visual attention. In Whiten, A. (ed.), *Natural Theories of Mind: Evolution, Development and Simulation of Everyday Mindreading*. Oxford: Basil Blackwell.

Butterworth, G. E. (1993) Dynamic approaches to infant perception and action: old and new theories about the origins of knowledge. In Smith, L. B and Thelen, E. (eds) (1993), *A*

Dynamic Systems Approach to Development: *Applications*. London: MIT Press/Bradford Books.

Butterworth, G. E and Bryant, P. (eds) (1990) *Causes of Development: Interdisciplinary Perspectives*. Hemel Hempstead: Harvester Wheatsheaf.

Butterworth, G. E and Harris, M. (1994) *Principles of Developmental Psychology*. Hove: Lawrence Erlbaum Associates.

Butterworth, G. E. and Light, P. (1982) *Social Cognition: Studies in the Development of Understanding*. Brighton: Harvester Press.

Butterworth, G. E., Rutkowska, J. and Scaife, M. (eds) (1985) *Evolution and Developmental Psychology*. Brighton: Harvester Press.

Butterworth, G. E., Verweij, E. and Hopkins, B. (1997) The development of prehension in infants. *British Journal of Developmental Psychology*, **15**: 223–36.

Butterworth, G. and Hopkins, B. (1997). In Bremner, J.G., Slater, A. and Butterworth, G.E. (eds), *Infant Development: Recent Advances*. Hove: Psychology Press, Erlbaum (UK) Taylor & Francis.

Byrne, R. (1995) *The Thinking Ape: Evolutionary Origins of Intelligence*. Oxford: Oxford University Press.

Carey, S. and Gelman, R. (eds) (1991) *The Epigenesis of Mind*: Essays *on Biology and Cognition*. Hillsdale, N.J.: Erlsbaum.

Cashdan, E. (1980) Egalitarianism among hunters and gatherers. *American Anthropologist*, **82**: 116–20.

Castillo, M. and Butterworth, G. E. (1981) Neonatal localisation of a sound in a visual space. *Perception*, **10**: 331–8.

Clark, A. (1997a) The dynamical challenge. *Cognitive Science*, **24** **(2)**: 461–81.

Clark, A. (1997b) *Being There: Putting Brain, Body and World Together Again*, A Bradford Book. London: MIT Press.

Clark, A. and Thornton, C. (1997) Trading spaces: computation, representation, and the limits of uninformed learning, *Behavioral and Brain Sciences*, **20**: 57–90.

Clark, J. E. and Philips, S. J. (1993) A longitudinal study of intra-limb coordination in the first year of independent walking: a dynamical systems approach. *Child Development*, **64**: 1143–57.

Clifton, R. K. Muir, D. W. Ashmead, D. H. and Clarkson, M. G. (1993) Is visually guided reaching in infancy a myth? *Child Development*, **64**: 1099–1110.

Cole, M. (1985) The zone of proximal development: where culture and cognition create each other. In Wertsch, G. (ed.) *Culture, Communication and Cognition*. Cambridge: Cambridge University Press.

Collett, T. S. and Zeil, J. (1998) Places and landmarks: an arthro-pod perspective. In Healy, S. (ed.), *Spatial Representation in Animals*. Oxford: Oxford University Press: 18–53.

Connolly, K. J. and Forssberg, H. (eds) (1997) Neurophysiology and neuropsychology of motor development. *Clinics in Developmental Medicine*, **143/144**. Cambridge: Cambridge University Press/MacKeith Press.

Cooper, R. P. and Aslin, R. N. (1990) Preference for infant-directed speech in the first month after birth. *Child Development*, **61**: 1584–95.

Cooper, R. P. and Aslin, R. N. (1994) Developmental differences in infant attention to the spectral properties of infant-directed speech. *Child Development*, **65**: 1663–77.

Costall, A. (1989) A closer look at 'direct perception'. In Gellatly, A. Rogers, D. and Sloboda, J. J. (eds), *Cognition and Social Worlds*. Oxford: Clarendon Press.

Crystal, D. (ed.) (1987) *The Cambridge Encyclopaedia of Language*. London: Guild Publishing.

Cutting, J. E. (1991) Four ways to reject directed perception. *Ecological Psychology*, **3(1)**: 25–34.

Dawkins, R. (1989) *The Selfish Gene*. Oxford: Oxford University Press.

Dawkins, R. (1982) *The Extended Phenotype*. Oxford: Oxford University Press.

DeCasper, A. J. and Fifer, W. P. (1980) Of human bonding: newborns prefer their mothers' voices. *Science*, **208**: 1174–6.

DeCasper, A. J. and Spence, M. J. (1986) Prenatal maternal speech influences newborns' perception of speech sounds. *Infant Behaviour and Development*, **9**: 133–50.

Dent-Reed, C. and Zukow-Goldring, P. (eds) (1997) *Evolving Explanations of Development Ecological Approaches to Organism – Environment Systems*. Washington, D.C.: American Psychological Association.

de Schonen, S. (1980) Développement de la coordination visuo-manuellet de la lateralisation manuelle des conduites d'atteinte et de prise d'objet. *Travaux du Centre D'Etude des Processus Cognitifs et du Langue*. Paris: Maison des Sciences de l'Hommes.

de Schonen, S., Mancini, J. and Liegeois, F. (1998) About functional cortical specialisation: the development of face recognition. In Simion, F. and Butterworth, G. (eds), *The Development of Sensory, Motor and Cognitive Capacities in Early Infancy: From Perception to Cognition*. Hove: Psychology Press, Taylor & Francis Group.

De Vries, J. J. P., Visser, G. H. A. and Prechtl, H. F. R. (1984). In Prechtl, H. F. R. (1984) (ed.), *Continuity and Development in Neural Functions*. Oxford: Blackwell Scientific Publications: 46–64.

Donald, M. (1993) *Origins of the Modern Mind: Three Stages in the Evolution of Culture and Cognition*. London: Harvard University Press.

Donaldson, M. (1978) *Children's Minds*. London: Fontana.

Dunbar, R. I. M. (1993) Coevolution of neocortical size, group size, and language in humans. *Behavioral and Brain Sciences*, **16**: 681–735.

Dziurawiec, S. and Ellis, H. (1986) Study reported in Johnson, M. and Morton, J., *Biology and Cognitive Development*. Oxford: Blackwell (1991).

Eilers, R. E., Gavin, W. J. and Oller, D. M. (1982) Cross-linguistic perception in infancy: early effects of linguistic experience. *Journal of Child Language*, **9**: 289–302.

Eimas, P. D. (1994) Categorization in early infancy and the continuity of development. *Cognition*, **50**: 83–93.

Eimas, P. D., Siqueland, E. R., Jusczyk, P. and Vigorito, J. (1971) Speech perception in infants. *Science*, **171**: 303–6.

Elderedge, N. and Gould, S. J. (1972) Punctuated equilibria: an alternative to phyletic gradualism. In Schopf, T. J. M. (ed.), *Models in Paleobiology*. San Francisco: Freeman: 82–115.

Ellis, A and Young, A. (1988) *Human Cognitive Neuropsychology*. Hove: Lawrence Erlbaum Associates.

Elman, J. (1993) Learning and development in neural networks: the importance of starting small. *Cognition*, **48**: 71–99.

Emde, R. N. and Koenig. K. (1969) Neonatal smiling and rapid eye movement states. *Journal of The American Academy of Child Psychiatry*, **11**: 177–200.

Emde, R. N. , Gaensbauer, T. J. and Harmon, R. J. (1976) Emotional expression in infancy. *Psychological Issues Monograph*, **37**, New York: International Universities Press.

Emlen, S. T. (1969) Bird migration: influence of physiological state upon celestial orientation. *Science*, **165**: 716–18.

Emlen, S. T. (1972) The ontogenetic development of orientation abilities. *Symposium of animal orientation: NASA special publications SP-62*: 191–210.

Etienne, A., Berlie, J., Georgacopoulos, J. and Maurer, R. (1998). In Healy, S. (ed.), *Spatial Representation in Animals*. Oxford: Oxford University Press: 54–68.

Fernald, A. (1992) Human maternal vocalisations to infants as biologically relevant signals: an evolutionary perspective. In Barkow, J., Cosmides, l. and Tooby, J. (eds), *The Adapted Mind: Evolutionary Psychology and the Generation of Culture*. New York: Oxford University Press.

Fernald, A. (1993) Approval and disapproval: infant responsiveness to vocal affect in familiar and unfamiliar languages. *Child Development*, **64**: 657–74.

Fernald, A. and Morikawa, H. (1993) Common themes and cultural variations in Japanese and American mothers' speech to infants. *Child Development*, **64**: 637–56.

Fernald, A. and Simon, T. (1984) Expanded intonation contours in mothers' speech to newborns. *Developmental Psychology*, **20**: 104–13.

Fernald, A., Kermanschachi, N. and Lees, D. (1984) The rhythms and sounds of soothing: maternal vestibular, tactile and auditory stimulation and infant state. Paper presented at the International Conference on Infant Studies, New York.

Fernald, A., Taeschner, T., Dunn, J., Papousek, M., Boysson-Bardies, B. and Fukui, I. (1989) A cross-language study of prosodic modifications in mothers' and fathers' speech to preverbal infants. *Journal of Child Language*, **16**: 477–501.

Ferrier, L. J. (1985) Intonation in discourse: talk between 12-month-olds and their mothers. In Nelson, K. (ed.) *Children's Language*, **5**. Hillsdale, N.J.: Erlsbaum: 35–60.

Fodor, J. A. (1983) *The Modularity of Mind*. Cambridge, Mass.: MIT Press.

Fogel, A. (1997) Information, creativity and culture. In Dent-Reed, C. and Zukow-Goldring, P. (eds), *Evolving Explanations of Development Ecological Approaches to Organism–Environment Systems*. Washington, D.C.: American Psychological Association.

Fogel, A. and Hannan, T. E. (1985) Manual actions of nine-to-fifteen week-old humans during fact-to-face interactions with their mothers. *Child Development*, **56**: 1271–9.

Fontaine, R. (1984) Initiative skills between birth and six months. *Infant Behaviour and Development*, **7**: 323–33.

Gabora, L. M. and Colgan, P. W. (1991) A model of the mechanisms underlying exploratory behaviour. In Meyer, J. A. and Wilson, S. W. (eds), *From Animals to Animals: Proceedings of The First International Conference on Simulation of Adaptive Behaviour*. Cambridge, Mass.: MIT Press: 475–84.

Gallistel, C. R. (1993) *The Organization of Learning*, A Bradford Book. Cambridge, Mass.: MIT Press.

Gardner, H. (1987) *The Mind's New Science: A History of the Cognitive Revolution*. New York: Basic Books.

Gibson, E. J. (1991) *An Odyssey in Learning and Perception*. London: MIT Press.

Gibson, E. J. and Walk, R. D. (1960) The 'visual cliff'. *Scientific American*, **202**: 64–71.

Gibson, J. J. (1950) *The Perception of the Visual World*. Boston: Houghton-Mifflin.

Gibson, J. J. (1966) *The Senses considered as Perceptual Systems*. Boston: Houghton-Mifflin.

Gibson, J. J. (1979) *The Ecological Approach to Visual Perception*. Boston: Houghton-Mifflin.

Gibson, K. R. and Ingold, T. (eds) (1993) *Tools, Language and Cognition in Human Evolution*. Cambridge: Cambridge University Press.

Gilmore, R. (1981) *Catastrophe Theory for Scientists and Engineers*. New York: Wiley.

Gilmore, R. O. and Johnson, M. H. (1998) Learning what is where: oculomotor contributions to the development of spatial cognition. In Simion, F. and Butterworth, G. (eds), *The Development of Sensory, Motor and Cognitive Capacities in Early Infancy: From Perception to Cognition*. Hove: Psychology Press, Taylor & Francis Group.

Goffman, E. (1974) *Frame Analysis: An Essay in the Organization of Experience*. New York: Harper & Row.

Goldbart, J. (1994) Playing in the zone: communication and cognition in the classroom. *The SLD experience, 10* (Autumn, Occasional Papers, **3**).

Goldfield, E. C. (1995) *Emergent Forms: Origins and Early Development of Human Action and Perception*. New York: Oxford University Press.

Goodwin, B. (1990) The causes of biological form. In Butterworth, G. E and Bryant, P. (eds), *Causes of Development: Interdisciplinary Perspectives*. Hemel Hempstead: Harvester Wheatsheaf.

Goodwin, B. (1995) *How the Leopard Changed its Spots: the Evolution of Complexity*. London and Phoenix: Orion Books.

Gopnik, A. and Meltzoff, A. (1986) Relations between semantic and cognitive development in the one-word state – the specificity hypothesis. *Child Development*, **57**: 1040–53.

Goren, C. C., Sarty, M. and Wu, P. Y. K. (1975) Visual following and pattern discrimination of face-like stimuli by new-born infants. *Pediatrics*, **56**, 544–9.

Goswami, U. (1998) *Cognition in Children*. Hove: Psychology Press.

Gottlieb, G. (1997) *Synthesising Nature–Nurture: Prenatal Roots of Instinctive Behaviour*. Mahwah, N.J.: Lawrence Erlbaum Associates.

Green, J. G. (1994) Gibson's affordances. *Psychological Review*, **101** (**2**): 336–42.

Haber, R. N. and Hershenson, M. (1980) *The Psychology of Visual Perception*. New York: Rinehart & Winston.

Hall, W. G. and Bryan, T. E. (1980) The ontogeny of feeding in rats. II Independent ingestive behaviour. *Journal of Comparative and Physiological Psychology*, **93**: 746–56.

Hartelman, P. A. I., van der Maas, H. L. J. and Molenaar, P. C. M. (1998) Detecting and modelling developmental transitions. *British Journal of Developmental Psychology*, **16**: 97–122.

Hayes, W. N. and Saiff, E. I. (1967) Visual alarm reaction in turtles. *Animal Behaviour*, **15**: 102–6.

Hayne, H. and Rovee-Collier, C. (1995) The organisation of reactivated memory in infancy. *Child Development*, **66**: 893–906.

Healy, S. (ed.) (1998) *Spatial Representation in Animals*. Oxford: Oxford University Press.

Hendriks-Jansen, H. (1996) *Catching Ourselves in the Act. Situated Activity, Interactive Emergence, and Human Thought*, A Bradford Book. London: MIT Press.

Hepper, P. G. (1991) An examination of fetal learning before and after birth. *Irish Journal of Psychology*, **12**: 95–107.

Hepper, P. G., Scott, D. and Shahidullah, S. (1993) Newborn and fetal response to maternal voice. *Journal of Reproductive and Infant Psychology*, **11**: 147–53.

Hinde, R. A., Perret-Clermont, A. and Stevenson-Hinde, J. (eds) (1985) *Social Relationships and Cognitive Development*. Oxford: Clarendon Press.

Hobson, R. P. (1993) Perceiving attitudes, conceiving minds. In Lewis, C. and Mitchell, P. (eds), *Origins of an Understanding of Mind*. Hillsdale, N.J.: Erlsbaum.

Hofsten, C. von, (1982) Eye–hand coordination in the newborn. *Developmental Psychology*, **18**: 450–61.

Hofsten, C. von (1986) Early spatial perception taken in reference to manual action. *Acta Psychologica*, **63**: 323–35.

Hofsten, C. von (1997) On the early development of predictive abilities. In Dent-Reed, C. and Zukow-Goldring, P. (eds), *Evolving Explanations of Development Ecological Approaches to Organism–Environment Systems*. Washington, D.C.: American Psychological Association: 163–94.

Hofsten, C. von and Spelke, E. S. (1985) Object perception and object directed reaching in infancy. *Journal of Experimental Psychology*, **28**: 158–73.

Hooker, D. (1952) *The Prenatal Origin of Behaviour*. Lawrence: University of Kansas Press.

Hopkins, B. and Butterworth, G. E. (1997) Dynamical systems approaches to the development of action. In Bremner, G., Slater, A. and Butterworth, G. E. (eds), *Infant Development: Recent Advances*. Hove: Psychology Press.

Inagaki, K. (1990) The effects of raising animals on children's biological knowledge. *British Journal of Developmental Psychology*, **8**: 119–31.

Ingold, T. (1996) Situating action VI: a comment on the distinction between the material and the social. *Ecological Psychology*, **8 (4)**: 183–7.

Isbell, B. J. and McKee, L. (1980) Societys' cradle: an anthropological perspective on the socialisation of cognition. In Sants, J. (ed.), *Developmental Psychology and Society*. London: Macmillan.

Johnson, M. and Morton, J. (1991) *Biology and Cognitive Development: The Case of Face Recognition*. Oxford: Basil Blackwell.

Johnson-Laird, P. N. (1988) *The Computer and The Mind*. Cambridge, Mass.: MIT Press.

Johnston, T. D. (1997). In Dent-Reed, C. and Zukow-Goldring, P. (eds), *Evolving Explanations of Development Ecological Approaches to Organism–Environment Systems*. Washington, D.C.: American Psychological Association.

Jones, S. S. and Smith, L. B. (1993) The place of perception in children's concepts. *Cognitive Development*, **8 (2)**: 113–40.

Jusczyk, P. W. (1997) *The Discovery of Spoken Language*, A Bradford Book. London: MIT Press.

Kalmeijn, A. J. (1974) The detection of electric fields from inanimate and animate sources other than electric organs. In Fessaro, A. (ed.), *Handbook of Sensory Physiology*, **III (3)**. New York: Springer.

Kaplan, H., Hill, K. and Hurtado, H. M. (1990) Risk, foraging and food-sharing among the Ache. In Cashdan, E. (ed.), *Risk and Uncertainty in Tribal and Peasant Economies*. Boulder: Westview Press.

Karmiloff-Smith, A. (1992) *Beyond Modularity: A Developmental Perspective on Cognitive Science*. London: MIT Press.

Kaye, K. (1977) Toward the origin of dialogue. In Schaffer, H.R. (ed.), *Studies in Mother–Infant Interaction*. New York: Academic Press.

Kaye, K. (1982) *The Mental and Social Life of Babies: How Parents Create Persons*. London: Methuen.

Kearsley, R. B. (1973) The newborn's response to auditory stimulation: a demonstration of orienting and defensive behaviour. *Child Development*, **44**: 582–90.

Kelso, J. A. S. (1995) *Dynamic Patterns: The Self-Organisation of Brain and Behaviour*. Cambridge, Mass.: MIT Press.

Kim, N. G., Turvey, M. T. and Carello, C. (1993) Optical information about the severity of upcoming contacts. *Journal of Experimental Psychology: Human Perception and Performance*, **19 (1)**: 179–93.

Knudsen, E. (1983) Early auditory experience aligns the auditory map of space in the optic tectum of the barn owl. *Science*, **222**: 939–42.

Kugiumutzakis, G. (1993) Intersubjective vocal imitation in early mother–infant interaction. In Nadel, J. and Camaioni, L. (eds), *New Perspectives in Early Communicative Development*. London: Routledge.

Kuhl, P. J. (1991) Perception, cognition and the ontogenetic and phylogenetic emergence of human speech. In Brauth, S. E., Hall, W. S. and Dooling, R. J. (eds), *Plasticity of Development*. London: MIT Press.

Kuhl, P. K. and Meltzoff, A. N. (1982) The bimodal perception of speech in infancy. *Science*, **218**: 1138–41.

Kuhl, P. K. and Meltzoff, A. N. (1988) Speech as an intermodal object of perception. In Yonas, A. (ed.), *The Development of Perception: Minnesota Symposia on Child Psychology*. Hillsdale, N.J.: Lawrence Erlbaum Associates: 236–66.

Kuhn, T. (1970) *The Structure of Scientific Revolutions*. Chicago: Chicago University Press.

Lee, D. N. (1993) Optic and acoustic constraints for action. In Neisser, U. (ed.), *The Perceived Self: Ecological and Interpersonal Sources of Self-knowledge*. Cambridge: Cambridge University Press.

Lee, D. N. and Reddish, P. E. (1981) Plummeting gannets: a paradigm of ecological optics. *Nature*, **293**: 293–4.

Lee, D. N., Reddish, P. E. and Rand, D. T. (1991) Aerial docking by humming birds. *Naturwissenschaften*, **78**: 526–7.

Lee, D. N., Young, D. S. and Rewt, D. (1992) How do somersaulters land on their feet? *Journal of Experimental Psychology: Human Perception and Performance*, **18 (4)**: 1195–1202.

Lee, D. N., Simmons, J. A., Saillant, P. A., Bouffard, F. (1995) Steering by echolocation: a paradigm of ecological optics. *Journal of Comparative Physiology A*, **176**: 347–54.

Lee, D. N., Weel, F. R., van der, Hitchcock, T., Matejofsky, E. and Pettigrew, J. (1992) Common principles of guidance by echolocation and vision. *Journal of Comparative Physiology A*, **171**: 563–71.

Lee, D. N., Davies, M. N. O., Green, P. R. and van der Weel, F. R. (1993) Visual control of velocity of approach by pigeons when landing. *Journal of Experimental Biology*, **180**: 85–104.

Lee, D. N., Young, D. S., Reddish, P. E., Lough, S. and Clayton, T. N. H. (1983) Visual 'iming in hitting an accelerating ball. *Quarterly Journal of Experimental Psychology*, **35A**: 333–46.

Lee, V. and Gupta, P. das (1995) *Children's Cognitive and Language Development*. Oxford: Blackwell, in association with The Open University.

Legerstee, M. (1991) The role of people and objects in early imitation. *Journal of Experimental Child Psychology*, **51**: 423–33.

Legerstee, M., Anderson, D. and Schaffer, A. (1998) Five-and eight-month-old infants recognise their faces and voices as familiar and social stimuli. *Child Development*, **69 (1)**: 39–50.

Leont'ev, A. N. (1981) The problem of activity in psychology. In Wertsch, J. V. (ed.), *The Concept of Activity in Soviet Psychology*. Armonk: M. E. Sharpe.

Lewis, M. and Freedle, R. (1977) The mother and infant communication system: the effects of poverty. In McGurk, H. (ed.), *Ecological Factors in Human Development*. New York: North-Holland.

Lewkowicz, D. J. and Turkewitz, J. (1980) Cross-modal equivalence in early infancy: auditory–visual intensity matching. *Developmental Psychology*, **16**: 597–607.

Light, P. and Butterworth, G. E. (eds) (1992) *Context and Cognition: Ways of Learning and Knowing*. London: Harvester Wheatsheaf.

Lock, A. J. (1980) *The Guided Re-invention of Language*. London: Croom Helm, in association with The Open University.

Lock, A. J. (1993) Language development and object manipulation. In Gibson, K. R. and Ingold, T. (eds), *Tools, Language and Cognition in Human Evolution*. Cambridge: Cambridge University Press.

Locke, J. L. (1996) Why do infants begin to talk: language as an unintended consequence. *Journal of Child Language*, **23**: 251–68.

Lockman, J. L. and Thelen, E. (1993) Developmental biodynamics: brain, body, behavioral connections. *Child Development*, **64**: 953–9.

Mandler, J. M. (1988) How to build a baby: on the development of an accessible representational system. *Cognitive Development*, **3**: 113–36.

Mandler, J. M. (1992) The foundations of conceptual thought in infancy. *Cognitive Development*, **7**: 273–85.

Mandler, J. M. (1993) On concepts. *Cognitive Development*, **8**: 141–8.

Mandler, J. M (1997) Development of categorisation: perceptual and conceptual categories. In Bremner, J. G., Slater, A. and Butterworth, G. E. (eds), *Infant Development: Recent Advances*. Hove: Psychology Press, Erlbaum (UK) Taylor & Francis: 163–89.

Mandler, J. M, Bauer, P. J. and McDonagh, L. (1991) Separating the sheep from the goats: differentiating global categories. *Cognitive Psychology*, **23**: 263–98.

Maratos, O. (1998) Neonatal, early and later imitation: same order phenomena. In Simion, F. and Butterworth, G. (eds), *The Development of Sensory, Motor and Cognitive Capacities in Early Infancy: From Perception to Cognition*. Hove: Psychology Press, Taylor & Francis Group.

Marler, P. (1993) The instinct to learn. In Johnson, M. H. (1993) (ed.), *Brain Development and Cognition: A Reader*. Oxford: Blackwell: 454–80.

Marr, D. (1982) *Vision*. San Francisco: W. H. Freeman.

Martin, D. D. and Meier, A. H. (1973) Temporal synergism of corticosterone and prolactin in regulating orientation in the migratory white-throated sparrow (*Zonotrichia albicollis*). *Condor*, **75**: 369–74.

Masataka, N. (1992) Motherese in a signed language. *Infant Behaviour and Development*, **15**: 453–60.

Masataka, N. (1994) Effects of experience with live insects on the development of fear of snakes in squirrel monkeys, *Saimiri sciurens*. *Animal Behaviour*, **46**: 741–6.

Masataka, N. (1996) Perception of motherese in a signed language by 6-month-old deaf infants. *Developmental Psychology*, **32**: 874–9.

Masataka, N. (1998) Perception of motherese in Japanese sign language by 6-month-old hearing infants. *Developmental Psychology*, **34 (2)**: 241–6.

Mataric, M. J. (1992) Integration of representation into goal-driven behaviour-based robots. *IEEE Transactions on Robotics and Automation*, **8 (3)**: 304–12.

Mataric, M. J. and Brookes, R. A. (1990) Learning a distributed map representation based on navigation behaviours. In *Proceedings of 1990 USA Japan Symposium on Flexible Automation*. Kyoto, Japan: 499–506.

Maurer, D. and Barrera, M. (1981) Infants' perception of natural and distorted arrangements of a schematic face. *Child Development*, **47**: 523–7.

Mayr, E. (1963) *Animal Species and Evolution*. Cambridge, Mass.: Harvard University Press.

McCrone, J. (1990) *The Ape that Spoke: How the Human Mind Evolved*. London: Macmillan.

McLean, I. and Snyder-McLean, L. K. (1984) Recent developments in pragmatics: remedial implications. In Muller, D. J. (ed.), *Remediating Children's Language: Behavioural and Naturalistic Approaches*. London: Croom Helm.

McMahon, T. A. (1984) *Muscles, Reflexes and Locomotion*. Princeton, N.J.: Princeton University Press.

Mehler, J., Lambertz, G., Jusczyk, P. and Amiel-Tison, C. (1986) Discrimination de la langue maternelle par le nouveau-né. *Comptes Rendes Academie des Sciences*, **303**, Serie III: 637–40.

Meltzoff, A. N. (1981) Imitation, intermodal co-ordination and representation, in Butterworth, G. E. (ed.), *Infancy and Epistemology: An Evaluation of Piaget's Theory*. London: Harvester Wheatsheaf: 85–114.

Meltzoff, A. N. (1985) The roots of social and cognitive development: models of man's original nature. In Field, T. M. and Fox, N. (eds), *Social Perception in Infants*. Norwood, NJ: Ablex: 1–30.

Meltzoff, A. N. (1988) Infant imitation and memory: nine-month-olds in immediate and deferred tests. *Child Development*, **59**: 217–25.

Meltzoff, A. N. and Borton, R. W. (1979) Intermodal matching by human neonates, *Nature*, **282**: 403–4.

Meltzoff, A. and Gopnik, A. (1993) The role of imitation in understanding persons and developing a theory of mind. In Baron-Cohen, S., Tager-Flusberg, H. and Cohen, D. (eds), *Understanding Other Minds – Perspectives from Autism*. Oxford: Oxford University Press.

Meltzoff, A. N. and Moore, M. K. (1977) Imitation of facial and manual gestures by human neonates. *Science*, **198**: 75–8.

Meltzoff, A. N. and Moore, M. K. (1983a) New born infants imitate adult facial gestures. *Child Development*, **54**: 702–9.

Meltzoff, A. N. and Moore, M. K. (1983b) Methodological issues in studies of imitation: comments on McKenzie and Over *et al*. *Infant Behaviour and Development*, **6**: 103–8.

Meltzoff, A. N. and Moore, M. K. (1992) Early imitation within a functional framework: the importance of person identity, movement and development. *Infant Behaviour and Development*, **15**: 479–505.

Messer, D. J. (1994) *The Development of Communication: From Social Interaction to Language*. Chichester: John Wiley.

Michel, G. and Moore, C. (1995) *Developmental Psychobiology An Interdisciplinary Science*, A Bradford Book. London: MIT Press.

Mills, M. and Funnell, E. (1983). In Meadows, S., (ed.), *Developing Thinking: Approaches to Children's Cognitive Development*. London: Methuen.

Mithen, S. (1996) *The Prehistory of the Mind: A Search for the Origins of Art, Religion and Science*. London: Thames & Hudson.

Morss, J. (1990) *The Biologising of Childhood*. Hove and London: Lawrence Erlbaum Associates.

Muir D. (1982) The development of human auditory localization in infancy. In Gatehouse, R. W. (ed.) *Localisation of Sound: Theory and Applications*. Groton, Conn.: Amphora: 22–46.

Muir, D. and Field, J. (1979) Newborn infants orient to sounds. *Child Development*, **50**: 431–6.

Muir, D., Abraham, W., Forbes, B. and Harris, L. (1979) The ontogenesis of an auditory localization response from birth to four months of age. *Canadian Journal of Psychology*, **33**: 320–33.

Nanez, J. E. and Yonas, A. (1994) Effects of luminance and texture motion on infant defensive reactions to optical collision. *Infant Behaviour and Development*, **17**: 165–74.

Nelson, K. (1986) *Event Knowledge, Structure and Function in Development*. Hillsdale, N.J.: Erlbaum.

Nelson, K. (1996) *Language in Cognitive Development: The Emergence of the Mediated Mind*. Cambridge: Cambridge University Press.

236   REFERENCES

Newell, A., Shaw, J. C. and Simon, H. (1958) Elements of a theory of human problem solving. *Psychological Review,* **65**: 151–66.

Newell, K. M. (1986) Constraints on the development of coordination. In Wade, M. G. and Whiting, H. T. A. (eds), *Motor Development in Children: Aspects of Coordination and Control.* Dordrecht: Martinus Nijhoff: 341–60.

Newell, K. M., Kugler, P. N., van Emmerick, R. E. and McDonald, P. V. (1989) Search strategies and the acquisition of coordination. In Wallace, S. A. (ed.), *Perspectives on the Coordination of Movement,* Amsterdam: Elsevier; 85–122.

Newman, D., Griffin, P. and Cole, M. (1989) *The Construction Zone: Working for Cognitive Change in School.* Cambridge: Cambridge University Press.

Newport, E. L. (1988) Constraints on learning and their role in language acquisition: studies of the acquisition of American Sign Language. *Language Sciences,* **10**: 147–72.

Newport, E. L. (1990) Maturational constraints on language learning. *Cognitive Science,* **14**: 11–28.

Nijhuis, J. G., Martin, C. B., and Prechtl, H. F. R. (1984) Behavioral states of the human fetus. In Prechtl, H. F. R. (ed.), *Continuity of Neural Functions from Prenatal to Postnatal Life.* Philadelphia: Lippincott: 65–78.

Ostwald, J., Schnitzler, H.-U. and Schuller, G. (1988) Target discrimination and target classification in echolocating bats. In Nachtigal, P. E. and Moore, P. W. B. (eds), *Animal Sonar: Processes and Performance.* New York: Plenum.

Oyama, S. (1985) *The Ontogeny of Information: Developmental Systems and Evolution.* Cambridge: Cambridge University Press.

Papousek, M. and Papousek, H. (1977) Mothering and the cognitive head-start: psychobiological considerations. In Schaffer, H. R. (ed.), *Studies in Mother–Infant Interaction: Proceedings of Loch Lomond Symposium.* New York: Academic Press: 63–85.

Papousek, M., Papousek, H. and Bornstein, M. H. (1985) The naturalistic vocal environment of young infants: on the significance of homogeneity and variability in parental speech. In Field, T. and Fox, N. (eds), *Social Perception in Infants.* Norwood, N.J.: Ablex.

Pfister, J. F., Cramer, C. P. and Blass, E. M. (1986) Suckling in rats extended by continuous living with dams and the preweaning litters. *Animal Behaviour,* **34**: 415–20.

Piaget, J. (1952) *The Child's Conception of Number.* London: Routledge & Kegan Paul.

Piaget, J. (1970) Piaget's theory. In Mussen, P. H. (ed.), *Carmichael's Manual of Child Psychology, 1,* 3rd edn: 703–32.

Piaget, J. (1971) *Biology and Knowledge*. Edinburgh: Edinburgh University Press.

Piaget, J. (1979) *Behaviour and Evolution*. London: Routledge & Kegan Paul.

Plunkett, K. and Sinha, C. (1992) Connectionism and developmental theory. *British Journal of Developmental Psychology*, **10**: 209–54.

Polka, L. and Werker, J. F. (1994) Developmental changes in perception of non-native vowel contrasts. *Journal of Experimental Psychology: Human Perception and Performance*, **20**: 421–35.

Port, R. F. and Gelder, T. van (1995) *Mind as Motion: Explorations in the Dynamics of Cognition*. Cambridge, Mass.: MIT Press.

Prechtl, H. F. R. (ed.) (1984) *Continuity and Development in Neural Functions*. Oxford: Blackwell Scientific Publications.

Querleu, D., Lefebvre, C., Renard, X., Titran, M., Morillion, M. and Crepin, G. (1984) Perception auditive et réativite du nouveau-né de moins de deux heures e vie à la voix maternelle. *Journal de Gynécologie, Obstètrique et Biologie de la Reproduction*, **13**: 125–34.

Quinn, P. C. and Eimas, P. D. (1996) Perceptual cues that permit categorical differentiation of animal species by infants. *Journal of Experimental Child Psychology*, **63**: 189–211.

Rader, N. (1997) Change and variation in responses to perceptual information. In Dent-Reed, C. and Zukow-Goldring, P. (eds), *Evolving Explanations of Development Ecological Approaches to Organism–Environment Systems*. Washington, D.C.: American Psychological Association.

Rader, N. and Stern, J. D. (1982) Visually elicited reaching in neonates. *Child Development*, **53**: 1004–7.

Reed, E. S. (1988) *James J. Gibson and the Psychology of Perception*. New Haven and London: Yale University Press.

Reed, E. S. (1991a) Cognition as the cooperative production of affordances. *Ecological Psychology*, **3 (2)**, 135–58.

Reed, E. S. (1991b) James Gibson's ecological approach to cognition. In Still, A. and Costall, A. (eds), *Against Cognitivism: Alternative Foundations for Cognitive Psychology*. Hemel Hempstead: Harvester-Wheatsheaf.

Reed, E. S. (1996) *Encountering the World: Towards an Ecological Psychology*. New York: Oxford University Press.

Reissland, N. (1988) Neonatal imitation in the first hour of life – observations in rural Nepal. *Developmental Psychology*, **24**: 464–9.

Reite, M. and Field, T. (eds) (1985) *The Psychobiology of Attachment*. London: Academic Press.

Richardson, K. (1998) *The Origins of Human Potential*. London: Routledge.

Richardson, K. G. (1991) Unpublished MA (Open) Final Report, *Interactive Approaches in Special Education*. University of Greenwich.

Richardson, K. and Bhavnani, K. K. (1984) How a concept is formed: prototype or contingency abstraction. *British Journal of Psychology*, **75**: 507–19.

Richardson, K. and Sheldon, S. (eds) (1988) *Cognitive Development to Adolescence*. Hove: Lawrence Erlbaum Associates, in association with The Open University.

Rochat, P. and Morgan, R. (1995) Spatial determinants in the perception of self-produced leg movements by 3-to-5 month-old infants. *Developmental Psychology*, **31 (4)**: 626–36.

Rollo, D. C. (1995) *Phenotypes: Their Epigenetics, Ecology and Evolution*. London: Chapman & Hall.

Ronnqvist, L. and Hopkins, B. (1998) Head position preference in the human newborn: a new look. *Child Development*, **69(1)**: 13–23.

Rovee-Collier, C. (1996) Shifting the focus from what to why. *Infant Behaviour and Development*, **19**: 385–400.

Saffran, J. R., Aslin, R. N. and Newport, E. L. (1996) Statistical learning by 8-month-old infants. *Science*, **274**: 1926–8.

Sameroff, A. J. (1991) The social context of development. In Woodhead, M., Carr, R. and Light, P. (eds), *Becoming A Person*. London: Routledge/The Open University.

Sants, J. (ed.) (1980) *Developmental Psychology and Society*. London: Macmillan.

Scaife, M. and Bruner, J. S. (1975) The capacity for joint visual attention in the human infant. *Nature*, **253**: 265.

Schaffer, H. R. (1984) *The Child's Entry into a Social World*. London: Academic Press.

Schaffer, H. R. (1992) Joint involvement episodes as contexts for development. In McGurk, H. (ed.), *Childhood Social Development*. Hove: Lawrence Erlbaum Associates.

Schank, R. C. and Abelson, R. P. (1977) *Scripts, Plans, Goals and Understanding*. Hillsdale, N.J.: Lawrence Erlbaum Associates.

Schiff, W. (1965) The perception of impending collision: a study of visually directed avoidant behaviour. *Psychological Monographs*, **79**: 604.

Seyfarth, R. M. and Cheney, D. L. (1986) Vocal development in vervet monkeys. *Animal Behaviour*, **34**: 33–61.

Sidaway, B., McNitt-Gray, J. and Davis, G. (1989) Visual timing of muscle preactivation in preparation for landing. *Ecological Psychology*, **1**: 253–64.

Siddiqui, A. (1995) Object size as a determinant of grasping in infancy. *Journal of Genetic Psychology*, **156 (3)**: 345–58.

Simion, F. and Butterworth, G. (eds) (1998) *The Development of Sensory, Motor and Cognitive Capacities in Early Infancy: From Perception to Cognition*. Hove: Psychology Press, Taylor & Francis Group.

Sinha, C. (1988) *Language and Representation: A Socio–Naturalistic Approach to Human Development*. London: Harvester Wheatsheaf.

Sitskoorn, M. M. and Smitsman, A. W. (1995) Infants' perception of dynamic relations between objects: passing through or support. *Developmental Psychology*, **31 (3)**: 437–47.

Slater, A. and Johnson, S. P. (1998) Visual sensory and perceptual abilities of the newborn: beyond the blooming, buzzing confusion. In Simion, F. and Butterworth, G. (eds), *The Development of Sensory, Motor and Cognitive Capacities in Early Infancy: From Perception to Cognition*. Hove: Psychology Press, Taylor & Francis Group.

Sleigh, M. J., Columbus, R. F. and Lickliter, R. (1998) Intersensory experience and early perceptual development: post natal experience with multimodal maternal cues affects intersensory responsiveness in Bobwhite quail chicks. *Developmental Psychology*, **34 (2)**: 215–23.

Smith, L. B. and Jones, S. S. (1993) Cognition without concepts. *Cognitive Development*, **8 (2)**: 181–8.

Smith, L. B and Thelen, E. (eds) (1993) *A Dynamic Systems Approach to Development: Applications*. London: MIT Press/Bradford Books.

Snyder-McLean, L. *et al.* (1984) Structuring joint action routines: a strategy for facilitating communication and language development in the classroom. *Seminars in Speech and Language*, **5(3)**: (August).

Souriau, J. (1990) The development of language. *Deaf–Blind Education* (July–December): 77.

Spelke, E. S., Kestenbaum, R., Simon, D. J. and Wein, D. (1995) Spatiotemporal continuity, smoothness of motion and object identity in infancy. *British Journal of Developmental Psychology*, **13**: 113–40.

Stehouwer, D. J. and Farel, P. B. (1984) Development of hindlimb locomotor activity in the bullfrog (*Rane catesbeiana*) studied in vitro. *Science*, **219**: 516–18.

Stern, D. (1977) *The First Relationship, Infant and Mother*. London: Open Books.

Stern, D. N., Spieker, S. and MacKain, K. (1982) Intonation contours as signals in maternal speech to infants. *Developmental Psychology*, **18**: 727–35.

Stewart, I. (1998) *Life's Other Secret: The New Mathematics of the Living World*. London: Allen Lane, The Penguin Press.

Still, A. and Costall, A. (1991) *Against Cognitivism: Alternative Foundations for Cognitive Psychology*. London: Harvester Wheatsheaf.

Struhsaker, T. T. (1967) Behaviour of vervet monkeys. *University of California Publications of Zoology*, **82**: 1–74.

Swenson, R. and Turvey, M. T. (1991) Thermodynamic reasons for perception–action cycles. *Ecological Psychology*, **3 (4)**: 317–48.

Tannen, D. (1981) *Analyzing Discourse: Text and Talk*. Georgetown: Georgetown University Round Table.

Thelen, E. (1985) Developmental origins of motor coordination: leg movements in human infants. *Developmental Psychobiology*, **18**: 1–22.

Thelen, E. (1986) Treadmill-elicited stepping in seven-month-old infants. *Child Development*, **57**: 1498–1506.

Thelen, E. and Fisher, D. M. (1982) Newborn stepping: an explanation for 'disappearing reflex'. *Developmental Psychology*, **18**: 760–75.

Thelen, E. and Smith, L. B. (1994) *A Dynamic Systems Approach to the Development of Cognition and Action*. Cambridge, Mass.: MIT Press.

Trehub, S. E. (1976) The discrimination of foreign speech contrasts by infants and adults. *Child Development*, **47**: 466–72.

Trevarthen, C. (1968) Two mechanisms of vision in primates. *Psychologische Forschung*, **31**: 299–337.

Trevarthen, C. (1980) Neurological development and the growth of psychological functions. In Sants, J. (ed.), *Developmental Psychology and Society*. London: Macmillan.

Turkewitz, G., Gardner, J. M. and Lewkowicz, D. L. (1984) Sensory/perceptual functioning during early infancy: implications of a quantitative basis of responding. In Greenberg, G. and Tobach, E. (eds), *Conference on Levels of Integration and Evolution of Behaviour*. Hillsdale, N.J.: Erlbaum: 167–95.

Ulrich, B. D. (1997) Dynamic systems theory and skill development in children. In Connolly, K. J. and Forssberg, H. (eds), Neurophysiology and neuropsychology of motor development. *Clinics in Developmental Medicine*, **143/144**. Cambridge: Cambridge University Press/MacKeith Press.

van der Maas, H. L. J. and Hopkins, B. (1998) Developmental transitions: so what's new? *British Journal of Developmental Psychology*, **16**: 1–13.

van der Maas, H. L. J. and Molenaar, P. C. M. (1992) Stagewise cognitive development: an application of catastrophe theory. *Psychological Review*, **99 (3)**: 395–417.

Veer, R. van der and Valsiner, V. (eds) (1994) *The Vygotsky Reader.* Oxford: Basil Blackwell.

Vintner, A. (1986) The role of movement in eliciting early imitation. *Child Development,* **57**: 66–71.

von Hofsten, C. (1997) Early development of predictive abilities. In Dent-Reed, C. and Zukow-Goldring, P. (eds), *Evolving Explanations of Development Ecological Approaches to Organism–Environment Systems.* Washington, D.C.: American Psychological Association: 163–94.

Vygotsky, L. S. (1960) *The Development of Higher Mental Processes.* Moscow: Academy of Pedagogical Sciences.

Vygotsky, L. S. (1978) (ed. Cole, M., John-Steiner, V., Scribner, S. and Souberman, E.) *Mind in Society: The Development of Higher Psychological Processes.* London: Harvard University Press.

Vygotsky, L. S (1994) The problem of the environment. In Veer, R. van der and Valsiner, V. (eds), *The Vygotsky Reader.* Oxford: Basil Blackwell.

Wade, M. G. and Whiting, H. T. A. (eds) *Motor Development in Children: Aspects of Coordination and Control.* Dordrecht: Martinus Nijhoff: 341–60.

Walk, R. D. and Gibson, E. J. (1961) A comparative and analytical study of visual depth perception. *Psychological Monographs,* **75**, no. **519**.

Wallman, J. (1979) A minimal visual restriction experiment: preventing chicks from seeing their feet affects later response to mealworms. *Developmental Psychobiology,* **12**: 391–7.

Walton, G. E., Bower, N. J. A. and Bower, T. G. R. (1992) Recognition of familiar faces by newborns. *Infant Behaviour and Development,* **15**: 265–9.

Wehner, R. (1982) Himmelsnavigation bei Ingexten. Neurophysiologie und verhalt. *Neujahrsblatt des Naturforschenden Gesselschaft* in Zurich, **184**: 1–32.

Wehner, R. and Wehner, S. (1990) Insect navigation: use of maps or Aviadne's thread? *Ethology, Ecology and Evolution,* **2**: 27–48.

Wertheimer, M. (1961) Psychomotor co-ordination of audio-visual space at birth. *Science,* **134**: 1692.

Wertsch, J. V., (ed.) (1981) *The Concept of Activity in Soviet Psychology.* Armonk: M. E. Sharpe.

Wertsch, J. V. (ed.) (1985a) *Culture, Communication and Cognition – Vygotskean Perspectives.* Cambridge: Cambridge University Press.

Wertsch, J. V. (1985b) *Vygotsky and the Social Formation of Mind.* London: Harvard University Press.

Wertsch, J. V. (1991) *Voices of the Mind: A Sociocultural Approach to Mediated Action.* London: Harvester Wheatsheaf.

Whiten, A. (ed.) (1991) *Natural Theories of Mind: Evolution, Development and Simulation of Everyday Mindreading*. Oxford: Basil Blackwell.

Wills, C. (1991) *The Wisdom of the Genes: New Pathways in Evolution*. Oxford: Oxford University Press.

Wimmers, R. H., Beek, P. J., Savelsburgh, G. J. P. and Hopkins, B. (1998) Developmental changes in action: theoretical and methodological issues. *British Journal of Developmental Psychology*, **16**: 45–63.

Wimmers, R. H., Savelsburgh, G. J. P., Beek, P. J. and Hopkins, B. (1998) Evidence for a phase transition in the early development of prehension. *Developmental Psychobiology*, **32 (3)**: 243–8.

Winnicott, D. W. (1965) *The Maturational Process and the Facilitating Environment*. London: Hogarth.

Wolff, P. H. (1959) Observations on newborn infants. *Psychosomatic Medicine*, **21**: 110–18.

Wolff, P. H. (1963) Observations on the early development of smiling. In Foss, B. M. (ed.), *Determinants of Infant Behaviour, 11*. London: Methuen: 113–34.

Woodhead, M., Carr, R. and Light, P. (eds) (1991) *Becoming a Person: Child Development in Social Context, 1*. London: Routledge.

Yonas, A., Bechtold, A. G., Frankel, D., Gordon, F. R., McRoberts, G., Norcia, A. and Sternfels, S. (1977) Development of sensitivity to information for impending collision. *Perception and Psychophysics*, **21**: 97–104.

Yonas, A., Petterson, L. and Lockman, J. J. (1979) Young infants' sensitivity to optical information for collision. *Canadian Journal of Psychology*, **33**: 268–76.

Zernicke, R. F. and Schneider, K. (1993) Biomechanics and developmental neuromotor control. *Child Development*, **64**: 982–1004.

Index